AF606029

MISSION TO MAO

Georgetown Studies in Intelligence History

Series Editors: Christopher Moran, Mark Phythian, and Mark Stout

Titles in the Series

Canadian Military Intelligence: Operations and Evolution from the October Crisis to the War in Afghanistan
David A. Charters

Crown, Cloak, and Dagger: The British Monarchy and Secret Intelligence from Victoria to Elizabeth II
Richard J. Aldrich and Rory Cormac

Spies for the Sultan: Ottoman Intelligence in the Great Rivalry with Spain
Emrah Safa Gürkan. Translated by Jonathan M. Ross and İdil Karacadağ

MISSION TO MAO

US INTELLIGENCE AND THE CHINESE COMMUNISTS IN WORLD WAR II

SARA B. CASTRO

GEORGETOWN UNIVERSITY PRESS / WASHINGTON, DC

Library of Congress Cataloging-in-Publication Data

Names: Castro, Sara B., author.
Title: Mission to Mao : US intelligence and the Chinese Communists during World War II / Sara B. Castro.
Other titles: US intelligence and the Chinese Communists during World War II
Description: Washington, DC : Georgetown University Press, 2024 | Series: Georgetown studies in intelligence history | Includes bibliographical references and index.
Identifiers: LCCN 2023035487 (print) | LCCN 2023035488 (ebook) | ISBN 9781647124502 (hardcover) | ISBN 9781647124519 (paperback) | ISBN 9781647124526 (ebook)
Subjects: LCSH: United States. Office of Strategic Services. | World War, 1939–1945—Secret service—United States. | World War, 1939–1945—Secret service—China. | Intelligence service—United States. | Intelligence service—China. | Communism—China. | United States—Relations—China. | China—Relations—United States.
Classification: LCC D810.S7 C4 2024 (print) | LCC D810.S7 (ebook) | DDC 327.1273009—dc23/eng/20230812
LC record available at https://lccn.loc.gov/2023035487
LC ebook record available at https://lccn.loc.gov/2023035488

♾ This paper meets the requirements of ANSI/NISO Z39.48-1992 (Permanence of Paper).

25 24 9 8 7 6 5 4 3 2 First printing

Printed in the United States of America

Cover design by Brad Norr
Interior design by BookComp, Inc.

To my family

CONTENTS

ABBREVIATIONS

AGAS	Air Ground Aid Service
AGFRTS	Air and Ground Forces Resources Technical Staff
CBI	China-Burma-India
CCP	Chinese Communist Party
CIA	Central Intelligence Agency
CIG	Central Intelligence Group
COI	Coordinator of Information
COMMO	OSS Communications Division
CT	China Theater
FBI	Federal Bureau of Investigation
FDR	Franklin Delano Roosevelt
FDRL	Franklin D. Roosevelt Presidential Library, Hyde Park, NY
FSO	Foreign Service Officer
G-2 / MID	US Army Military Intelligence Division
G-3	US Army Operations and Training Division
GMD / KMT	Guomindang/Chinese Nationalist Party
HSTL	Harry S. Truman Presidential Library, Independence, MO
IIC	Interdepartmental Intelligence Committee
JCS	Joint Chiefs of Staff
JICA	Joint Army-Navy Intelligence Collection Agency
KMT / GMD	Kuomintang/Chinese Nationalist Party
MID / G-2	US Army Military Intelligence Division
MO	OSS Morale Operations Branch
NARA	US National Archives and Records Administration, College Park, MD
NKVD	Soviet intelligence organization, precursor to KGB
ONI	Office of Naval Intelligence
OSS	Office of Strategic Services
OWI	Office of War Information
PRC	People's Republic of China

R&A	OSS Office of Strategic Services Research and Analysis Branch
RG	Record Group
SACO	Sino-American Special Technical Cooperative Organization
SEAC	Southeast Asia Command
SI	OSS Secret Intelligence Branch
SO	OSS Special Operations Branch
SSU	War Department Strategic Services Unit
X-2	OSS Counterespionage Branch
YENSIG	Radio operation in Yan'an

DRAMATIS PERSONAE

US ARMY OBSERVER MISSION TO YAN'AN (DIXIE MISSION) PERSONNEL

Personnel Deployed July 1944–January 1945 (rank order)

Col. David D. Barrett: First commanding officer of Dixie Mission, representing Army G-2 Intelligence Division; served in Yan'an July–December 1944; former US attaché to China

John "Jack" S. Service: Foreign Service Officer detailed to Stilwell's CBI staff; first political officer

Raymond Ludden: Foreign Service Officer; second political officer

Maj. Melvin A. Casberg: Army Medical Corps medic

Maj. Ray Cromley: OSS officer; order of battle expert; under AFGRTS and G-2 covers

Maj. Charles R. Dole: Army Air Corps; weather officer

Maj. Wilbur J. Peterkin: Army Infantry; third commanding officer (February 1944)

Capt. Jack Champion: Army C-47 pilot

Capt. John C. Colling: OSS; operations and demolition

Capt. Brooke Dolan II: OSS; AGAS cover

Capt. Paul C. Domke: Signal Corps; supply officer

Capt. Charles C. Stelle: OSS R&A Branch; under AFGRTS cover

Lt. Louis M. Jones: Army Air Corps

Lt. Henry C. Whittlesey: Army Infantry/Air Ground Aid Service; KIA in China, 1944

Sgt. William E. Cady: Army Air Corps; weather officer

Sgt. Anton H. Remenih: OSS radio tech; under Signal Corps cover

Sgt. Walter Gress: OSS radio tech; under Signal Corps cover

Lt. Herbert Hitch: US Navy; ONI representative

George I. Nakamura: Office of War Information; POW debriefing

John K. Emmerson: Foreign Service Officer detailed to Stilwell's CBI staff; Japanese linguist and expert in propaganda

Personnel Deployed to Yan'an after January 1945

Col. Morris DePass: US attaché prior to January 1945; mission commanding officer (replaced Barrett); declared persona non grata by CCP and forced to leave in February 1945

Col. Ivan D. Yeaton: Mission commanding officer July 1945–April 1946

Capt. Julius Pomeranze: Army Medical Corps medic (replaced Casberg)

Capt. Clifford F. Young: Mission final commanding officer; executive officer to Yeaton

Col. John Sells: Last commanding officer posted at Yan'an, April 1946–March 1947

OTHER US GOVERNMENT OFFICIALS AND MILITARY OFFICERS

US Army

Gen. Claire L. Chennault: Commander, Fourteenth Air Force

Gen. George C. Marshall: US Army chief of staff, 1939–45; special envoy to China, 1945–47; US secretary of state, 1947–49

Gen. Robert B. McClure: Chief of staff to Albert Wedemeyer, October 1944–August 1945

Gen. John Magruder: G-2 intelligence officer in China; detailed to OSS in 1941

Gen. Joseph Stilwell: Chief of staff to Chiang Kai-shek; Commander, American Forces, China-Burma-India Theater, February 1942–October 1944

Gen. Alfred C. Wedemeyer: Commander, China Theater, October 1944–August 1945

Col. Joseph Dickey: Army G-2 representative

Col. Frank "Pinky" Dorn: Army G-2 representative; former executive officer to Stilwell

State Department/US Embassy in China Personnel

James F. Byrnes: US secretary of state, July 1945–January 1947

John Paton Davies: Foreign Service Officer detailed to Stilwell

Clarence E. Gauss: US ambassador to China; resigned November 1944

Patrick Hurley: US ambassador to China, January–September 1945
Cordell Hull: US secretary of state, 1933–44
Edward R. Stettinius Jr.: US secretary of state, December 1944–June 1945
Henry Stimson: US secretary of state, 1929–33; US secretary of war, 1911–13 and 1940–45
F. McCracken Fisher: OWI propaganda specialist

Office of Strategic Services (OSS) and Other US Intelligence Officers

Gen. William J. Donovan: Coordinator of information, July 1941–June 1942; OSS director, June 1942–October 1945
Col. John Coughlin: OSS China director in 1944
Col. Ilia Tolstoy: OSS mission lead to North China in 1944; OSS mission lead to Tibet with Brooke Dolan
Lt. Col. Willis Bird: Deputy chief, China Theater, 1945
Lt. Col. Robert Hall: OSS China deputy branch chief under Coughlin, 1944
Maj. Joseph Spencer: OSS R&A Branch
Capt. Evans Carlson: US Marine who campaigned with CCP's Eighth Route Army and founded Carlson's Raiders; corresponded with FDR about 1938 visit to Yan'an
Lauchlin Currie: Harvard University economist and assistant to FDR who served as special envoy to White House, 1941 and 1942
Burton Fahs: OSS director of R&A Branch, Far East Section
John King Fairbank: OSS R&A Branch, Far East Section; renowned historian of China and Harvard University professor
Richard Heppner: Head of OSS China Theater under Wedemeyer
William Langer: OSS R&A Branch director
Herbert Yardley: American cryptologist, Black Chamber founder

CHINESE PLAYERS

Chinese Nationalist Party (Guomindang) Leaders

Chiang Kai-shek (Jiang Jieshi): Generalissimo of Chinese National Government and China's national army
Dai Li (Tai Li): Head of intelligence and secret police
Soong Tse-vung "T.V" (Song Ziwen): Brother-in-law of Chiang Kai-shek; Nationalist government deputy premier and foreign minister
Soong Mei-ling Chiang: Fourth wife of Chiang Kai-shek; First Lady of the Republic of China

CCP Leaders and Staff

Mao Zedong: Chairman
Zhou Enlai: Vice chairman; member of Central Revolutionary Military Council
Gen. Zhu De: Commander, Eighth Route Army
Gen. Ye Jianying: Chief of staff, Eighth Route Army
Gen. Peng Dehuai: Vice commander, Eighth Route Army
Chen Jiakang: Secretary to Zhou Enlai
Marsh. Lin Biao: Division commander, Eighth Route Army
Marsh. He Long: Division commander, Eighth Route Army
Marsh. Nie Rongzhen: Deputy division commander under Lin Biao, Eighth Route Army

PREFACE

My professional career began a little over twenty years ago and has involved several different occupations. The theme that has been a constant through all of them has been my interest in Chinese history and culture. I have tried to serve as a cultural intermediary, explaining America to Chinese people and vice versa, ever since I had the privilege to first visit China. I do not perform this work at the same level as the people I describe in this book, but I have attempted to make my own small difference. In the space of my career this work has significantly changed. US-China relations are now at the point of greatest tension that I have observed.

I have often heard both Chinese and American speakers refer in different ways to the special relationship between our countries. My work on this project has led me to think more deeply about the meaning of the phrase "special relationship" and its history in US-China relations. Michael H. Hunt, who wrote a very important book on the countries' special relationship, was an early mentor for this project. His thoughts on how ideology has affected American attitudes and behaviors toward China have significantly influenced both my attitude and this work. Hunt's book focuses on the Open Door era and primarily pre-twentieth-century bilateral contacts. However, the Open Door paternalism that Hunt describes certainly survived that era. It was a pernicious force in the World War II era, as this book demonstrates. Reviewed from today's vantage point, the examples of paternalism in the 1940s that this book describes appear obvious and outdated. I hope exposure to them makes readers more sensitive to persistent paternalism in US-China relations.

Like all books, this one is far from a solitary effort. An army of mentors, friends, and family supported me through its creation, and my gratitude extends far beyond the space available to thank people individually. These are just the highlights. This book would not be possible without the academic and financial support I received from the University of North Carolina at Chapel Hill. Michael Tsin, Michelle King, Joseph Cadell, Wayne Lee, and Michael Hunt were vital doulas for this work, as were Margaret Martin, Mary Beth Chopas, Rachel Levandoski, and Elizabeth Lundeen. Support from all my friends and colleagues in the Department of History at the US Air Force Academy has been essential to bringing this book into the world. I also owe a huge debt of gratitude to the Wilson Center for supporting my research through its generous China Fellows program.

The Society for Intelligence History was an essential incubator for this project; I am forever indebted to Mark Stout, Sarah Jane Corke, Calder Walton, and Nicholas Reynolds for bringing me into the fold of spy historians. Thank you to Donald Jacobs at Georgetown University Press and the editors of the Studies in Intelligence History series, who helped me elevate my manuscript beyond the potential that I had hoped for it. The entire team of editing, production, and marketing staff are true heroes who have played a significant role in bringing this book to readers. To Pablo Garcia Loaeza, thank you for the fantastic map. Lastly, to my family: without your support and devotion my work would be both impossible and no fun.

Although this book had so much help to bring it to fruition, there may still be errors. If you find one, rest assured that the fault is all mine. The views expressed in this book are those of the author and do not reflect the official policy or position of the US Department of Defense, the US Government, the US Air Force Academy, the US Air Force, or the Central Intelligence Agency.

A NOTE ON NAMES AND SPELLINGS

This book documents the social history of US Army–led operations known colloquially as the "Dixie Mission" that occurred at the Chinese Communist headquarters area in Yan'an (延安), China, from July 1944 to March 1947. Over the course of time that people have been documenting the Dixie Mission, conventions for writing and romanizing Chinese have changed significantly. In almost all cases this book defaults to the simplified characters and Pinyin romanization that the People's Republic favors today. Direct quotes from older sources include variations, the most common being the spelling "Yenan" for "Yan'an."

The "Dixie Mission" was a nickname for the US delegation based at Yan'an, which went by many different official names during its brief time of operation, including (but not limited to) US Army Observer Mission to Yan'an, US Army Observer Group to Yan'an, US Army Observer Section in Yan'an, the Yan'an Observer Group, and Yan'an Liaison Group. Declassified records about this delegation are mostly informal, operational correspondence among relatively low-ranking military and intelligence officials. The documents rarely note the name changes or describe the reasons for them. Moreover, not all actors within the installation adopt the name changes in their correspondence. This book uses either the Dixie Mission nickname or the names given to the US operation in contemporaneous sources when referring to the mission.

Chinese names typically begin with a surname followed by a given name. Many Chinese leaders during the World War II era used "courtesy names" or noms de guerre. This book attempts to use the most widely recognized names and spellings for such leaders. For example, numerous historical sources refer to the Guomindang leader as Chiang Kai-shek, using the Cantonese pronunciation of his preferred courtesy name, 蒋介石, instead of its Mandarin Pinyin version, Jiang Jieshi. To avoid confusion, in this book he is Chiang Kai-shek.

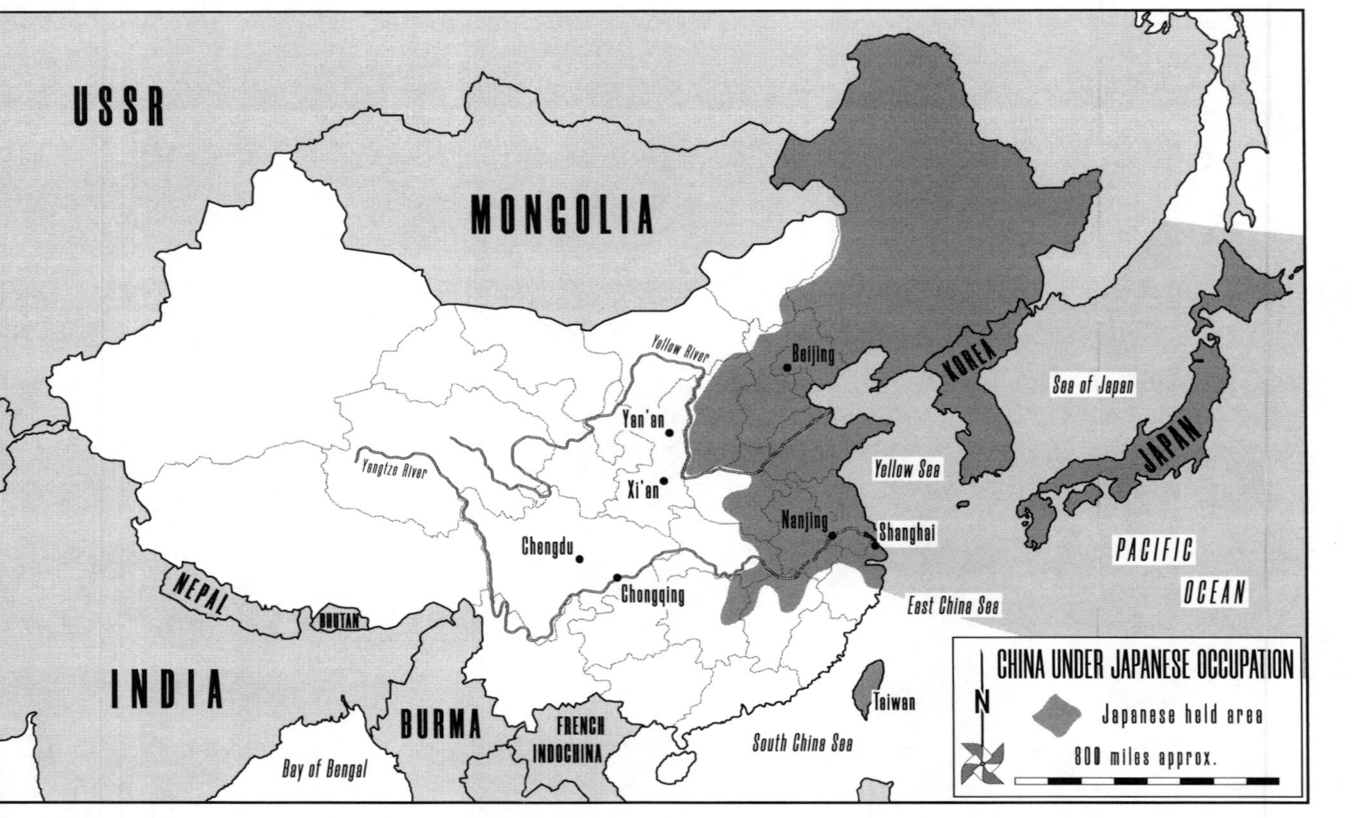

Map of China and Surrounding Countries in World War II. *Cartography by Pablo Garcia Loaeza*

INTRODUCTION

December 7, 1944. Exactly three years after the Japanese military bombed Pearl Harbor, Col. David Barrett, US Army, sat on a US military plane next to Zhou Enlai, one of the most important leaders in the Chinese Communist Party (CCP), who later became the first premier of the People's Republic of China and the architect of much of its diplomacy. Barrett was the leader of the so-called Dixie Mission to the CCP headquarters at Yan'an. The mission's official title—the US Army Observer Group in Yan'an—was a mouthful to say and cumbersome for telegrams. Early planners conjured imagery from the US Civil War and the lyrics of a popular song to assign the informal codename "Dixie" to the group, hinting at its assignment to CCP "rebel" territory.[1]

Barrett and Zhou were attempting to return north to Yan'an from Chongqing, wartime capital of China's central government. Chiang Kai-shek and his political party, the Nationalist Party, were leading the government and had been attempting to eliminate the CCP, their primary political opposition, since the 1920s.[2] The two parties agreed to cooperate in the war against Japan, but by this point in the war they had settled into an uneasy and distrustful truce. Barrett and Zhou traveled to Chongqing for frustratingly unproductive meetings between Chinese central government leaders and the recently named American ambassador regarding China's war effort against the occupying Japanese. In late November Zhou had asked Barrett to arrange the plane for his return to Yan'an and the chance to regroup with other CCP leaders.

Weather conditions in Chongqing had not been cooperating. Their plane, piloted by American Jack Champion, had been attempting to leave for more than a week. They had taken off several times but always turned back before clearing the tall mountains that surround Chongqing. In the damp and cold Sichuan winter, ice had formed on the plane's propellers and broken off in chunks after each takeoff, slamming into the windshield and fuselage. Champion was spooked. He told Barrett he had "already used up too many points flying around China."[3] He was not taking the chance that the C-47 could make it through the dangerous weather.

Chongqing was unfriendly to pilots. A blanket of low clouds often hovered above the chaotic city, which Westerners spelled (and mispronounced) "Chungking." Its dim and steamy streets were home to more than one million souls in 1944. Chiang Kai-shek had relocated the Chinese central government to the city in late 1937 after the Japanese Army had pushed his government out of the previous capital, Nanjing. The Generalissimo, as Chiang preferred people call him, chose Chongqing precisely because it was difficult for enemies to access. Four separate mountain ranges form a basin around the main urban area, which sprawls out around the confluence of the Jialing and Yangtze Rivers. In the 1940s Chongqing was unconnected to China's railroad network, due to the mountains. Near-permanent cloud cover regularly obscured visibility. The Tibetan plateau loomed to the west of Chongqing, and the Japanese occupied most cities and railways beyond the mountain ranges on the city's east side. The geography did not ultimately stop the Japanese from launching more than two hundred bombing runs on it before 1942, but the attacks had slowed to nothing by 1943.[4] The main dangers to pilots after that point were weather and visibility.

Improved weather had granted a promising start to the flight on December 7. Barrett reported a gleeful mood aboard the plane upon takeoff. High spirits reigned for the first two-thirds of the flight, until Zhou glanced out the window. "Colonel," he then said to Barrett, "it seems to me something is wrong. The terrain outside looks definitely unfamiliar to me, and we should be in Yenan by now. I think we are flying west instead of north."[5]

Barrett described Zhou as calm in this moment, which is difficult to believe. The sparsely populated desert and mountain areas below the plane offered no airstrips and little anticipated help for any plane attempting a crash landing or seeking fuel for a return trip to Chongqing. Moreover, overcorrecting the plane's bearing could likewise cost the group their lives. A lost American plane would have provided an extremely tempting target for Japanese anti-aircraft artillery, to which the plane could have easily fallen prey, depending on where it veered off-course. Barrett, Zhou, and Champion all would have recognized these dangers.

Barrett had come to respect Zhou over the previous few months working together. He and Zhou together convinced Champion to turn the plane. Based on memory and landmarks, Zhou peered through the small windows and helped navigate the plane back to the makeshift airstrip in Yan'an. Barrett later recalled that without Zhou's guidance, the plane likely would have run out of fuel and crash-landed "somewhere in the marshes of Tibet."[6]

The story of Barrett and Zhou on this plane at this time, like many other anecdotes from the Dixie Mission's three-year existence, highlights America's growing pains and vulnerability: a flash of humility and exposure in all the hubris that characterized US intelligence and military operations in China in the 1940s. In the century leading up to World War II, the United States had embraced a paternalistic approach to foreign relations that leaders in East Asia, the Philippines, and across the Caribbean recognized as American imperialism. During the years of the Dixie Mission, this American imperialist impulse was fusing with the self-determined mantle of responsibility for global security that was later ensconced in Harry Truman's National Security Act.[7] The combination would require the United States to undertake significant bureaucratic expansion and improve intelligence practices that had developed on the fly during the war. This process not only caused a spectrum of violence upon local populations where the United States was operating but it was also chaotic for individual American officials grappling with and attempting to execute it on behalf of their government. Individuals who represented the US government in China during World War II, particularly those who had positions within the nascent US intelligence regime, reflected US ideologies and perspectives in direct interactions with Chinese leaders and influenced the messages US policymakers received about China. Recent scholarship has overlooked these historical actors.

The Dixie Mission brought a group of US officials to Yan'an under army auspices but also included personnel from various other agencies to meet with and learn about the CCP leaders. It was the first sustained official engagement between US government officials and the CCP. Chiang Kai-shek strongly opposed it. Contacts began in the summer of 1944 and outlasted the war; US officials did not withdraw from Yan'an completely until March 1947, when negotiations to mediate the civil war between the Nationalists and the Communists in China completely failed. At every point, the US installation in Yan'an was closely linked to an American resolve to remake the world in the liberal image of the United States—a project that US policymakers had realized required the development of modern intelligence practices, which the Dixie Mission attempted to develop and implement. It was one of numerous examples in World War II of US officials venturing forth with confidence into territory they found unfamiliar and dauntingly complex, buoyed by determination that morality favored the Allies and the high stakes of the global war justified drastic measures.

A fresh look at the Dixie Mission reveals that in China (as elsewhere), US officials often created their own obstacles. They were ultimately reliant on the compliance, support, and expertise of local hosts, who frequently saw the terms of global security much differently than their American counterparts did, whether or not the Americans ever noticed. Some US officials, such as Barrett and the first Dixie cohort that accompanied him, came to appreciate this dynamic, even as they acted upon intrinsic impulses toward imperialism. By the 1950s the Dixie Mission members' appreciation of the expertise of their CCP hosts had caused some in Washington to question their loyalty to the American cause. Dixie Mission participants who seemed too charitable to the CCP faced scrutiny from Sen. Joseph McCarthy and suffered subsequent career consequences.[8]

Chinese allies in the war, including the CCP leaders, had much to teach US officials about China, and the Americans in Yan'an had something to offer the CCP as well: access to airpower. US officials would not have been able to supply or operate the Dixie Mission—or virtually any of the rest of the positions the US military held in China—without planes. Planes carried equipment, supplies, mail, documents, and people across China, from Xi'an to Chongqing, and from India into China over the Himalayas. Yan'an was in a remote location, with Japanese troops occupying nearby areas. Roads to it were unpaved and took weeks to traverse, when they were even passable. Access to US planes for travel and cargo boosted CCP leaders' legitimacy in Yan'an. Transporting items and people on US planes saved the CCP cadre the treacherous land travel between their remote base and the CBI headquarters. Even without the ability to own, lease, or operate the American planes, Chinese leaders saw the advantages of access to American planes. It was a powerful incentive for cooperation with the United States.

NEW LESSONS FROM THE DIXIE MISSION

This book is far from the first study of the Dixie Mission, but it takes a fresh look at the operation from the ground up, focusing on the individual US officials involved. The scope of this study includes Chinese actors, but the focus of its intervention is directed at the US actors, especially those serving the US government and military from lower officer ranks. It intends to incorporate the actions of the US Observer Group at Yan'an into current scholarly debates on the history of US-China relations and the history of US intelligence since the beginning of World War II. Previous studies of the Dixie Mission have focused almost exclusively on evaluating the mission's role in the outcome of the Chinese Civil War that ended in 1949 with the establishment of the People's Republic under Communist leadership. This discursive thread proceeded through decades of Western historical scholarship with no recognition of American imperialism or the hubris driving the deployment of Americans to Yan'an. Instead, controversy often stemmed from emotions about the perceived failures of US ideology in China. The Communists' rise to power in China met with such outrage in Washington that it spurred a debate that historian Maochun Yu has aptly described as "partisan and bitter."[9] Historical analysis of US intervention in China in World War II morphed into "a smoke-ridden political battleground" particularly focused on evaluating the attitude of Dixie Mission participants toward Communist ideology.

Policymakers, journalists, and scholars in the 1950s and 1960s frequently linked the activities of the Dixie Mission with the Americans' "loss of China" to the Communists. In this view, which historian Barbara Tuchman later called "one of the most damaging campaigns of vilification in recent public life," the participants of the Dixie Mission were accused of being both culpable, for not using their expertise on China to make US-led negotiations more successful, and disloyal to American-style liberalism, for their charitable views of CCP capabilities.[10] A constituency of US intellectuals essentially argued that if the Dixie Mission personnel had not worked against their own government's interests, US policy in China might have brokered mediation between the Nationalists and the Communists and ushered in a capitalist, multiparty liberal government into power.[11] The anti-Communist intellectual atmosphere of the time was discouraging to scholars whose studies could be perceived to portray Chinese Communism in a complimentary manner. This effect complicated initial efforts at producing an objective study of CCP ideology, goals, and intentions. On the other hand, the foreign policy interests and anti-Communist agenda of the United States government leaders and, to some extent, Western European leaders in this period probably encouraged the study of contemporary Chinese politics as a means of contextualizing and advancing anti-Communist foreign policy goals.[12]

A new wave of academic interest in the role of the Dixie Mission in US-China relations developed in the 1970s due to a confluence of factors. Sufficient time had passed since the war to allow the US government to declassify and release many documents from the Office of Strategic Services (or OSS, the US intelligence agency established during World War II). The release of these documents raised public awareness of previously secret US wartime intelligence activities. Scholars and the public were already observing the effects of global decolonization and critiquing US actions in Vietnam at this time. At the same time, the aging and retirement of many Americans who participated in World War II encouraged a period of their public reflection in the form of published memoirs, interviews, and articles.[13] The combination of these elements encouraged Western intellectuals to reevaluate and debate post–World War II US foreign policy. Based on the newly released government sources and the participant memoirs, studies emerged suggesting that instead of the loss of China, the actions of the Dixie Mission represented a "lost *chance* in China," whereby US statesmen squandered opportunities for engagement with the CCP in lieu of an exclusive partnership with what the scholars determined to be the corrupt and dysfunctional (but non-Communist) government led by Chiang Kai-shek.

At the core of this argument was an idealized assessment of the actions of Gen. Joseph W. Stilwell, who commanded US forces in the CBI Theater and served as Chiang Kai-shek's chief of staff from 1942 until his removal from the job by President Franklin Roosevelt in October 1944. In this view, Stilwell was an American military hero, a friend to the Chinese people, and an expert on China who tried but failed to save China from Chiang Kai-shek's flaws. Ironically, Tuchman, who critiqued the politicization of the earliest Dixie Mission histories, was the historian most famous for this view of Stilwell. Her book, *Stilwell and the American Experience in China, 1911–1945* (1970), won the Pulitzer Prize in Nonfiction and captivated American readers.[14] Another significant book frequently associated with the "lost chance" argument is journalist E. J. Kahn's *The China Hands,* published in 1976. Like earlier studies conveying the "loss of China" argument, both books today appear significantly flawed and politicized, but they also record important facts about the events that might otherwise have been lost. Tuchman and Kahn each engaged in extensive interviews with members of Stilwell's network and former Dixie Mission participants. They also reviewed documents from the personal papers of their interview subjects—material that likely will never make it into official archives.

Two more recent historiographic developments exposed the need to reevaluate the Dixie Mission's history. The first is that historians have appropriately concluded that China's choice of political system was not up to the United States to win or lose, as the earlier studies implied. China's period of reform and opening up under Deng Xiaoping's leadership offered scholars new access to Chinese official documents and initiated the inclusion of Chinese scholars in historical debates happening in the West. Combined with new methodological approaches that incorporate cultural and social history, historians began to recognize and document the imperial hubris of the US approach to China in World War II. A wave of studies effectively denied that the US government possessed the agency necessary to shape the course of Chinese politics to the degree that previous scholars suggested.

Historians such as Chen Jian and Michael Sheng argued that by the mid-1940s, political and ideological reasons would have prevented CCP leaders from entertaining any serious diplomatic accommodations to the United States. In 1997 Chen argued that, "contrary to the assumption of the advocates of the 'lost chance' thesis, Chinese materials now available demonstrate that in 1949–50, Mao Zedong and the CCP leadership were unwilling to pursue Western recognition, let alone to establish diplomatic relations with Western countries."[15] Chen's article was a more forceful articulation of suggestions by Michael Sheng that the CCP ideology in the 1940s allowed for some flexibility to achieve short-term goals, but its anti-imperialist agenda would have ultimately prevented a US-CCP partnership in 1949. Chen and Sheng separately referred to the idea of a squandered diplomatic opportunity as a "myth" that is both arrogant and "American-centered."[16]

The second crucial historiographic development was the recognition of political factors that encouraged studies in the twentieth century to build up the narrative of General Stilwell's heroism by criticizing the wartime actions of Chiang Kai-shek. Newer empirical scholarship about Chiang Kai-shek and other Nationalist Party leaders such as Gen. Dai Li, now incorporating Chinese sources, reveals a significantly more nuanced view of Nationalist policy and strategy in the 1930s and 1940s than previously accepted.[17] At the same time, historians such as Hans J. van de Ven compared the nuanced assessments of Chiang to previous Western scholarship and offered a revised view of Stilwell. Van de Ven describes what he calls the "Stilwell myth," which entailed the idea that the Nationalists "were a militarist, corrupt, and authoritarian regime" whose loss in the war resulted from "their myopic refusal" to "reform their armies and mount offensives against the Japanese" as Stilwell had instructed them to do.[18] Van de Ven argues that this view of Stilwell and Chiang first emerged to deflect criticism from FDR when the war in China was facing setbacks just before the 1944 presidential elections.[19] Under President Harry Truman the Stilwell myth served the interests of American constituencies who were arguing over whether and how to intervene on behalf of the Nationalists in China's civil war.[20] Van de Ven argues that the Stilwell narrative covered up Stilwell's pervasive paternalism toward China that was also widespread among American personnel in China during World War II and an outdated emphasis on infantry offensive, which led to some dramatic military failures under Stilwell's watch.

This book fills an important gap in the history of US-China relations by incorporating the story of the Dixie Mission into a narrative that reflects the significance of van de Ven's findings. Van de Ven's work influenced scholarship on US-China relations that has emerged in the past two decades. However, few of the key books about the history of US-China relations published during this time frame make more than a passing mention of the Dixie Mission. In fact, the most recent academic studies that have included a significant focus on the Dixie Mission predate van de Ven's intervention. Maochun Yu's *OSS in China: Prelude to Cold War* was the first book-length effort to disentangle the politicized and contradictory historical records about how the OSS operated in China. Yu shouldered the challenge of being one of the first historians to plow the voluminous declassified records. *OSS in China* is an important reference of lasting value that analyzes US intelligence in China primarily from the OSS perspective. This book builds on Yu's work by incorporating the findings of scholars like van de Ven about the broader philosophical basis of US military efforts in China during World War II. It also seeks to center the Dixie Mission as the locus of first official contact between the United States and the CCP and as an example of an interagency intelligence mission during World War II.

Another study of the Dixie Mission published in the 1990s, *Mission to Yenan: American Liaison with the Chinese Communists, 1944–1947* by Carol Carter, is a synthesis of extensive oral history interviews the author performed with the Dixie Mission participants.[21] Carter's book succeeds in humanizing the Dixie Mission participants and brings to light the stories they remembered of what happened during the time they served. The details and anecdotes the book contains are unique and of tremendous value to historians. However, one risk of relying on oral histories is that memories are slightly imperfect. Carter's book shows the vulnerability of this effect when memories of the Dixie participants contradict each other and sometimes contradict the declassified government records. *Mission to Yenan* focuses on the people in the Dixie Mission, but it does not seek to change the trajectory of the historiographical debates about either the policy outcomes or the intelligence processes involved.

Since *OSS in China* and *Mission to Yenan* were published, only a few authors have dipped into declassified OSS and State Department records about US-CCP relations during World War II. The most important monographs have done so with the specific intention of updating accounts of US-China relations in the 1940s for popular audiences. Their authors are prominent journalists who did not seek to intervene in scholarly debates. The best of these monographs include Richard Bernstein's *China, 1945*, Kevin Peraino's *A Force So Swift: Mao, Truman, and the Birth of Modern China, 1949*, and Daniel Kurtz-Phelan's *The China Mission: George Marshall's Unfinished War, 1945–1947*. These books take a top-down approach focused on the role of policymakers in shaping the bilateral relationship.

SOURCES AND METHODS

The Dixie Mission case presented here embarks from two theoretical and methodological influences: both a cultural historian's approach and a compelling argument for scholars to reinvoke the social historian's tool kit to expand the boundaries of intelligence history. My reasoning embraces historian Richard Aldrich's theoretical argument that the evolution of American national security institutions in the aftermath of World War II, particularly the procedures used in the collection of foreign intelligence and covert actions abroad, are intricately related to changing American attitudes about the implications of global decolonization in the postwar decades.[22] Aldrich has demonstrated that conflicting, volatile, and frequently subconscious American attitudes about international human rights, democratization, and imperialism's potential for violence shaped both policy motivations and intelligence practices in East Asia in World War II.

Records from the Dixie Mission put a personal face on Aldrich's ideas. The Dixie Mission reveals important tangible examples of how individual American intelligence officials attempted to make decisions about communications and resources that could either reinforce or undermine American philosophical priorities for which the ranking was in flux. These ranged from expelling the Japanese occupiers from China to establishing a liberal representative democracy in China to rejecting the visible corruption of the Chinese central government in the early 1940s. *Mission to Mao* is a social history of US intelligence focused on the role of human relationships, social networks, factions, rivalries, and personalities involved in the Dixie Mission—a roots-up, everyday perspective on events. This approach pushes presidents, ministers, secretaries, and ambassadors to the periphery. It instead focuses on the routine activities of the individual US officials who ate watermelon with Mao Zedong and coped with a lack of plumbing and heat in order to research and compose intelligence reports in Yan'an in the mid-1940s.

This book thus contributes to the growing body of studies that seek to bring the benefits of the so-called social and cultural turns firmly into the study of intelligence—a pivot that is long overdue. Christopher Richard Moran and Andrew Hammond make a powerful argument for a social turn in intelligence studies in an article in a special issue of *Cambridge Review of International Affairs* devoted to the topic.[23] They suggest that intelligence historians often act as "refugees" from official diplomatic history, which usually privileges archives, policies, leaders, and major operational successes and failures. These topics are important, but they are also threatening to make intelligence history a stale subfield, squandering the vibrancy of what are essentially true spy stories. Moran and Hammond admit that social history is difficult to precisely define. The diversity within the approach is part of its value to this project.

My work borrows several techniques from social historians. I use a bottom-up rather than top-down approach. My emphasis is on US intelligence officials, including those at the lowest levels of their respective organizations. This work both moves beyond the archives and reads the archives in a new way. Declassified records from official archives are an important part of US intelligence history, but these are not the only interesting and relevant sources for a full understanding of the historical situation. Furthermore, archival documents related to intelligence from the Chinese perspective are not always available or accessible. The personal papers and memoirs of former Dixie Mission participants are the backbone of this project, and I put these in conversation with official records. To perform this task, I use both vertical and horizontal perspectives on the US government in China during World War II. The vertical approach takes readers from the point of information collection in Yan'an through Chongqing to New Delhi, to the White House, and back.

The horizontal approach facilitates analysis of collaboration and rivalries that affected the ability (or lack thereof) for US intelligence officials in China to conduct their work. In these ways, this project performs the paradigm shift that Moran and Hammond recommend: "Bringing the social in from the cold" and "moving from the upstairs to the downstairs of international relations."[24]

This book draws upon a carefully curated mosaic of sources written in English and in Chinese, but American sources outnumber Chinese sources by a wide margin. This is mostly due to the book's scope and its narrow focus on individual American intelligence officials who visited Yan'an between 1944 and 1947. *Mission to Mao* is the story of US intelligence officials getting in their own way in Yan'an and Chongqing. Because the book's core argument is focused on US actors, it has not required the same kind of comprehensive engagement with archival materials produced by Chinese counterparts of the American subjects that a book on a broader aspect of US-CCP relations would.

Rather than welcoming scholars into archives, the Chinese government has long preferred to curate records into published volumes that are widely available in university libraries. I have cited English translations of these materials, when they exist, to facilitate further study by the broadest likely audience of this book. Researchers have been largely unable to investigate the potential for lacunae in these volumes because archival access is severely limited. Policies and norms have prevented both Chinese and foreign researchers from exploring archives in China for decades. Pandemic policies and rising tension between the United States and China have further reduced archival permits for US scholars. Chinese researchers also face various kinds of censorship. Perhaps for this reason, secondary sources published in Chinese did not offer more or different insight on the Dixie Mission than studies published in English. I have cited Chinese sources only when they offer a unique perspective beyond what is available in the English language sources.

US government records and personal papers related to the US officials who staffed the Dixie Mission and conducted intelligence in China during World War II present a sharp contrast to Chinese-language material in their sheer abundance. The controversy surrounding the Dixie Mission has led policymakers, journalists, and scholars throughout the twentieth century to lobby successfully for the declassification and release of volumes of documentary material about its activities.[25] The Dixie Mission included the participation of virtually every US agency involved in intelligence collection at the time. Thus, declassified documents offer a rare opportunity to compare the reactions of each agency to events and to the activities of other agencies as well as to review how and to what extent the agencies communicated with each other. As these official documents have surfaced, individuals implicated in the documents often have produced their own explanations and recorded their memories in the form of memoirs, personal letters, and interviews.[26] All these materials form the rich and extensive source base undergirding this work.

A HUMAN-CENTERED INTELLIGENCE HISTORY

By turning the lens to US intelligence officials, particularly those serving in remote field locations and from an interagency—not exclusively OSS—approach, this book forms an important new bridge between recent scholarship on the history of US-China relations in World War II and emerging studies that are adapting theoretical methodologies from social and cultural history to benefit US intelligence history. *Mission to Mao* moves beyond the accepted twentieth-century historiography of the Dixie Mission to examine the case through a new line of inquiry: the history of US intelligence activities in World War II from the bottom up. The Dixie Mission's history has important lessons still to reveal, not just about US-China relations but also about the people who Michael H. Hunt calls "cultural intermediaries" in their intelligence roles in World War II. US leaders in the 1940s initially addressed their knowledge gap on China by seeking personnel who had extensive experience living in China and who spoke the language. This cohort of Americans had collective characteristics that influenced how they conducted intelligence operations, especially in Yan'an.

The Dixie Mission failed to live up to the potential its architects had imagined for either intelligence or diplomacy. The initial members of the Dixie Mission ultimately became victims of the immature intelligence system of which they were a part because their policymaker audience was unfamiliar with Chinese politics and unprepared for their messages. Moreover, their ad hoc solutions to ambiguous orders and remote conditions triggered fear, rivalry, and risk aversion among their superiors. When the activities of US officials at Yan'an created controversy in the winter of 1944–45, US leaders took the opposite approach to recruitment. Starting in 1945 they dispatched to Yan'an mostly US officials who had no special expertise on China. This had the effect of making the US outpost there less collegial to the CCP and less effective at collecting actionable intelligence. The dysfunction and disunity that the American delegation to Yan'an displayed in its three-year existence distanced and betrayed Chinese leaders in both the Guomindang and the CCP.

Previous scholarly debates about the implications of the Dixie Mission have prioritized the analysis of high-level policy outcomes and the actions of top leaders as well as the fervent anti-Communism of the time as contributing influences on American strategic behavior. Consequently, historians have generally assumed that anti-Communism was the most important factor shaping US intelligence about the CCP in the 1940s. This focus on anti-Communism is outdated. It oversimplifies the evolution of attitudes about Communism among

American strategic decision-makers, it undervalues what US officials in China evaluated to be the temptations of their liberal ideology for China counterparts, and it overstates the influence of anti-Communism in US-China policy prior to the late 1940s.

In fact, evidence from the Dixie Mission demonstrates that inefficiency and unprofessionalism within the US intelligence process were equally important, if not more influential, than anti-Communism in determining what information top US leaders received about China's Communists throughout World War II. This inefficiency and unprofessionalism resulted from inexperienced personnel, interagency friction, policymakers who were unaccustomed to handling strategic intelligence, and a dramatic and abrupt expansion of the American national security regime under the Truman administration. The ideology that mattered more than Communism to the Dixie Mission was American-style imperialism, which inflected the intentions of US officials dispatched to Yan'an. The details of the Dixie Mission point to the implications of the asymmetry between what top US diplomatic and military leaders were asking intelligence officials to do in the field in service of that ideology and what services the rudimentary US intelligence bureaucracy could realistically provide.

NOTES

1. US National Archives and Records Administration (hereafter NARA), RG 226, entry 146, box 192, folder 2723; and David D. Barrett, *Dixie Mission: The United States Army Observer Group in Yenan, 1944* (Berkeley: Center for Chinese Studies, University of California, Berkeley, 1970).
2. The ruling party in China during World War II was named 国民党, rendered in the Roman alphabet as either "Guomindang" or "Kuomintang" and translated as "Nationalist Party."
3. Barrett, *Dixie Mission,* 69. All direct quotes related to this tale are Barrett's.
4. See Edna Tow, "The Great Bombing of Chongqing and the Anti-Japanese War, 1937–1945," in *The Battle for China: Essays on the Military History of the Sino-Japanese War*, ed. Mark Peattie, Edward Drea, and Hans van de Ven (Stanford, CA: Stanford University Press, 2010), 256–82.
5. Barrett, *Dixie Mission,* 69. This direct quote uses an older spelling of the CCP headquarters city. 延安 is written as "Yan'an" in the Pinyin romanization system used in the People's Republic of China today.
6. Barrett, *Dixie Mission,* 69.
7. Several recent studies of US foreign relations in the late nineteenth century and the interwar period have clarified the effects of US imperialism in East Asia and the Caribbean, such as Mary A. Renda, *Taking Haiti: Military Occupation and the Culture of U.S. Imperialism, 1915–1940* (Chapel Hill: University of North Carolina Press, 2004); and, specifically related to China, Zach Fredman, *The Tormented Alliance: American Servicemen and the Occupation of China, 1941–1949*

(Chapel Hill: University of North Carolina Press, 2022). Among others, see also Alan McPherson, *The Invaded: How Latin Americans and Their Allies Fought and Ended U.S. Occupations* (Oxford: Oxford University Press, 2014); and Ellen D. Tillman, *Dollar Diplomacy by Force: Nation-Building and Resistance in the Dominican Republic* (Chapel Hill: University of North Carolina Press, 2016).

8. After coming under the scrutiny of McCarthy, Davies and fellow Foreign Service Officer John S. Service both faced legal and professional consequences from their work in the Dixie Mission. See E. J. Kahn, *The China Hands: America's Foreign Service Officers and What Befell Them* (New York: Viking, 1976), 56.
9. Maochun Yu, *OSS in China: Prelude to Cold War* (Annapolis, MD: Naval Institute Press, 1996), xii.
10. Barbara Tuchman, *Stilwell and the American Experience in China, 1911–45* (New York: Macmillan, 1970), xii.
11. Regardless of their startling degree of politicization, some of the studies published in the 1950s and 1960s about the US intervention in China in the 1940s remain useful to today's scholars for their ability to accurately preserve contemporaneous historical details. For example, Herbert Feis's Pulitzer Prize–winning book, *The China Tangle: The American Effort in China from Pearl Harbor to the Marshall Mission* (Princeton, NJ: Princeton University Press, 1953), and works by Charles F. Romanus and Riley Sunderland about Stilwell's actions in China, e.g., *United States Army in World War II: China, Burma, India Theater* (Washington, DC: Office of the Chief of the Army, US Department of Defense, 1953), remain in some ways the definitive texts for establishing the timeline of events in US-China relations in World War II.
12. Examples of such studies include Benjamin I. Schwartz, *Chinese Communism and the Rise of Mao* (Cambridge, MA: Harvard University Press, 1951); and Stuart R. Schram, *Mao Tse-tung*, reprt. ed. (Baltimore: Penguin, 1967). For more on the sources and effects of politicization on Cold War–era studies of the early PRC and the changes in the past two decades that have increased scholarly interest in early PRC history, see Julia Strauss, "Introduction: In Search of PRC History," *China Quarterly* 188 (December 2006): 856–57.
13. Relevant memoirs, either autobiographical or ghost-written, published in this period include Barrett, *Dixie Mission*; John S. Service, *Lost Chance in China: The World War II Despatches of John S. Service*, ed. Joseph E. Esherick (New York: Random House, 1974); and Ivan D. Yeaton, *Memoirs of Ivan D. Yeaton* (Stanford, CA: Hoover Institution Press, 1976). Memoirs and biographies continued to appear throughout the 1980s and 1990s.
14. Kahn, *The China Hands.*
15. Chen Jian, "The Myth of America's 'Lost Chance' in China: A Chinese Perspective in Light of New Evidence," *Diplomatic History* 21, no. 1 (Winter 1997): 77–86; and Michael M. Sheng, "Chinese Communist Policy toward the United States and the Myth of the 'Lost Chance' 1948–1950," *Modern Asian Studies* 28, no. 3 (July 1994): 475–502.
16. Chen, "The Myth of America's 'Lost Chance,'" 77.
17. For examples, see Hans van de Ven, *War and Nationalism in China, 1925–1945* (London: RoutledgeCurzon, 2003); Frederic Wakeman Jr., *Spymaster: Dai Li and the Chinese Secret Service* (Berkeley: University of California Press, 2003); Jay Taylor, *The Generalissimo: Chiang Kai-shek and the Struggle for Modern China*

(Cambridge: Belknap Press of Harvard University Press, 2009); and Alexander V. Pantsov, *Victorious in Defeat: The Life and Times of Chiang Kai-shek, China, 1887–1975* (New Haven, CT: Yale University Press, 2023).

18. Hans van de Ven, "Stilwell in the Stocks: The Chinese Nationalists and the Allied Powers in the Second World War," *Asian Affairs* 34, no. 3 (2003): 243.
19. Van de Ven, 244.
20. Van de Ven, *War and Nationalism in China*, 3.
21. Carolle J. Carter, *Mission to Yenan: American Liaison with the Chinese Communists, 1944–1947* (Lexington: University Press of Kentucky, 1997).
22. Richard J. Aldrich, *Intelligence and the War against Japan: Britain, America, and the Politics of Secret Service* (Cambridge: Cambridge University Press, 2000).
23. Christopher Richard Moran and Andrew Hammond, "Bringing the 'Social' In from the Cold: Towards a Social History of American Intelligence," *Cambridge Review of International Affairs* 34, no. 5 (2021): 616–36.
24. Moran and Hammond, 622, 632.
25. The US National Archives and Records Administration makes available to researchers the declassified records associated with the OSS in the CBI Theater as well as the separate records of various agencies serving there. Additional Dixie Mission records were declassified and published by the US government as *China White Paper: U.S. Relations with China, with Special Relations to 1944–1949* (Washington, DC: Government Printing Office, 1949), which was intended to support the congressional hearings regarding the "loss" of China and failure of US China policy; and *The Amerasia Papers: A Clue to the Catastrophe of China* (Washington, DC: Government Printing Office, 1970) was prepared as part of investigations into the activities of John S. Service and other US Foreign Service Officers who were suspected of leaking sensitive official information.
26. In addition to a long list of memoirs published by individuals involved in the US Observer Group at Yan'an, many personal letters between Dixie Mission participants that circulated in the 1970s and 1980s have been preserved in archival collections of the participants' papers. Some of these letters are held at the Bancroft Library at the University of California, Berkeley, and at the Hoover Institution at Stanford University. The letters often offer more candid analysis and opinions than the contemporaneous official records, but they also introduce the historian's challenge of analyzing memory—a very imperfect source.

1

THE ROOTS OF AMERICAN INTELLIGENCE ON CHINA

This habit of trying to make other lands just like our own is a major failing of many American minds.

—Milton "Mary" Miles

The Yongding River is a silty stream that curves through Beijing. A thousand years of Chinese rulers have attempted to tame the river's unfixed flow with hydraulic inventions, canals, and bridges. The fierce carved lions and eleven strong granite arches that comprise the Lugou Bridge (卢沟桥) already spanned the river when Marco Polo crossed it in the thirteenth century. David Barrett, then a US Army major, thus knew it as the Marco Polo Bridge. On July 8, 1937, Barrett was serving as an assistant to Joseph Stilwell, who was then a colonel and the US military attaché to China. That day Stilwell dispatched Barrett to the bridge to check out rumors of a Sino-Japanese skirmish. Some in Beijing were saying the Japanese had destroyed the bridge. Barrett drove the 1929 Dodge used by the attaché's office for such tours to investigate.[1]

Barrett was something of an authority at running down such rumors. At age forty-five in 1937, he had spent more than a decade in the Beijing area doing such work. Barrett had interviewed warlords all over northern China, using fluency in the Chinese language that he had developed in rigorous study and practice since the early 1920s.[2] In the spring of 1937 Barrett had been closely following Japanese maneuvers around the main railway that connected Beijing and the major port city of Tianjin. Japanese troops had gathered near this railway, which ran parallel to the Marco Polo Bridge, less than fifteen miles west of Beijing. The small stretch of railway was the last route out of Beijing that the Japanese did not control. Yet.

Barrett arrived at the bridge on the morning of July 8 to find it intact and unexpectedly quiet. Morning sun glared off the carved stone lions that decorated the bridge, so Barrett had to move toward the Japanese platoon gathered further down the bridge. Looking between the troops to see what they were guarding, Barrett found the body of a Japanese soldier, shot dead the night before, presumably by the Chinese troops on the other side of the bridge. Barrett knew the death would serve as the pretext that the Japanese needed to invade the city. All hell was about to break loose.

People in China remember the incident at Marco Polo Bridge as the trigger point that touched off Japan's occupation of China. Barrett was one of a relatively small number of Americans living in China while working for the US government or military in the 1930s, and he was one of the first witnesses to this event. He, Stilwell, and his colleague and lifelong friend Frank "Pinky" Dorn got busy writing up what they had observed, to send back to Washington, DC.[3]

Barrett, Dorn, and Stilwell were what American intelligence collectors in China looked like before World War II. A handful of diplomats and attachés reporting out gossip from Beijing, Nanjing, and Shanghai plus a few naval officers with US Office of Naval Intelligence (ONI) billets were all that comprised the US system for gathering intelligence in China after World War I. They had been drafted into intelligence duties that served a different demand than the intelligence work that World War II required. World War II changed US intelligence, expanding the definition of what US intelligence meant in Washington, DC, and how policymakers planned to use it. The transition was messy, competitive, sometimes unfriendly, and even violent, but performed out of necessity.

In the late 1930s US general William Donovan recognized that the United States' requirements for global intelligence were changing and expanding. By 1941 he had convinced President Roosevelt to sponsor the creation of a dedicated US intelligence service—the Office of Strategic Services—that could perform intelligence duties deliberately, with personnel, bureaucratic systems, a philosophy, and a budget designed to match the new demands and new US vision of future responsibilities for global security. But the OSS did not replace the intelligence work that America's agencies were already performing. Instead, the OSS competed with, cooperated with, integrated with, or gave way to these older intelligence practices. Understanding the nexus of US policy and intelligence regarding China—and *who* the intelligence officers were—in the period between the world wars is essential for explaining the transition in US intelligence practices from what transpired between the Marco Polo Bridge incident in 1937 and the departure of the US military from Yan'an in 1947.

CULTURAL INTERMEDIARIES AND US INTELLIGENCE IN CHINA

Barrett and other Americans involved in gathering intelligence in China in the 1920s and 1930s were what historian Michael H. Hunt would call "cultural intermediaries" between the United States and China. Cultural intermediaries operate comfortably in two worlds, communicating in a foreign language, observing and carrying messages between a host location and their home countries. Individuals like Barrett who had spent years in China were important in US-China relations in World War II for their role "facilitating access to the other culture and interpreting it to their fellows."[4] Just prior to World War II the intermediaries serving in US government or military jobs with intelligence duties were a small cohort, but Barrett was far from alone. Others were diplomats in the US Foreign Service, such as John Paton Davies, John S. Service, and Raymond "Ray" Ludden. The Office of Naval Intelligence employed a few, such as Milton "Mary" Miles. When the OSS was established, a few intermediaries went to work there, including Charles Stelle. Of these men, Barrett, Service, Ludden, and Stelle were among the first group of Americans in Yan'an, and Davies was the primary architect of the Dixie Mission.

American cultural intermediaries already living in China in the first decades of the twentieth century were somewhat insulated from mainstream US social and intellectual trends, and yet they played an outsize role in influencing US policy and attitudes toward China. Diverse repositories of American cultural attitudes, some antiquated or heavily influenced by Protestant Christianity, informed their actions. Hunt explained that, as a cohort, American intermediaries in China tended to hold fast to "the belief in American-directed reform."[5] At times these attitudes perpetuated a form of cultural imperialism that warped the trajectory of US-China relations, especially as the intermediaries took up military and civilian service to the US government. On the other hand, having roots in China sometimes made the opinions of these individuals easy for the Washington, DC, and New York metropoles to ignore or dismiss. American cultural intermediaries in China, and their Chinese counterparts in the United States, in the nineteenth and early twentieth centuries "occupied a potentially vulnerable, even perilous position."[6] In moving between two cultures, they were not entirely *of* either.

PREWAR AMERICAN INTELLIGENCE OFFICERS IN CHINA

Most Americans who ended up performing intelligence duties in China prior to the Japanese attack on Pearl Harbor came to the work in one of two ways: either they were the adult children of Christian missionaries who had spent part or all of their childhood in China—so-called mish kids—or they were part of the US military presence in China. Both situations had roots in the paternalistic US policies and imperialist ideologies arising in the nineteenth and early twentieth centuries, particularly the so-called Open Door policy. Starting in 1898 the US secretary of state negotiated with European imperial powers that were threatening to carve up China into fiefdoms to ensure that trade with China would be defined by a policy of "fair field and no favor"—an open door. Tariffs would be standardized, and the crumbling Qing state bureaucracy would collect them. The ideological impetus behind the policy included "long-established ideas of westward expansion and moral and material uplift," which Americans saw themselves as bringing to China for mutual benefit.[7] This ideological impetus was both tenacious and subconscious. It was carried forth into US policy toward China in the twentieth century, as much via policymakers as through US diplomatic, military, and intelligence personnel. Open Door paternalism inspired many of the Americans who lived and worked in China in the nineteenth and early twentieth centuries, and it dominated US government and military institutions operating in China in that time.

Mish Kids in US Diplomacy and Intelligence in China

American children of Protestant missionaries in China from the 1910s and 1920s were frequently attracted to federal public service and diplomacy as young adults. From the perspective of the US government, they were desirable resources of knowledge about China. Scholars in recent years have demonstrated that people who participated in Protestant missions in Asia, Africa, and the Middle East in the late nineteenth and early twentieth centuries, and their progeny, formed a core constituency of the subject matter experts within the US government diplomatic and intelligence workforce in the 1930s through the Second World War.[8] Moreover, this constituency of Americans directly influenced US intelligence, which was in transition during their time of service.

The children of American Protestant missionaries in China closely observed how their parents projected American moral and ideological values in the places where they went. This served as a powerful example for many of them as they entered public service in the first decades of the twentieth century. Historian Matthew Sutton has demonstrated that missionaries and their families "often worked at the vanguard of American imperialism," becoming "an unofficial foreign service" for their tendency to represent America and American values among communities of people who had never met any others from the United States.[9] Missionaries were frequently the first Americans, sometimes even the first foreigners, that Chinese people who encountered them had ever met. These first impressions carried weight, and the missionaries took the responsibility seriously. Protestant values were intertwined with American moral, social, and political values for the missionaries, and they hoped to spread ideas about democracy, self-determination, and humanitarianism around the globe.

Protestant missionaries in China differed from expatriates who were in the country for business, journalism, or military affairs, primarily because they established more permanent connections for the purpose of helping Chinese people. The specific ideas that the missionaries held about morality, human rights, justice, and democracy became a platform of ideas and organizations abroad, which Sutton has called a unique brand of imperialism that eschews force and armies but embraces transculturation.[10] In China this transculturation was inseparable from the Open Door paternalism that Hunt identified. The missionaries' philanthropic work required communicating with people, so they frequently became fluent in Chinese, often in several dialects. Compared to the most widely spoken form of Mandarin Chinese, regional dialects range from having slight accent differences to being completely distinct from Mandarin, with unique spoken vocabulary. Once established, Protestant missions and the social welfare services they provided would sometimes last years or decades, so families established homesteads in China. New family members were born in China. Missionaries frequently set up posts deep in China's interior, where they thought people needed their help and their message the most.

American Protestant missionaries in China founded some of the most prominent social welfare organizations operating in late nineteenth- and early twentieth-century China. Missionary efforts and donations from Americans in the collection plates every Sunday funded schools, orphanages, and hospitals around China. Some of these institutions still exist; some morphed into other famous Chinese organizations. For example, Yenching University merged four Christian colleges to form a modern university in Beijing in 1915. One famous president of Yenching University, John Leighton Stuart, who later became US ambassador to China, was the son of Protestant missionaries. In the Communist era, newer universities absorbed various faculties of Yenching University, so parts of it live on at Beijing University and Tsinghua University today. Being able to translate one culture into another and back was a necessary skill for Christian missionaries in China; they were cultural intermediaries.

Historians studying missionary communities in Asia, Africa, and the Middle East have found that children of missionary families naturally transferred this aptitude for translating cultures into public service, diplomacy, and, eventually, intelligence work in the twentieth century. Many mish kids ended up in government and military jobs in World War II. Protestant missions in China, Africa, and the Middle East contributed to creating the world we know as "modern," according to a persuasive cultural study of American missionaries by David A. Hollinger.[11]

Protestant missionaries developed resilience and empathy from their exposure to the broader world, and they brought these qualities home to their American communities when they returned to collect funds and visit extended family. Despite the many luxuries missionary families had in China that the communities around them did not enjoy, life in China between 1840 and 1940 was not especially easy. Americans in these situations had to adapt and assimilate as best they could, which they did by learning about Chinese language and culture. Sutton demonstrates how missionaries themselves experienced what he calls "missionary cosmopolitanism": a lived experience of inclusion, exclusion, and identity that contributed to their impulses toward cross-cultural community-building and understanding of others.[12] Mish kids brought into government the cosmopolitanism and empathy that Hollinger has found in all missionary communities. These characteristics influenced the "mish kids" in the Dixie Mission in the 1940s. They again found themselves far from home, exposed to ideologies and customs that were new to them (in this case, Chinese Communism), and needing to explain it all to other Americans.

John Service, who went by "Jack," is a good example of a mish kid in US government service before and during World War II. Service was born in China to missionary parents who directed the Chengdu branch of the YMCA.[13] Chengdu, the capital of Sichuan province in China's far west, was about two hundred miles northwest of the Chinese wartime capital, Chongqing. Though it was a major regional hub, Chengdu was also quite remote. In his memoirs Service notes that Chengdu was much more urban and connected to the world than Yan'an, but the locations were similarly remote and unfamiliar to most Americans.

Service spoke several dialects of Chinese and had spent much of his life in China by the time the Japanese bombed Pearl Harbor. His family rotated back to the United States when he was a teenager, enabling him to graduate from high school in northern California and attend an American university. But Service had a deep personal connection to China and to the Open Door ideology that led him to seek work with the State Department. Service worked as a diplomat in China for nearly a decade prior to the Dixie Mission, was an aide to Stilwell in 1943, and was among the first Dixie Mission members to arrive in Yan'an in July 1944.

Another US Foreign Service Officer in China, John Paton Davies, had a slightly different family background than Service. He grew up in a family serving the China Inland Mission, which was decidedly more politically conservative than American enclaves operating YMCA missions or in other educational or medical missions elsewhere in the country, according to Hollinger.[14] Despite this difference in their families' efforts, Davies and Service bonded over their similarities and expertise during the war years. After the war they continued to be lifelong friends.[15]

The needs of the American expatriate community in China were different than what others experienced in most parts of the world, which in turn meant that diplomatic and attaché services in China took unique forms. The US Foreign Service dispatches a cadre of diplomats to American embassies globally.

In some parts of the world prior to World War II these posts were a political perk for elites who were close with a sitting president or cabinet member. In China, on the other hand, Foreign Service Officers tended to be heavily professionalized. Many were mish kids like Service and Davies: raised in China and bilingual. Others dedicated their careers to deepening their understanding of China. They spent years learning the language. It was rare for them to rotate to other places, and they formed a closed network, with few new diplomats rotating in unless they had or planned to acquire expertise on the region. Foreign Service Officers serving in China were "special among specialists," and China was "the only spot on Earth where career diplomats were not normally assigned to consulates unless they spoke the local language," according to E. J. Kahn, a staff writer for the *New Yorker* who documented personal narratives of Dixie Mission officials in his book in 1972.[16]

Mish kids such as Charles Stelle also found their way into the nascent US intelligence community via the OSS. Stelle worked for the OSS Research and Analysis (R&A) Branch, which he represented in the Dixie Mission in 1944. The OSS had evolved from the Coordinator of Information (COI), the first US organization devoted to strategic intelligence since the Revolutionary War, which FDR established in July 1941 under Donovan's leadership. By June 1942 the COI was split into two separate agencies: the Office of War Information (OWI) and the OSS. The OWI officially handled public diplomacy for the United States, known in some circles as "white" propaganda. These activities were made separate and distinct from other more covert forms of "black" propaganda that the OSS was assigned to handle. Roosevelt also tasked the OSS to collect and analyze strategic information the military required for fighting the war and to conduct special operations that were not assigned to other agencies. Donovan became its first and only director.[17]

Donovan went searching for personnel like Stelle because he believed that the American government bureaucracy lacked the talent, flexibility, speed, and creativity needed to meet the US demands for wartime strategic intelligence. He sought to correct the problem by hiring a collection of diverse experts and empowering them to enact their creative ideas for winning the war. One of Donovan's most celebrated ideas to improve US intelligence collection was to involve new blood in government work, and he famously raided Ivy League schools and top Wall Street firms for staff. In addition to many borrowed military personnel, the OSS workforce included actors, lawyers, professors, and socialites that Donovan recruited to do whatever unconventional tasks were necessary. Donovan envisioned a nimble new organization staffed by people to replace or override some of the diplomatic and military personnel who were performing strategic intelligence activity within a calcified and old-fashioned bureaucracy—people like Service, Davies, Barrett, and Dorn.

Once the OSS began to operate around the world, a few high-profile failures convinced Donovan that the organization had to recruit people who had a solid understanding of how things abroad worked. For China operations, the OSS ultimately hired many China mish kids, who had what Sutton has called a useful "skill set" for tracking spies, including fluency in the language, a deep understanding of China's geography and culture, and experience with trying to persuade people to change their minds.[18] Stelle was one such person.

Stelle was a career intelligence officer and public servant who started the work during World War II. He served in the China headquarters of the OSS R&A Branch China in the China-Burma-India (CBI) Theater campaign before joining the Dixie Mission. Stelle's family on both sides had been in China for decades. His relatives had performed such services as helping create one of the first Chinese typewriters, establishing the famous Lu He School, and even serving as English language interpreter to the Qing Empress Dowager Cixi, in addition to the typical service-related functions of American Protestants in China.[19] In the OSS China records, Stelle's reports to CBI headquarters in Chongqing—destined also for Washington—stand out as particularly eloquent and astute assessments of both the CCP and the internal bureaucratic obstacles to American strategic success in that front of the war.

US Military Attachés in China

Mish kids were one source of personnel for intelligence jobs in China in the 1920s and 1930s. They were distinct from the other primary source of personnel—military officers—because they chose to be in China. Barrett was typical of the cohort of American military officers in China before the war, but he was an atypical active-duty member of the US Army because he was an attaché. In his generation, attachés in general were viewed as outside the mainstream of the army or the navy. Attachés in China were even weirder.

Barrett came from an ordinary working-class family in a small mining town in Colorado. A degree earned at the University of Colorado in 1915 qualified him to teach English at a high school near Durango as the Great War picked up steam. Barrett left teaching and joined the army in 1917. He arrived in China in 1924 after short stints in Zion, Utah, and the Philippines. There he entered a Military Intelligence Division training program for Chinese language. The program eventually became what is known today as the Foreign Area Officer Program. Its first student, when it began in 1919, was Joseph Stilwell. Barrett later told his biographer that the teachers the program hired were all former Manchu elites of the sort that would have studied the canon of Chinese classical literature in their youth, with aspirations of joining the Qing civil service. American officers in the language training program spent their full duty day studying, with the first five hours of the day in conversation with a teacher or two and the rest reserved for memorizing, reading, and writing Chinese characters.[20] Learning Chinese this way had the bonus effect of educating the officers in the Chinese classics, which served as the teaching materials, in the traditional style of Chinese pedagogy. Barrett later became well known among Chinese leaders for his ability to reference these stories in conversations.

The army chose China as Barrett's posting, and he went there as part of the Fifteenth Infantry Regiment. A substantial cohort of US military attachés to China in the 1930s and 1940s had served in the regiment, which was based in Tianjin from 1912 to 1938. In the 1920s Stilwell, then a major, served as the commander of the Second Battalion, of which Barrett was a member. Above the two of them, George Marshall, then a lieutenant colonel, served as executive officer of the regiment. Marshall, Stilwell, and Barrett would all play highly visible and significant roles in advising and implementing US strategic policy in China in the 1940s.[21]

The Fifteenth Infantry was among the regiments that first came to China to help resolve the Boxer Rebellion and to protect American business interests in the Open Door era. The regiment today boasts that it has more years of overseas service than any other army regiment, including twenty-six years in China.[22] Elements of the regiment stayed on after the Boxers ceased to be an issue, intending to depart when Chinese politics settled down. This never really came to pass. Instead, the rulers of the Qing Dynasty, China's last ruling monarchy, abdicated the throne. The Xinhai Revolution in 1911 transformed China into a modern nation-state, and the former Qing subjects became its citizens. This revolutionary impulse failed to form itself into a stable, functioning, and unified government, however. China after 1911 remained too lucrative for American businesses to abandon but too volatile to embrace without the security of an active American legation to provide security and consular services.

Officers such as Barrett and the soldiers who comprised the Fifteenth Infantry were technically on active-duty deployment, but the United States was never at war with China. Their work and presence in China required them to learn the language, which resulted in the language training programs that Marshall and Stilwell attended and helped develop. Military service members in China also assumed a particularly active role as observers of political and military conflict occurring in China that would later be of interest to top brass and policymakers in Washington—the bread and butter of attaché work.

US military attachés in China before World War II invested considerable energy into developing linguistic and cultural expertise, and they possessed a unique depth of knowledge about China. By definition, a military attaché is a military officer posted abroad and based in the embassy of his or her sponsoring country to serve as an overt intelligence officer, contacting local counterparts, tracking intentions and resources of the host country, and informing his or her sponsoring government unit about information learned that could have strategic significance. The attaché typically relies on all available sources, including reports and gossip from contacts in the host country, observations of host country events and exercises, review of host country mass media, and any other relevant information that can be collected. In the 1930s US attachés in China reported information through Army, Navy, and War Department channels via the communications systems available at the US embassy (mostly telegrams or physical messages that official couriers transported in the diplomatic mail pouch system).

Officers from the army's G-2 (the staff division focused on intelligence) comprised most of the attaché positions with assistance from the navy's ONI. Stilwell became the US military attaché in China from 1935 to 1938, and Barrett was an assistant attaché at the same time. When Stilwell left the position in 1938, Barrett was promoted. Stilwell was a West Point graduate in 1904, which earned him an elite status and credibility that Barrett lacked. Stilwell began his military career serving as an intelligence officer in World War I. In his time as attaché to China in the 1930s he observed at close range the intensifying Japanese aggression in China as well as China's response to it. Barrett was at his side.

US government bureaucrats outside the bubble of China expatriates likely would not have expected attachés to be as capable as they were. This level of expertise was far from universal in the US embassy system worldwide. The US government did not send its first attachés abroad until 1894, first to Japan and then to Mexico.[23] The practice slowly expanded, and by the beginning of World War I twenty-three army and eight navy attachés were posted to US embassies worldwide—a significant increase by percentage but still a small global footprint. In the 1920s and 1930s the attaché position tended to be held by officers ranked lieutenant colonel or colonel. The position lacked prestige and rarely led to promotions, particularly for those who served in posts outside Europe. Other army personnel viewed attaché service as shirking "real" military duties, and some suggested attachés were selected "based on their good looks and social graces."[24] In the first few decades of the twentieth century, attaché billets in East Asia were among the few that did not require applicants to be independently wealthy, because the cost of living was sufficiently low that officers could live on their salaries alone.[25]

While attachés posted to China may have had a poor reputation among other military officers outside Asia, for Americans in China, developing expert attachés made sense. Consular duties—those related to taking care of Americans and their interests within a foreign country—took on a much larger share of the diplomatic effort in China than in many other parts of the world. It would be too much to call the China attaché post a meritocracy, but the US embassy in China did help develop a cadre of military officers proficient in Chinese who could support consular efforts, collect and report intelligence about military affairs, and potentially participate in the physical protection of Americans in China, if circumstances required it.

As a former attaché, Barrett possessed the linguistic and practical skills needed to function well as a professional intelligence officer and the head of the Dixie Mission. The same was true of Davies, Service, and Stelle. At the same time, their abilities were closely linked to their personal commitment to the US prewar policy in China and the paternalism of the Open Door ideology. Their experience of China had occurred in the context of them going to China to help people there and to protect US interests, both economic and moral. These values came with them into wartime intelligence as US policy in China transformed.

US POLICY TOWARD CHINA IN THE 1930s

Japan's initial incursion into northern China via Manchuria in 1931 occurred when the intensifying Great Depression and related domestic issues dominated the attention of US officials, which masked the increasing need for improved US intelligence on the region. The passage of the resolution that became known as the Hoover-Stimson Doctrine in January 1932 made clear that the United States would not recognize any territory that Japan or other aggressors seized, particularly in Manchuria. However, President Herbert Hoover failed to support Secretary of State Henry Stimson's efforts to back US opposition to Japanese aggression through military force—a policy that changed little until the 1940s.[26] The army's Fifteenth Infantry regiment was monitoring developments and sending reports to Washington, but they had orders to avoid involvement unless specific American interests were threatened.

When FDR came into the White House in 1933, he viewed China's situation with sympathy and concern but concluded that the United States could not be responsible for China's security at the time.[27] US State Department officials based in China and Washington continued to closely monitor Sino-Japanese relations in the mid-1930s, but the United States maintained a consistent policy toward China without any major developments for the next five years, until Japanese aggression in China increased dramatically in 1937 with the Marco Polo Bridge incident.

When officials in Washington received Barrett's reports about the bridge incident, they recognized that China stood on the brink of full-scale war with Japan. Chinese president Chiang Kai-shek consolidated his best German-trained troops near Shanghai, preparing for a major offensive by the Japanese. Officials at the US embassy in Nanjing—the Chinese capital city at the time—were aware of Chiang's plans, having received reports from local informers and press correspondents.[28]

Despite reports coming in from China about heightened tensions, Secretary of State Cordell Hull definitively reiterated the American policy of noninterference in a press statement delivered on July 16, 1937. Hull recognized that there "can be no serious hostilities anywhere in the world which will not one way or another affect interests or rights or obligations of this country," but he emphasized the US commitment to "revitalizing and strengthening" international law, meaning that beyond diplomatic efforts, it would not intervene in international conflicts between sovereign states such as China and Japan.[29] Domestic political will in the United States did not support military alliance with China against the Japanese.

When diplomatic channels failed to resolve tensions in August 1937, Chiang independently led the Chinese forces in a major offensive against the Japanese in Shanghai. Although Chinese troops outnumbered their Japanese counterparts, the Japanese eventually overcame them, in part due to a dramatic amphibious attack. By December the Japanese held Shanghai, and they soon took Nanjing in an infamous streak of violence in which Japanese soldiers assaulted or killed many unarmed Chinese civilians.[30] Because Japanese forces occupied key cities in China's northern and eastern regions, Chiang retreated into China's southwestern interior and reestablished the capital of the Chinese government in Chongqing.

As US diplomats and policymakers observed Japan's behavior and reassessed Japan's intentions from 1938 to 1940, American political will shifted toward supporting China for two reasons. First, emerging reports of the atrocities in Nanjing and other Chinese cities disgusted Americans and stoked public sympathy for China. Second, the violence of the Japanese occupation forces began to impinge directly on US interests in the region. For just one example, Japanese forces in December 1937 attacked and sunk the US Navy gunboat *Panay*, which was guarding merchant vessels on the Yangtze River. The incident made a strong impression on US government officials. However, the US government's initial reaction to the *Panay* incident was restrained. Although American diplomats immediately doubted whether the incident was accidental, as Japanese diplomats claimed, US officials chose to resolve the issue diplomatically rather than responding with force. The United States withdrew other navy gunboats operating in the area to avoid additional conflict.[31]

As time passed, US officials came to view the sinking of the *Panay* as both deliberate and part of a growing number of actions demonstrating Japan's vision of a pan-Asian empire that did not include the influence of the United States or the Open Door trade privileges to which the United States had become accustomed.[32] Throughout 1938 US officials in the State, Treasury, and War

Departments and the various military branch offices expressed increasing concern about Japan's actions in China, but they could not agree on the best course of action. Treasury Secretary Henry Morgenthau developed a controversial proposal to provide economic aid to Chiang Kai-shek's troops in 1938, which met with considerable bureaucratic bickering.[33] Officials from the State and War Departments and the military were unsure that economic aid would help the Chinese forces, and some officials questioned Chiang's military and governance practices. Conversely, Morgenthau was concerned about the rising threat to global economic security that he perceived from Nazi and Japanese ambitions, starting with Japan's domination of China.

Against this divisive backdrop, the combination of two other external factors finally determined the outcome of debates over US China policy: the Japanese released a declaration in November 1938 specifying a "new order" for East Asia that rendered the Open Door policy moot, and concern was growing over Soviet aid.[34] The declaration, taken together with the growing body of reporting from American diplomats and military attachés in Asia in the late 1930s and early 1940s, informed the consensus among US officials that Japan's ambitions were a serious threat to the future of US and European interests in East Asia. Policymakers were further concerned that Soviet aid would shift Chinese loyalties away from the United States.[35]

From 1939 to 1941 the United States provided economic and materiel aid to Chiang Kai-shek's military, including a cache of military equipment and supplies worth $45 million in fall 1941.[36] By December 1941 China was receiving supplies and weapons as part of the Lend-Lease policy; Gen. Claire Chennault was commanding a unit of Chinese airmen, the Flying Tigers; and American military advisers were assisting Chinese forces.[37]

EARLY PROBLEMS WITH US WARTIME INTELLIGENCE IN CHINA

The US military alliance with China intensified the need for strategic intelligence within the US government's executive branch. In this policy environment, the existence of a network of capable American experts within the embassy could help US policymakers to only a limited extent. Moreover, the policymakers themselves were not necessarily prepared consumers of intelligence. No matter what their reports said, US diplomats and attachés in China found it extremely difficult to penetrate the Washington bureaucracy or reach those in Roosevelt's administration who were able to shape China policy. In fact, bureaucrats who were outside of the China network found excuses to dismiss information from area experts on China who had lived there, calling them disloyal or oblivious to norms or political issues that affected Washington. The

American system for collecting, analyzing, and disseminating intelligence had not yet taken a cohesive form, and procedures for recognizing warnings and alternate views did not exist.

Prior to 1941 the US government had no independent agency dedicated to the collection and dissemination of strategic foreign intelligence. The Japanese occupation of China and the spread of European fascism challenged US foreign policy decision-makers throughout the late 1930s. American intelligence analysis and dissemination were performed by various agencies within the US executive branch, namely, the State and War Departments, the army, and the navy.[38] Existing foreign intelligence organizations, such as the navy's ONI and the army's G-2 divisions, were nestled underneath larger parts of the US executive branch and subject to executive branch budgetary interests. The Federal Bureau of Investigation (FBI) was independent, but it focused on domestic investigations and criminal justice under the framework of the US constitution—a completely different agenda than the collection of foreign strategic intelligence. The United States also relied heavily on intelligence shared by the British.

Although US diplomats and attachés in China were reporting potentially useful information to their sponsoring agencies, few regularized channels existed to convey the information to the White House or other relevant principals or agencies. Beyond the conversations that occurred at the White House, norms for communication between US government agencies on matters of strategic intelligence and national security were often highly personalized, malleable, caustic, or nonexistent. Rather than collaborating on intelligence matters, the government agencies that were performing intelligence-gathering duties tended to see each other as competition. Although US foreign policy, defense, and military officials were ostensibly working toward the same goal of protecting American domestic and foreign interests, they also operated out of a sense of loyalty to and pride in their own agencies and offices, reinforced by the eternal competition for budgetary resources that exists within all bureaucratic governments.[39]

Most American policymakers opposed the creation of an independent strategic intelligence agency, especially in peacetime. They were concerned that support for "shadow warfare," as the application of strategic foreign intelligence was often called, would present a conflict of interest with liberal values and protections of civil liberties. As historian Bradley F. Smith explains, "As long as the protective oceans, the fleet, and the capacity for quick mobilization did their work, it was assumed that there was little need to establish an early warning system or to accept the political hazards of setting up a European-type central intelligence service."[40] Leaders of the Army, Navy, and State Departments opposed new agencies that would reduce their influence or budget. What is today known as the US intelligence community did not exist in the 1930s, nor did a discrete legal framework that could provide oversight and institutional boundaries.

World War II and the Pearl Harbor bombing highlighted the inadequacy and inefficiency of US intelligence practices of the 1930s: no officials pursued intelligence as a full-time job, and all agencies and organizations routinely failed to communicate necessary intelligence information to each other in a timely manner (when they communicated at all).[41] The State Department's diplomats dispatched reports based on local contacts they met and news they overheard. Senior State Department officials occasionally distilled important reports and shared them with the White House. Similarly, attachés abroad would send reports to army and navy branches that were focused on intelligence: the US Army Military Intelligence Division (MID) or G-2, and the ONI, respectively. These branches concentrated on tactical and operational intelligence, given their organizations' needs.[42]

As the war in China intensified, US leaders began to recognize the inadequacy of the intelligence they were receiving from and about China. US officials tasked with intelligence collection in China felt pressure to rectify the problem quickly, not only because the information was essential to fighting the Pacific War but also because the organization that successfully collected actionable intelligence in China would gain an edge over all the rest. Donovan saw intelligence gaps in China and attempted to maneuver around other agencies to fill them, but the approach backfired. The creation of the COI and the OSS initially did little but exacerbate turf wars that had been brewing between agencies competing for intelligence opportunities, budgetary resources, and Roosevelt's attention.

THE CHALLENGE OF ROOSEVELT'S LEADERSHIP STYLE

Compounding the problem of systemic intelligence gaps facing the United States on the brink of World War II, Roosevelt's leadership style and highly personalized approach to foreign affairs undermined the creation of a cooperative and symbiotic US intelligence bureaucracy. Roosevelt tended to bypass advice from within his bureaucracy and rely instead on a few key advisers, personal contacts, and his own instincts. He regularly appointed such individuals to serve as his personal representatives or liaisons, circumventing bureaucratic protocols.[43] This type of personalized approach to leadership has strengths and weaknesses. The main strengths are often speed and decisiveness in statecraft—two characteristics that were associated with Roosevelt, to be sure. However, the value placed on high-profile outsiders to perform tasks for which those within government bureaucracies have been developing expertise through years of work can also be demoralizing for the workforce. Moreover, this leadership style can encourage excessive competition for the president's attention, and because interagency communication is not necessarily valued, duplication of efforts is common.

These drawbacks can have significant negative effects on intelligence work. The leader may not be receiving all the relevant information, and other decision-makers with a stake in statecraft actions may not be aware of all the information that the top leader knows. Bradley F. Smith cites this phenomenon as one reason FDR particularly enjoyed using emissaries. According to Smith, "in both domestic and foreign affairs, Roosevelt delighted in skirting regular channels and establishing himself as the only person who had *all* the information on a given issue."[44] Historian Miles Maochun Yu, author of the most comprehensive history of OSS activities in China, has demonstrated that Roosevelt's unilateral and personalized decision-making style had far-reaching consequences for the development of US intelligence practices, including in China.[45]

THE MAGRUDER MISSION

In a revealing example of the competitive behavior among and between US agencies operating in China, on the same day that Roosevelt established the COI (July 11, 1941), the G-2, under George Marshall, officially established an American military intelligence mission in China. Known as the Magruder Mission, after Brig. Gen. John L. Magruder, who was chosen to lead it, the mission was a deliberate attempt to preempt COI intelligence operations in China using army personnel. Brig. Gen. Sherman Miles, head of the G-2 and a known rival of Donovan, told Magruder the purpose of his mission was to "advise the Chinese government in all military matters, particularly in the use of Lease Lend [*sic*] credits or Lease Lend material which they may receive from us" and "keep the Chinese Government informed as to such military plans or progress made here as we may want them to have," such that "when we get into this war actively, the mission will be the liaison for strategic planning and cooperation with our ally, China."[46]

Magruder arrived in China in October 1941 and began serving as the official US intelligence liaison with the Nationalist-led Chinese government, a role he kept until he was supplanted by Stilwell in 1942.[47] Magruder, an army intelligence officer who spoke Chinese and had served several tours in China, including a stint as attaché (1926–30), made contacts with Chiang Kai-shek and the Guomindang's de facto intelligence czar, Dai Li.[48] Both the navy's ONI and the nascent COI requested the ability to post personnel to the Magruder Mission, but G-2 headquarters denied these requests. The Chinese government's first

US intelligence contacts were army G-2 intelligence officers. Magruder began dispatching a daily intelligence summary on December 13, 1941, only days after the beginning of the US Pacific War.[49] Incidentally, Magruder was so angered at his poor treatment following Marshall's decision to unify command of all US intelligence and military operations in China under Stilwell in March 1942 that he quit the army and began working for the G-2's major rival, Bill Donovan.

Effective foreign intelligence operations typically require the support and resources provided by intelligence liaison relationships. Cut off from such relationships in China by the army, Donovan and ONI leaders both sought other opportunities to get a foothold in China intelligence collection in 1941. Initial COI operations in East Asia flopped spectacularly, alienating officials in the State Department, such as Stanley Hornbeck, the State Department's chief policy adviser on East Asia at the time, and Ambassador Clarence Gauss, who served in the US Embassy in China (at the time located in China's wartime capital of Chongqing).[50] It was not a positive China debut for the OSS.

The Japanese attack on Pearl Harbor jolted US policy on China in a new direction. The United States and China shared an enemy. For Roosevelt, a first step was supporting China in its own fight against Japan, but without engaging US troops in that fight. The Allies appointed Chiang Kai-shek supreme commander of forces in the China Theater. George Marshall sought a high-ranking US military representative who could assist Chiang. He found his old colleague Joseph Stilwell in Carmel, California, preparing for a tour in Africa. Stilwell and Marshall brainstormed who might go to Chiang's aide. They ran through and dismissed several names. Finally, Marshall gave Stilwell "24 hours to think up a better candidate, otherwise it's you."[51] The next day Stilwell and Dorn began making their way back to China.

NOTES

Epigraph: Milton E. Miles, *A Different Kind of War* (New York: Doubleday, 1967), 491. Miles was a naval officer who served as the first head of operations in China for the Office of Strategic Services.

1. This description of the Marco Polo Bridge investigation borrows from Frank Dorn, *The Sino-Japanese War, 1937–41: From Marco Polo Bridge to Pearl Harbor* (New York: Macmillan, 1974), chap. 1.
2. See David D. Barrett, "The Guest of a Chinese War Lord: A Side-Light on War in China," *Coast Artillery Journal* 75, no. 2 (March–April 1932): 119–22.
3. Alexander V. Pantsov, *Victorious in Defeat: The Life and Times of Chiang Kai-shek, China, 1887–1975*, translated from Russian by Steven I. Levine (New Haven, CT: Yale University Press, 2023), 268; and Barbara Tuchman, *Stilwell and the American Experience in China, 1911–45* (New York: Macmillan, 1970), 164–68.

4. Michael H. Hunt, *The Making of a Special Relationship: The United States and China to 1914* (New York: Columbia University Press, 1983), 301.
5. Hunt, 307.
6. Hunt, 302.
7. Hunt, 177.
8. Important recent scholarship has explored the influence of Protestant Christianity and the Protestant missionary experience on US foreign policy and intelligence in the twentieth century. See David A. Hollinger, *Protestants Abroad: How Missionaries Tried to Change the World but Changed America* (Princeton, NJ: Princeton University Press, 2017); Matthew Avery Sutton, *Double Crossed: The Missionaries Who Spied for the United States during the Second World War* (New York: Basic, 2019); and Michael Graziano, *Errand into the Wilderness of Mirrors: Religion and the History of the CIA* (Chicago: University of Chicago Press, 2021).
9. Sutton, *Double Crossed*, 5.
10. Sutton, 5.
11. Hollinger, *Protestants Abroad*, 6.
12. Hollinger, 22–23.
13. E. J. Kahn, *The China Hands: American Foreign Service Officers and What Befell Them* (New York: Viking, 1972), 58–64.
14. Hollinger, *Protestants Abroad*, 13–14.
15. The personal papers of both these men contain boxes full of decades of swapped Christmas cards, wedding invitations, and long personal correspondence between the two.
16. Kahn, *The China Hands*, 35.
17. For a comprehensive history of the evolution of OSS, see Bradley F. Smith, *OSS and the Origins of the CIA* (New York: Basic, 1983).
18. Sutton, *Double Crossed*, 27–29.
19. Author email correspondence with son of Charles Stelle, 2021. For further on the typewriter designed by Devello Zelotes Sheffield, see Jing Tsu, *Kingdom of Characters: The Language Revolution That Made China Modern* (New York: Riverhead, 2022).
20. John N. Hart, *The Making of an Army "Old China Hand": A Memoir of Colonel David D. Barrett* (Berkeley: University of California, Center for China Studies, 1985), 7.
21. See Hart, *The Making of an Army "Old China Hand,"* chap. 1. For further on the Fifteenth Infantry, see the works of Alfred E. Cornebise: *The United States 15th Infantry Regiment in China, 1912–1938* (Jefferson, NC: McFarland, 2004) and *The United States Army in China, 1900–1938: A History of the 9th, 14th, 15th and 31st Regiments in the East* (Jefferson, NC: McFarland, 2015). See also Charles G. Finney, *The Old China Hands* (New York: Doubleday, 1961), a partially fictionalized account of the activities of the 15th, which includes comprehensive factually correct rosters for the division.
22. Fifteenth Infantry Regiment Association, "About Us," accessed May 15, 2022, www.15thinfantry.org/aboutus.php.
23. For more on the traditional role of the US military attaché and the history of the position, see Alfred Vafts, *The Military Attaché* (Princeton, NJ: Princeton University Press, 1967).
24. Hart, *The Making of an Army "Old China Hand,"* 4.
25. Hart, 5.

26. For more on US foreign policy in northeast Asia in the 1930s and the Stimson-Truman Doctrine, see George C. Herring, *The American Century & Beyond: U.S. Foreign Relations, 1893–2014* (Oxford: Oxford University Press, 2005), 190–93.
27. Michael Schaller, *The U.S. Crusade in China, 1938–1945* (New York: Columbia University Press, 1979), 6–7.
28. US Department of State, Councilor of Embassy in China Peck to Secretary of State, July 12, 1937, *Foreign Relations of the United States* (hereafter *FRUS*), *Diplomatic Papers 1937: The Far East* (Washington, DC: Government Printing Office, 1937), 138–39.
29. US Department of State, "Statement by the Secretary of State," July 16, 1937, *FRUS, Diplomatic Papers 1937: The Far East*, 699–700.
30. For a brief but clear summary of the events of this period, see Jonathan Spence, *In Search of Modern China*, 2nd ed. (New York: W. W. Norton, 1999), 419–25. See also Richard B. Frank, *Tower of Skulls: A History of the Asia-Pacific War* (New York: W. W. Norton, 2020).
31. US State Department records describe American diplomats' efforts to determine if the sinking of the *Panay* was deliberate, as well as communications regarding the eventual diplomatic response. US Department of State, "Diplomatic correspondence regarding the *Panay*" (multiple letters), August 1937, *FRUS, Diplomatic Papers 1937: The Far East*, 488–506.
32. For further on the Open Door policy or the reasons the last Chinese emperors found it advantageous, see Warren I. Cohen, *America's Response to China: A History of Sino-American Relations*, 5th ed. (New York: Columbia University Press, 2010), 11, 71.
33. This section briefly summarizes a much more detailed account of the controversy that Michael Schaller meticulously researched in the National Archives and the FDR Presidential Library in Hyde Park, New York. See Schaller, *The U.S. Crusade in China*, 17–38.
34. US Department of State, Statement by the Japanese Government, November 3, 1938, *FRUS, Diplomatic Papers 1931–1941: Japan, Vol. 1* (Washington, DC: Government Printing Office, 1943), 477.
35. Although Chinese connections with the Soviets were one factor in US decision-making about China policy in 1938 and 1939, Soviet aid to the Chinese temporarily ended in 1939 due to Stalin's signing of a non-aggression pact with Hitler. Because Japan was part of the Axis Powers, the Soviet Union had agreed not to interfere in Japan's actions in China. See Maochun Yu, *OSS in China: Prelude to Cold War* (Annapolis, MD: Naval Institute Press, 1996), chap. 2.
36. Rana Mitter, *Forgotten Ally: China's World War II, 1937–1944* (Boston: Houghton Mifflin Harcourt, 2013), 235.
37. Chennault became Chiang Kai-shek's air force adviser in 1937 after resigning from the US Army in the belief that helping Chiang through his volunteer air force would keep the United States out of the war in China. Richard Harris Smith, *OSS: The Secret History of America's First Central Intelligence Agency* (Berkeley: University of California Press, 1972), 243.
38. The key studies on this topic are still Bradley F. Smith, *The Shadow Warriors: O.S.S. and the Origins of the C.I.A.* (New York: Basic, 1983); and R. Smith, *OSS: The Secret History*. See also Jeffrey Dorwart, *Eberstadt and Forrestal: A National Security Partnership, 1909–1949* (College Station: Texas A&M University Press, 1991.

39. Conflicts between the army and the navy were particularly legendary. For further details, see Dorwart, *Eberstadt and Forrestal.*
40. See B. Smith, *The Shadow Warriors.*
41. William R. Corson, *The Armies of Ignorance: The Rise of the American Intelligence Empire* (New York: Dial, 1977), 150–65.
42. Tactical and operational intelligence focuses on issues important to the successful use of military force, including geography, weather conditions, appropriate military targets, and the strength and capabilities of opponents. Strategic intelligence typically refers to nonpublic foreign information that influences geopolitics and foreign policy, such as leadership intentions, political stability, economic affairs, and social issues within a foreign country. For further on basic definitions of foreign intelligence, Jeffrey T. Richelson, *The U.S. Intelligence Community,* 6th ed. (Boulder, CO: Westview, 2012), 1–14.
43. The characteristics of Roosevelt's leadership style are well known and well studied. See Joseph E. Persico's *Roosevelt's Secret War* (New York: Random House, 2001), an excellent detailed study of the effects of Roosevelt's leadership on US intelligence practices during his presidency. Christopher Andrew covers some of the same ground more succinctly in his chapter on Roosevelt in his book, *For the President's Eyes Only: Secret Intelligence and the American Presidency from Washington to Bush* (New York: HarperCollins, 1995). For discussion of Roosevelt's leadership style as it pertained to China, see Schaller, *The U.S. Crusade in China,* 99; and Robert Messer, "Roosevelt, Truman, and China: An Overview," in *Sino-American Relations, 1945–1955: A Joint Reassessment of a Critical Decade,* ed. Harry Harding and Yuan Ming, eds. (Wilmington, DE: SR, 1989), 64–66.
44. B. Smith, *The Shadow Warriors,* 27.
45. Yu, *OSS in China,* 5–6.
46. Yu, 8.
47. For more on Magruder, see Yu, *OSS in China,* 27–29.
48. Dai Li's official title was director of the Bureau of Investigation and Statistics. The bureau was the Nationalist Party's intelligence arm.
49. Yu, *OSS in China,* 8–9.
50. Gen. Douglas MacArthur had been opposed to the creation of OSS and he banned them from operating in the South Pacific region under his command. R. Smith, *OSS: The Secret History,* 250–51.
51. Tuchman, *Stilwell and the American Experience,* 243.

2

THE STILWELL FACTION

Can Do.

—Motto of the US Army Fifteenth Infantry Division

"You know, General Stilwell, we're just getting around to studying your reports on China," the Washington-based army G-2 staff officer said to Stilwell and Stilwell's loyal aide-de-camp, Frank "Pinky" Dorn. "How right you were in your conclusions." It was early in 1942, and Stilwell and Dorn were preparing to depart for China. President Roosevelt had made a deal with Chiang Kai-shek that the United States would support China's fight against Japan with financial and materiel support as well as training of Chinese troops. But China had to provide the troops for the fight. Roosevelt had assigned Stilwell to serve as Chiang's aide while simultaneously commanding the US forces in the CBI Theater and overseeing the distribution of US Lend-Lease supplies to China. Stilwell, an army officer through and through, was determined to help the Chinese troops mount an offensive to retake land in Myanmar that had fallen to the Japanese. He thought this would be important to fortifying roads for ferrying in Allied supplies. Stilwell turned for a quiet aside with Dorn. "My God, Dorn," Stilwell said. "Some of those reports are six years old. No wonder we're in this mess now."[1]

Dorn's memoirs relate this exchange as emblematic of the rift he perceived between war planners in the Army G-2 offices in Washington and those, like Stilwell and himself, who had spent time in China and perceived themselves to be experts on the Chinese situation. Stilwell, Dorn, and the other American military officers and diplomats who had staffed the US government outposts in China through the 1920s and 1930s were used to observing events in remote parts of China and translating what they had seen into written reports for superiors in the US embassy and in Washington. Considering the disorganized state of US intelligence collection in this period, the job required ingenuity and adaptability, with no real expectation of an audience. US government procedures for the dissemination of reports from foreign outposts were particularly relevant to each leader, office, and agency in 1942. Today's observers would recognize the reports as intelligence, but the norms for producing them and distributing them across the affected agencies were not yet codified during World War II.

As producers of intelligence reports in China, Stilwell's staff bonded over feeling underappreciated and isolated from both the main front of the war and the main strategists making decisions from afar. They believed it was up to them to invent their own means for carrying on US goals in China. This philosophy was familiar to Americans who had worked for the US government in China, as characterized by the "Can Do" motto of the China-based Fifteenth Infantry Regiment in which Stilwell and many of his CBI subordinates served. These perceptions bonded them as a group and exacerbated their assuredness that they were the only Americans in government who truly understood China—an assessment that subsequent historical analysis has discredited.

From a position of confidence in his own expertise, Stilwell led his staff cohort to subscribe to two crucial—and ultimately problematic—assumptions: first, that China's leadership was helpless to stop Japan without US support, including training and mentoring that would enable Chinese forces to mirror the structure and capabilities of US forces, and second, that Chiang Kai-shek should and would eventually agree to taking US help in whatever form it came. Time has revealed these assumptions to be flawed and symptomatic of a particular kind of paternalistic and injurious hubris. Moreover, when Chiang disagreed with Stilwell's strategies, Stilwell diagnosed the problem as Chiang's ignorance and corruption, even though historians have subsequently revealed the cause of the friction between these two military leaders to be significantly more complicated.[2] Most important for this study, Stilwell's distrust in and frustration with Chiang primed Stilwell's curiosity about ways to circumvent him. Thus, when Foreign Service Officer John Paton Davies Jr. suggested the idea of sending US officials to Yan'an to learn more about the capabilities of the Chinese Communist Party, the plan held appeal.

STILWELL'S STRATEGY IN CBI

In March 1942, Stilwell, then age sixty and newly promoted to the rank of lieutenant general, arrived in Chongqing to serve as Chiang Kai-shek's official chief of staff and simultaneously the commander of US Army efforts in China. Stilwell considered the Allied air route over the Himalayas to bring supplies into China from India as unnecessarily precarious and expensive.[3] He instead focused on helping train Chinese troops for a series of ill-fated campaigns to retake and secure a land-based route for supplies through Southeast Asia.

Stilwell took the liberty of assuming that China would be eager to receive this kind of aid. Not only was this not the case, but the campaigns failed dramatically. In one instance, Stilwell sent Chiang's infantry troops into a battle with the Japanese in Myanmar in spring 1942 that resulted in the encirclement of China's only mobile division.[4]

Stilwell aimed to design and lead reforms of the Chinese infantry forces that he thought would make them more effective in land battle against the Japanese Army. His belief in this goal emerged organically from his combat experience, military education, and the philosophy of war that emphasized infantry tactics. The problem was that Stilwell never updated his views of this approach as warfare became more mechanized in World War II and airpower became a game changer for the Allies. Instead of adapting, Stilwell fell into the grooves of his mentor's ideas and his own experiences. Gen. George C. Marshall had attempted similar reforms to amplify the offensive tactics of the infantry with the US Army just after World War II while stationed at Fort Benning, where Stilwell also served.[5] Like Marshall, Stilwell's approach to war bore the heavy influence of the American warrior ethos dominant in World War I. Jack Snyder, one of the first scholars to document the belief in this World War I approach, dubbed it "the ideology of the offensive."[6] Historian Hans van de Ven has demonstrated how this ideology negatively influenced US Army strategy in China during World War II, especially under Stilwell's leadership, and ultimately eroded Stilwell's relationship with Chiang. Van de Ven convincingly argues that Stilwell and his protégés combined the ideology of the offensive with Orientalist attitudes about Chinese civilization in their approach to wartime strategy. Stilwell operated from a view of the world in which "modern offensive warfare was associated with modernity, industrialization, honesty, manly vigor, science, initiative, mastery of nature, and progress, while defensive strategies stood for emasculation, backwardness, degeneration, passivity, traditionalism, lack of discipline, and deceit."[7] Stilwell's beginnings in the military as a West Point cadet in 1913 introduced him to this offensive warfare ideology. His experiences in World War I reinforced it, even though many infantry battles in that war were unsuccessful. Positions in army intelligence and training programs punctuated the bulk of his résumé in the 1920s and 1930s, which meant that he had lived through few actual battlefield experiences that perhaps would have forced him to rethink.

Stilwell designed his plans to support the broader Allied strategy. The Allies' plan counted on the Chinese forces to resist the Japanese until the war in Europe was complete, at which point they would discuss increasing US and British troops, support, and intervention in China.[8] US concerns in Asia took second place to activities on the European front, even after the bombing of Pearl Harbor. British and American leaders agreed on this approach at the

Arcadia Conference in 1942, when Allied leaders summarized their grand strategy for the war as "Europe First, Asia Second."[9] While the main Allied resources focused on Europe, the Allies envisioned a simultaneous "cordon of defense" with one "anchor" in Australia and the other in India and Myanmar. American airpower and Chinese forces would cooperate to expel the Japanese military from China while European allies protected India, Australia, and the parts of Southeast Asia not under Japanese control.[10] Allied leaders believed that assisting the Chinese in mounting a strong, continuous defensive position would weaken Japanese forces overall. US officials also perceived China's military to be a crucial part of a campaign to encircle Japan's forces and strangling their ability to expand further. US war planners feared that if Japanese occupiers successfully overwhelmed or co-opted Chinese forces, it would severely damage the United States' ability to bring its forces to bear in other parts of the war. Moreover, the possible defeat of China by Japan would free 600,000 Japanese troops to pursue Allied targets elsewhere.[11]

The Allies' Man in China

The Allies' plan required a strong partnership with Chiang Kai-shek, and the US military was prepared to work closely with him. Although China had experienced challenges in the 1920s with governance and unification, the world in 1942 recognized Chiang as the head of China's central government with whom alliances would form. Motivated by the nationalist, democratic, and anti-imperialist values of Sun Yat-sen and the 1911 Xinhai Revolution, Chiang's political party, the Guomindang, had established the Republic of China. China's new republic inherited some of the administrative vestiges of late Qing imperial bureaucracy. Though crumbling, this system included traditional levers of state power such as conventional military forces and an ancient tax-collection system that empowered a decentralized network of local officials that could collect taxes. These traditional measures of political power offered the Guomindang legitimacy among the Chinese population. However, the party's popularity was uneven, transitory, and not consolidated countrywide.[12] Regional warlords who had accumulated political and military power in the waning days of the Qing dynasty bristled against the unification of China under Chiang's Republican government into the mid-1920s. Chiang's authority was strongest in the urban areas, especially in the eastern portions of China—the same areas that Japan sought to occupy in the 1930s.

Chiang himself had been both a political leader and military leader for his entire adult life. He preferred foreigners to address him as "Generalissimo," referencing his position as commander in chief of China's National Revolutionary Army, the official forces of the Guomindang-led Chinese central government.

Stilwell and many others in the US government abbreviated this title "GIMO" in their communications. Chiang's fourth wife, Soong Mei-ling, assisted him in diplomatic outreach to the West. Soong, sometimes known as Madame Chiang Kai-shek, was one of several daughters of a wealthy Methodist businessman on China's eastern coast. Her father sent her to the United States to attend college at Wesleyan University, where she learned English and American social customs. Chiang Kai-shek became a Methodist after they were married.

Soong's glamorous brand of diplomacy captured the attention of the American public, particularly when she visited the United States in 1943. She addressed the US Congress. Henry Luce, the famous American journalist and media tycoon, had grown up in similar social circles with Soong as the son of missionary parents in China. Luce brought both Soong and Chiang the attention of the American public by placing them on the cover of *Time* magazine multiple times.[13] To the extent that Americans thought of China at all in the 1930s and early 1940s, they often associated it with Chiang and his sophisticated wife.[14]

The politics of Stilwell's appointment to Chiang's staff were delicate. Marshall, at the time serving as chief of staff of the army, was among those who advised Roosevelt on the choice. Marshall thought it prudent to make a dramatic gesture that would demonstrate the extent to which the United States stood in solidarity with the Chinese against Japan's invasion. However, Marshall harbored some of the same paternalistic attitudes as Stilwell. He did not trust Guomindang leadership to administer US aid directly and opposed issuing Chiang a blank check. Instead, Marshall urged Roosevelt to make US financial support contingent upon Chiang's acceptance of US military advisers.

Upon Marshall's recommendation, Roosevelt persuaded Chiang to allow him to appoint a US officer to serve as Chiang's official chief of staff, advising him on strategy, troop training, logistics, and resource allocation. Roosevelt negotiated an agreement between China, Britain, and the United States in early 1942 that recognized Chiang's command of China's war efforts and formalized the appointment of an American aide to assist Chiang with decision-making and logistics.[15] Marshall then placed Stilwell in charge of American forces in China and Southeast Asia, but he also specified that "General Stilwell himself will always be under the command of the Generalissimo."[16] Stilwell firmly believed that the arrangement ultimately put him in a difficult position to accomplish what he perceived to be his task in China. He bristled at the job from the beginning and thought he should be in charge. Marshall's time serving as Stilwell's superior at other times in their careers, including while deployed to China, should have tipped him off to the potential lack of chemistry between Stilwell and Chiang. If Marshall had these instincts, he ignored them, perhaps because army generals possessing Stilwell's experience living in China were rare.

VINEGAR JOE

Stilwell was a divisive figure, despised by his rivals as ardently as he was admired by loyal colleagues and immediate subordinates. Historian Rana Mitter has noted that Stilwell operated from "a particular way of viewing the world, and anything that ran counter to the assumptions that shaped that view was dismissed as irrelevant, or worse, maliciously intended to undermine him."[17] Stilwell's single-minded insistence in 1944 that Chinese troops should be directly under his own control is a good example of this pigheadedness. The idea that a Chinese leader would yield control of troops to a "foreign devil," even under the auspices of an alliance, was beyond audacious, especially for someone who presumed to know China as well as Stilwell claimed he did. Even Foreign Service Officer Davies, who worked closely with Stilwell during the war and who generally counted himself among Stilwell's supporters, suggested that "Stilwell's unwillingness to dissemble, to conceal his low opinion of pomposity, hypocrisy, and the sacrifice of military considerations to political expediency aroused the resentment of those he held in contempt."[18] Stilwell's personality, combined with his stubbornness and his Open Door imperialist ideology, would lead to trouble in US-China relations.

Stilwell's frustration with others who disagreed with him spilled over into a confrontational rivalry with Claire Chennault, an army aviator who commanded the Fourteenth Air Force in China from 1943 to 1945. In the late 1930s Chennault had helped train the pilots in the Chinese Air Force who became known as the Flying Tigers. As an aviator Chennault had a radically different attitude than Stilwell about US airpower and its role in combat. He also expressed doubt—appropriately—about the practicality and feasibility of Stilwell's plans to retake northern Myanmar in spring 1943.[19] This touched off a rivalry between them that was mostly instigated by Stilwell. Chiang showed favor to Chennault over Stilwell, which further stoked Stilwell's ire. The rift between the two US generals affected the delivery of communications and materiel around China during the war years, which on a regular basis directly affected the Americans posted to Yan'an.[20]

Conversely, Stilwell had fans and supporters elsewhere in the government, such as Secretary of War Henry Stimson. Stimson shared his confidence in Stilwell with Roosevelt in May 1943: "I had a good deal to do with the selection of Stilwell to go to China because of my very high opinion of him. I thought then and I am confirmed now in my belief that he is one of the very best officers we have got anywhere. For the job he holds in China I know of no other man who is anywhere near as good." Stimson appreciated Stilwell's attitude. He wrote, "I have had to deal with so many other men who sought after the good and easy things in life and war and were prompt to shuffle off responsibilities for evil fortune that Stilwell's readiness to acknowledge defeats and take the blame for situations that were not his fault has been most refreshing."[21]

Although he had support within the Roosevelt administration, particularly within army channels, many peers and observers throughout Stilwell's career did not appreciate his personality or way of communicating. Stilwell's lifelong tendency to speak his mind in an acerbic and direct fashion when teaching cadets at West Point just after World War I earned him the nickname "Vinegar Joe," which stuck with him throughout his career, as did his barbed tongue.[22] However, Stilwell's sharp style of speech reflected his personality and philosophy rather than a lack of sophistication or education. Davies emphasized that Stilwell "was often an abusive vulgarian in his speech and writing. And yet—he was also a man who had a discriminating command of the English language and who possessed refined perceptions and tastes."[23] This combination of refinement and vulgarity is apparent from his personal motto, in creative Latin, as recorded by historian Barbara Tuchman: "*Illegitimati non carborundum*," which he translated as "Don't let the bastards grind you down."[24] The motto also illuminates an attitude of superiority Stilwell frequently exhibited during his time in China. Perhaps it was easier for him to rationalize the failure to achieve his strategic goals in the way he imagined by blaming Chiang rather than by testing his own assumptions. This approach certainly helped support the "Stilwell myth" during and after the war. As van de Van writes, Stilwell "began to think of himself as the one man who could save China."[25]

EARLY SETBACKS IN THE CBI CAMPAIGN

Stilwell's position in CBI was well underway before the idea of reaching out to the Chinese Communists surfaced. When Stilwell's land-based campaigns failed to meet quick success, instead of interrogating the plans for weaknesses, he blamed the problems on Chiang and his troops and asked his staff to think of alternative counterparts in China. Stilwell identified two factors he faced when cooperating with Chinese Nationalist allies. The first was that Chinese troops and their leadership refused to take the kind of offensive positions against the Japanese that Stilwell advised. The most recent historical analysis, which includes Chinese records, suggests that Chinese troops definitely *did* resist Stilwell's advice to pursue offensive positions in infantry formations because they usually ended up being unsuccessful bloodbaths motivated by Stilwell's outdated World War I combat philosophy. Stilwell perceived that the failure of these tactics was not due to the planning but to the low modernization and motivation of the Chinese troops, which led them to fail at executing the offensive campaigns.

Stilwell's relationship with Chiang was the second reason he offered for the slow pace of Allied progress in pushing the Japanese out of China in 1942 and 1943. Chiang proved himself to be a recalcitrant partner. He did not appreciate Stilwell's condescending attitude nor his World War I–era tactics. Chiang expressed to Roosevelt and others that he deserved more respect from Stilwell, hinting that the American general's behavior and words bordered on insubordination. Stilwell's preserved statements and writings regularly display an intrinsic imperial hubris that gives credence to Chiang's complaints. Stilwell once remarked to a journalist, "If I can prove the Chinese soldier is as good as any Allied soldier, I'll die happy."[26] Stilwell diagnosed the challenge in getting the Chinese military to fight according to his recommended plans was as much a problem with the leadership as with the troops. The issue went from the troops all the way up to the Generalissimo himself, in Stilwell's mind. Stilwell and protégé David Barrett were both quoted as saying, "The Chinese soldier is excellent material, wasted and betrayed by stupid leadership."[27] Chiang probably never intended to carry out Stilwell's plans. However, Stilwell never appears to have doubted the nature of the plans themselves. The United States was coming to help China, whether China wanted the help or not.

Efforts to motivate Chinese counterparts and their troops toward the efforts Stilwell designed seemed to Stilwell and his network to grow more futile as the war ground on, which inflamed frustrations within the US Army and with those who backed Stilwell. Many, but not all, American leaders shared Stilwell's assumptions that China needed and would accept military help from the United States. Stilwell experienced his first significant clash with Chiang over the retreat of Chinese troops from a 1943 battle with the Japanese in what is now Myanmar.[28] Troops were fighting over one of the major supply lines through Indochina that would allow whichever army controlling it to transport materiel and personnel to the front lines. Without this land-based route, all Allied aid would need to enter China by air, which was more expensive and riskier. Stilwell wanted the Chinese to stand and fight over the route, despite being outnumbered. Chiang appropriately thought retreat or greater use of airpower were the wiser courses of action. Lacking complete control of the airpower options, he defaulted to lagging and retreat.

By this time Stilwell had surrounded himself with a cohort of capable aides who seemed to share many aspects of his worldview. Pinky Dorn was at his side. Dorn had requested from the State Department and received a detail of Foreign Service Officers: John Paton Davies, Jack Service, John Emmerson, and Ray Ludden. Stilwell's aides shared his disappointment with the war's progress in China, which they attributed directly to Chiang's leadership, or lack thereof.

Davies wrote a detailed report on his observations in China, dispatched to colleagues at the State Department in 1943: "It would be naive in the extreme to suggest that all he [Stilwell] has to do to make China an aggressive factor in the war against Japan is to place lend-lease arms in Chinese hands and in consultation with the Generalissimo issue orders for the attack."[29] In fact, Davies explained, Stilwell's only options were to "argue, plead and bargain." Reconsidering outdated tactics or embracing airpower were not among the possibilities that Davies mentioned.

Two competing versions of cultural essentialism emerged in discussions of how to work with Chiang. Roosevelt learned of Stilwell's carrot-and-stick approach to dealing with Chiang and became angry. According to Davies, the president informed Marshall in 1943 that when it came to working with Chiang, stern bargaining was "exactly the wrong approach in dealing with Generalissimo Chiang."[30] This was because, being "a Chinese," the "Gimo" could not be expected "to use the same methods that we do." Davies and others in the Stilwell network at the time fumed at this perception. As Davies explained, "the fact of the matter, of course, was that being a Chinese, Chiang was from childhood habituated to bargaining—and maintained himself in such power as he possessed domestically through bargaining."[31]

The opposing assumptions of both Roosevelt and Davies on Chiang's character and how it related to the culture that birthed him were sufficiently sweeping and radicalized generalizations to seem downright offensive by twenty-first-century standards. The difference in their views nonetheless reflects two conclusions that affect the history of the Dixie Mission and US relations with the CCP: that the White House and US "subject matter experts" on China did not operate from a consensus opinion about China's leadership, and that Stilwell was in a very difficult position for achieving the orders he had been given but not in the way he thought the work should be done. Seemingly incapable of self-reflection that would lead him to question his plans and the real reasons behind challenges, Stilwell instead became open to alternatives to working with Chiang at all.

INTELLIGENCE STRUGGLES IN CHONGQING

Although improved intelligence reporting might have helped resolve some of the problems that emerged during the US military's cooperation with China, the methods for collecting, analyzing, and disseminating such information were in development. As an attaché earlier in his career, Stilwell had participated in intelligence collection. When he arrived in Chongqing in March 1942, Stilwell was more prepared to be a consumer of intelligence than a collector. His position in CBI required him to oversee intelligence operations within CBI from a high level, and he became increasingly interested in the process. Within days of Stilwell's arrival in Chongqing, the first officer dispatched by the Coordinator of Information to collect intelligence in China also arrived. The COI was the predecessor to the Office of Strategic Services, led by William Donovan. The COI had sent Esson Gale to recruit Korean exiles living in Chongqing to participate in the collection of secret intelligence and conduct sabotage throughout East Asia in a plan modeled after standard British intelligence practices of the time. Gale, chairman of the Department of Far Eastern Studies at the University of California at Berkeley prior to joining the COI, was part of Donovan's R&A Branch and had no previous intelligence experience.[32] Gale's orders were to circumvent State Department and G-2 personnel already operating in the region and instead cooperate directly with the British intelligence officers based at the British embassy in Chongqing.

The plan reflected the COI's lack of awareness of the situation in China, where seasoned officials from the US Army G-2 Intelligence Division, military attachés working in the US embassy, and Foreign Service Officers had cultivated their own social networks and norms. Donovan had difficulty recruiting a staff with deep expertise on China who were not already part of one of these other government agencies by the early 1940s. The sensitive nature of the work required US citizens to staff the organization, but the work itself required intensive cultural knowledge of foreign places. Donovan found support for intelligence operations in Europe from scholars of European history and politics at American universities, but when it came to China and Japan, those same universities lacked a similar deep bench of experts.[33] East Asian studies at American universities did not pick up momentum until after the Second World War. Indeed, many of the scholars who founded the academic field in the United States had been OSS officers during the war, such as John Fairbank, Harvard University's famous historian of China.

In creating a new intelligence agency, Donovan and Roosevelt had imagined the COI and the OSS to base norms and procedures on the British example, at times even shadowing British operations. This approach had poor outcomes in China, where British intelligence officers suffered from their status as representatives of an imperialist power. The British had a much different historical relationship with the Chinese leaders than the Americans had, but Chinese leaders distrusted both. Even so, Chiang and the rest of the Nationalist Party targeted significant portions of their anti-imperialist leanings toward the British. Chiang disliked and distrusted British intelligence organizations; the feelings of Chiang's intelligence chief, Dai Li, went far beyond dislike. He expelled all British intelligence officers from China in 1942 upon learning that they were coordinating elaborate intelligence operations within China without his knowledge or consent. Thus, OSS personnel made a mistake in modeling their tactics upon British intelligence methods and teaming up with British intelligence officers in China.[34]

Upon arrival in Chongqing, Gale demonstrated poor discretion, flaunting his connections to the British intelligence officers and establishing an office for himself at the Jialing Hotel, where most foreign correspondents and other foreign observers stayed. Word of Gale's intentions quickly spread, stoking vehement reactions from US and Chinese officials alike.[35] Dai was among the most infuriated. The episode was one among many catalysts that prompted Dai to "invite" the British intelligence officers to leave Chongqing. By April the entire Gale mission had been scuttled. Having attempted and failed to establish intelligence operations in China unilaterally and facing the loss of British officers who could mentor his newly recruited personnel, Donovan had little choice but to partner with Stilwell. The incident laid the groundwork for some friction between the army's G-2, the navy's Office of Naval Intelligence, and OSS officers in China.

THE SACO SUCK

After learning of several attempts by OSS officers to follow in British footsteps and organize intelligence operations completely independent of their Chinese hosts, Dai required a firm agreement from the United States to share plans and responsibilities for intelligence operations in China. Roosevelt and Chiang negotiated an agreement between the US and Chinese governments to create the Sino-American Special Technical Cooperative Organization. American and Chinese officials referred to both the agreement and the organization it created by the same acronym: SACO. The SACO agreement, signed in July 1943, prevented intelligence collection by US officials in China without the awareness and express permission of Chiang Kai-shek. This agreement restrained the ability of most US government agencies, particularly the OSS, to independently collect any information that Chiang Kai-shek did not want them to learn. SACO forbade all US intelligence collection on the Chinese Communist Party. The Dixie Mission violated this agreement 100 percent.

The SACO agreement specified that a US military official would be appointed to coordinate intelligence efforts in East Asia. Operating from his typical hubris, Stilwell viewed the agreement as limiting the opportunities for the United States to achieve its goals in China. He thus distanced the army's G-2 from the collaboration by allowing the OSS and the ONI to appoint US liaison personnel to SACO from their ranks instead of sending army personnel. Adm. Milton "Mary" Miles thus assumed the role of intelligence coordinator within SACO. Miles was a Naval Academy graduate who had served the navy by patrolling the Yangtze River from 1922 to 1927. He was a contemporary of

Barrett, and they both learned to speak Chinese around the same time. Miles worked closely with Dai Li to implement joint "guerrilla training, espionage, sabotage, and radio interception."[36] The Chinese offered the human resources, and the United States contributed the funds and materiel for intelligence work under the SACO agreement.

Donovan and Stilwell did not agree on much, but they did recognize the intrinsic drawbacks of requiring Dai Li's approval for all US intelligence work in China, and together they attempted to develop legal ways to circumvent elements of the SACO agreement. Stilwell granted Miles the responsibility for overseeing the actions of the OSS in China—an action of some significance, given the broader ongoing turf wars about intelligence responsibilities and funding. Unlike Donovan, Miles deeply distrusted US officials who had previous experience in China because he believed they were greedy imperialists. He insisted that these "old China hands" be banned from participating in OSS activities in China and SACO. Miles observed that Americans who had spent time living in China before the war tended to look down on Chinese people instead of seeing them as equals. They also tended to have large social networks of other expatriates, which made it difficult for them to keep secrets, as intelligence work required.[37] Most of Stilwell's trusted aides were exactly the type that Miles shunned.

Stilwell gave over the ONI and OSS operations in China to SACO to take the pressure of Dai Li's gaze off the G-2. This effort ultimately failed due to Dai Li's excellence in performing his duties and his advanced level of "barbarian handling," as the Chinese sometimes referred to foreign relations speaking among themselves. Donovan began to see SACO as a means for wedging the OSS into China and limiting the intelligence work the G-2 could perform. Donovan thus favored maintaining SACO even though his subordinates in OSS opposed it.[38] It is worth noting that SACO was successful in the intelligence operations it undertook. It developed a poor reputation in Western historiography of US-China relations during the war for the same reasons that motivated what van de Ven called the "Stilwell myth": since Stilwell and Donovan could not control the activities of SACO, it was important to disparage it.

ASSESSING CHIANG'S INTENTIONS

As the war progressed it became more difficult for Stilwell and other US officials to cooperate with Chiang Kai-shek. By 1943 and 1944 US diplomats and attachés in Asia were suggesting that friction between the CCP and the Nationalist Party was distracting Chinese attention and resources away from their Japanese target. US officials in Stilwell's network believed that Chiang hoped to rely on American airpower to win the war and was behaving in ways that would conserve his own military resources. They claimed that he effectively intended to wait out the war against the Japanese so that he could later use his forces and materiel to fight the civil war with the CCP that he believed was inevitable.[39]

Historians have discredited this view of Chiang, but US officials in China reported numerous demonstrations of such thinking to their counterparts in Washington. In one instance, the US embassy reported that a Nationalist Party blockade preventing visitors to Yan'an in the winter of 1943–44 had tied up 400,000 of Chiang's best troops.[40] Clarence Gauss, US ambassador to China, described the problem explicitly in a January 1944 telegram: "The presence of Chinese Communist forces in North China, whose positions are expanded as the Central Government abandons them, constitutes a barrier to Central Government penetration northward; and the Chungking [Nationalist] forces are unwilling to use their scanty military resources against the Japanese when they feel the Communist problem still exists. Many military and civil officials stating that the Japanese are the secondary enemy and the Communists the primary one."[41] In the face of this rampant line of analysis among the US legation, some US officials became curious about the activities of the CCP guerrillas, who were rumored to be running successful operations against the Japanese.

THE US INTELLIGENCE GAP ON THE CCP

Learning about the CCP was no easy enterprise for US officials in any agency prior to the dispatch of the Dixie Mission in 1944. Chiang Kai-shek and his Guomindang subordinates forbade and, to the best of their ability, actively prevented the CCP from engaging with the outside world. Chiang appropriately feared that contact with foreign observers would legitimize the CCP or enable them to independently solicit foreign aid. As a result of the Generalissimo's physical blockade around the CCP base area and his prohibition on foreigners visiting Yan'an, the Communist lands were "largely a terra incognita" for foreigners, according to Barrett.[42] From 1937 to 1944 the US government lacked any regular, reliable official contact with the CCP. Foreign Service Officers based in China relied mostly on secondhand information they learned from local contacts and journalists to inform their assessments.[43]

Nationalist efforts to combat the CCP had been highly effective, particularly in the CCP's early years, when the Communists attempted to base their political movement on Soviet strategies that did not fit the demographic realities of China in the 1920s. A Bolshevik-style revolution required fomenting rebellion among China's urban working population. Urban workers in China were a much smaller fragment of the total politicized population of China than the urban workers who had comprised Russia prior to the Soviet revolution. Many of the factories that employed such workers were owned by imperial powers—British, French, German, and Japanese—that brought in military legations for protection of their interests. Furthermore, the Guomindang had consolidated political power in the cities where they were fighting the CCP. By the time the first CCP leaders collectively recognized that their urban strategy was failing, the Guomindang had decimated urban Communist enclaves and pushed the survivors out of Shanghai (where the CCP was founded) into China's southeast. Chiang's final assault to wipe out the CCP communes in 1935 prompted the famous Long March. The remaining CCP members who were sufficiently dedicated to their cause moved, often on foot, six thousand miles to the base area the party had established at Yan'an. CCP leadership remained at Yan'an until the late 1940s.

The intricacies of Chinese domestic politics at this level were beyond the scope of interest of most Americans in the 1930s and into the early 1940s. The concept of "Chinese leaders" conjured up an exclusive image of Chiang Kai-shek, if it conjured any image at all.[44] In correspondence with Roosevelt's aide Harry Hopkins in 1943, Davies wrote, "The Generalissimo is probably the only Chinese who shares the popular American misconception that Chiang Kai-shek is China."[45] Learning more about Chinese politics than this one leader's name was not a venture that most ordinary Americans pursued.

The Americans who were able to interact with the CCP in the 1930s were mostly journalists. Reporters who sought the adventure of traveling to Yan'an at this time tended to be left leaning and possessed of an idealized image of the Communist cause, which they then transmitted back to the United States in their reporting. American journalists Earl Browder, Anna Louise Strong, and Agnes Smedley all had Communist sympathies and individually visited Chinese Communists—often at great personal risk—in the mid-1930s, then wrote about their experiences for American audiences. Rather than convey descriptive details about the Chinese Communists or their base camp, their books romanticized the Chinese Communist cause and how it extended the ideological project of the Soviets' Communist International (Comintern). The accounts were often approving of the Communists to the point of appearing to be propaganda.

This sensationalism had the dual effect of attracting limited curiosity and sympathy from American readers and encouraging US officials to avoid taking many of their reports seriously. The lack of any alternate information emerging about the CCP to corroborate or contradict the tone of these reports made it easier for many US officials to dismiss the CCP's importance within Chinese domestic politics, thus underestimating the implications of partisan conflict for the anti-Japanese war.

SNOW'S SENSATIONAL VIEW OF YAN'AN

From 1936 to 1938 the CCP maintained a poorly publicized policy of welcoming foreign visitors, at least those brave and fortunate enough to evade the Nationalist efforts to isolate the CCP base areas. Few foreigners took up the CCP invitation. Among those who visited in that period, two were extremely important for the future of US relations with the CCP because their reporting alerted both American officials and the American public to their ignorance about Chinese Communism and hinted that learning more about the CCP might prove useful to crafting an East Asia policy that preserved US interests.

The first such visitor to the CCP base area, Edgar Snow, produced reporting on the CCP that reached mainstream American audiences. Snow and his wife, Helen Foster Snow (who published her own observations under the pseudonym Nym Wales), visited the CCP's top leaders beginning in 1936. Many Americans learned for the first time about Chinese Communism by seeing Snow's photo essays in *Life* magazine.[46] Snow followed the magazine articles a few months later with the publication of his book, *Red Star over China*, which describes his conversations with Mao Zedong.

Red Star over China appeared only a short time after the brutal Japanese invasion of Nanjing in December 1937, just when American public interest in China's political situation was gradually increasing. In the book and the magazine articles Snow portrays the CCP leaders as brave and committed patriots, willing to endure tremendous personal strain on behalf of their country who also happened to adhere to a socialist ideology. Snow reported a quote, which he attributed to Mao: "For a people being deprived of its national freedom, the revolutionary task is not immediate Socialism, but the struggle for independence. We cannot even discuss Communism if we are robbed of a country in which to practice it."[47] Observations such as this appealed to American values and willingness to root for the underdog. Although the sympathetic impulse would not last in America into the early years of the Cold War, Snow's work offered Americans a positive first impression of the Chinese Communist movement. Snow portrayed the CCP guerrillas as cowboy freedom fighters taking on the Japanese with little more than their wit and bare hands.

The work of Snow and other journalists had broad public exposure and may have influenced US government bureaucrats as well. However, journalism is no substitute for actual intelligence reporting. Intelligence reporting on the CCP in the late 1930s was rare and subject to the same decentralized and informal procedural norms as all US strategic intelligence at the time.

In the absence of a formalized process for intelligence collection and dissemination, one of Roosevelt's main sources of information on the CCP was

Evans Fordyce Carlson, a US Marine who had visited Yan'an in the late 1930s. Carlson received much less popular attention than Snow, but his reports of meetings with CCP members found an influential audience within the US government and the White House. Carlson had served as a language and intelligence officer in Shanghai in the mid-1930s, and he became the first American military observer to study the CCP's Red Army in 1937.[48] Carlson is also credited with introducing the mistranslated Chinese phrase "Gung ho" into the American lexicon, initially used as a US Marines battle cry. Carlson is more well known for introducing into the Marine Raider Battalion that he commanded during World War II an organizational structure and training methods he observed being used by a squad in the CCP's Eighth Route Army. The system was adopted by other battalions and became a standard operating procedure for Marine units for decades. Inspired by reading a manuscript version of *Red Star over China,* Carlson visited with Red Army leaders to better understand how the Japanese were able to defend against the CCP's guerrilla war tactics.[49] Carlson negotiated with Mao, Chiang, and US officials to make the visit happen, and he arrived in Shaanxi in November 1937.

Carlson was a charismatic, scholarly, and very religious person who identified with the egalitarian aspects of the socialist ideology explained to him by the CCP leaders he met. He found his CCP hosts at Yan'an to be cordial, and he soon became friends with Gen. Zhu De, the commander in chief of the Red Army. The CCP made an extremely positive impression on Carlson. He recorded his impressions and later published them.

Carlson's observations might have easily fallen into the morass of US government documents streaming into Washington bureaucracies were it not for one serendipitous fact: Carlson had served for a brief time in 1935 as second-in-command of Roosevelt's military guard unit at Warm Springs, Georgia.[50] Roosevelt took a personal interest in Carlson's China experiences. Prior to his departure for China in July 1937, Carlson met with Roosevelt, and the president requested that Carlson personally write to him to inform him about his observations of the CCP; Roosevelt also asked that the correspondence be kept confidential, which it was.[51] Roosevelt apparently read the letters closely and used them to inform his own impressions of Chinese domestic politics.[52] It is impossible to know for sure, but Carlson's positive portrayal of the CCP appears to have influenced Roosevelt's receptivity to the idea of the Dixie Mission when his advisers first proposed it in 1943.

After Carlson's visit to Yan'an, US government officials had only brief and sporadic visits with CCP officials. Few desired increased contact until Stilwell's frustration reached a boiling point. The small network of US officials serving Stilwell, such as Davies, became more interested in contacting the CCP in 1942 and 1943. By this time several of the factors that had prevented the

United States from seeking more regular contact with and information about the CCP had changed. Stilwell's aides were aware that CCP guerrilla units deep in China were successfully defeating Japanese units and disrupting Japanese supply chains. The Guomindang attempted conventional and guerrilla military engagements, but these were rumored to be less successful than the CCP operations. Stilwell's network of aides began to lobby for the ability to engage the CCP. Getting American officials anywhere near Yan'an would be difficult and likely impossible under the constraints of the SACO agreement. Access to Yan'an would require direct White House intervention.

LOBBYING FOR A MISSION TO YAN'AN

As resentment between Chiang and Stilwell festered in late 1943 and early 1944, a small but vociferous contingent of American officials within Stilwell's cohort in CBI headquarters and the US embassy were advocating the idea of sending staff to Yan'an. Barrett credited Davies with the initial idea for sending an American group to Yan'an. Several other Stilwell aides who had watched the CBI struggle warmed up to it immediately. Davies himself may have gotten the original idea from Zhou Enlai, who thought that engagement with Americans might help legitimize the CCP cause.[53] Richard "Dick" Heppner, OSS China, was also involved on the ground floor of the idea, and in its earliest iteration the plan even became known as the Davies-Heppner plan within OSS circles. John Fairbank in the OSS likewise supported the trip.[54] Stilwell had briefed Donovan on the idea in late 1943 and soon had his support.[55] According to Barrett, "what deeply concerned Americans was the feeling that China's effort, and the war effort in general, would benefit if all of China's strength could be directed against the Japanese, instead of a part of it being devoted to containing, and sometimes fighting, the Chinese Communists."[56] They started referring to the Communist base area as "Dixie."

Records disagree on the precise origins of the nickname. Most credit Davies with its first use in cables. Davies is known to have assembled a long list of unofficial code words for various aspects of Stilwell's plans. These code words were not meant to deceive enemies' espionage, as later OSS and CIA operational security efforts typically intended when using official code words. Rather, these names were intended to conceal certain American plans from the Guomindang officials who were present in CBI workspaces, to avoid the consequences of violating the restrictive SACO agreement. Davies, Ludden, and Service created the code words to use among themselves for plans they knew were unpopular with Chiang Kai-shek and Dai Li. Asked about the etymology of the "Dixie" term years later, Davies and Service both referenced the US Civil War. "Dixie" evoked the idea of rebel-held turf, which Yan'an was. Barrett later said he thought the name came from both this reference to the Confederacy and the tremendously popular 1930s song "Is It True What They Say about Dixie?" Jimmy Dorsey's big band version of the song skyrocketed to number one on the music charts in 1936, and the American Forces Network played it regularly long into the war years.[57]

In January 1943 Jack Service drafted the first memo to General Donovan suggesting that a US military and intelligence mission to the CCP base area would be advantageous. Service suggested that the United States send one or two Foreign Service Officers with expertise on China to "combine moderately long-term residence at Yenan or its vicinity with fairly extensive travel in the guerrilla area."[58] Stilwell's aides sent several similar memos throughout 1943 and into early 1944. Almost all received no response.[59] Distracted by the Casablanca Conference and dubious of Service's recommendation, Washington officials ignored the memos. Although Stilwell's subordinates supported the idea of sending Americans to Yan'an, the idea was unpopular with counterparts in Washington, particularly those with little expertise on China who believed that Chiang Kai-shek strongly opposed the plan. Angering the recognized leader of China, on whom the United States was relying for holding back Japanese advancement in the China Theater, was sufficient to make an American Yan'an visit out of the question.

Finally, in early 1944 one memo stirred action. In December 1943 Davies wrote to Stilwell and the Department of State, identifying several reasons why US observers must visit Yan'an.[60] The memo explained that though Carlson was the only US official to visit the CCP base, the Communists had extended an open invitation to other American observers. Davies suggested that the invitation could expire, particularly if the CCP's lack of contact with the United States led them to become more dependent on the Soviet Union.

Recognizing that most US intelligence on the CCP was secondhand or worse, Davies then wrote,

> In Communist China there is: (1) a base of military operations in and near Japan's largest military concentration and second largest industrial base, (2) perhaps the most abundant supply of intelligence on the Japanese enemy available to us anywhere, (3) the most cohesive, disciplined and aggressively anti-Japanese regime in China, (4) the greatest single challenge in China to the Chiang Kai-shek government, (5) the area which Russia will enter if it attacks Japan, and (6) the foundation for a rapprochement between a new China and the Soviet Union.[61]

On this basis he advocated that the US government negotiate with Chiang Kai-shek for permission to send a group of American military and political observers to meet the Chinese Communists at Yan'an and report back regarding their capabilities.

Davies deliberately kept his January 1944 memo brief so that it could easily be shown to Roosevelt.[62] He attached to the memo a draft of correspondence that he recommended should be sent directly to Chiang Kai-shek. This approach finally penetrated the Washington foreign policy bureaucracy. Roosevelt did see Davies's memo and within days set in motion negotiations with a very reluctant Chiang Kai-shek to allow the American observers' visit. Chiang begrudgingly agreed in correspondence with Roosevelt but delayed the mission by withholding his approval of the required personnel transfers that had to occur first.

It took several more months until consent "was extracted" from Chiang (as Davies put it). The consent only came during the visit of Vice President Henry Wallace to China in June and July 1944, where he and Chiang met face-to-face.[63] According to OSS official Charles Stelle, who was one of the first participants in the Dixie Mission, Roosevelt penned a letter for Chiang that Wallace hand delivered, requesting a military mission "in such terms that the Generalissimo found it impolite to refuse."[64] By late July 1944 the first members of what was officially known as the US Army Observer Group were on their way to Yan'an.

The late spring of 1944 marked a turning point in the US engagement in China for several reasons. The summer began just as the tide was turning in the war in Europe, opening the door for the president and US policymakers in Washington to begin focusing more on the Pacific War. US officials who had been focused on China and the CBI Theater since the Pearl Harbor attacks were becoming frustrated. Ambassador Gauss, Stilwell, and Davies recognized that their plans and strategies were failing, and they lacked the necessary intelligence to determine and implement policy adjustments that might alter the outcomes of their actions. Reforms to US intelligence practices designed to help the war effort, particularly the creation of the OSS and its early missions, had proven successful in Europe but had been embarrassing failures in China. Admitting the intelligence gap on Chinese Communist efforts was an essential first step toward recalculating how China could effectively fit into US plans to defeat the Japanese in Asia. The question remained whether the US intelligence bureaucracy in 1944 could adapt to fill the gap in time.

EXPERT PERSONNEL ASSEMBLED FOR THE DIXIE MISSION

Davies assembled his dream team of US intelligence officials who would proceed to Yan'an. The initial roster of participants in the Dixie Mission boasted the most expertise on Chinese culture, language, politics, and history of any

Americans who had cycled through Yan'an before the American offices there permanently closed in 1947. They also had experience in military and political intelligence roles regarding field conditions in China. Expertise did not immunize this crew from Open Door paternalist ideology, however. On the contrary, many were steeped in these views while living in the expatriate communities in China. With Stilwell's approval, Davies selected the US personnel initially posted to Yan'an based on their language ability and level of understanding of China in addition to their functional skills as intelligence collectors. By selecting officials for Yan'an who did not require Chinese translators, CBI Theater commanders also sought to avoid the need for Chiang Kai-shek's "liaison officers"—a euphemism for spies—to accompany the mission as translators. Stilwell placed a high value on area expertise, particularly among intelligence officers serving in the China Theater.[65] This emphasis was one of the few areas where Stilwell and Donovan agreed.

Many officials who met Stilwell's qualifications had already worked with Stilwell in China during or prior to the war. The group included a small team of dedicated and professional American officials who had frequently collaborated in the past and who had formed credible contacts with CCP leaders, even though they were slightly asymmetric in rank (Colonel Barrett was the highest-ranking member of the group). Davies calculated that sending lower-ranked US officials to Yan'an would make the mission seem less important to intelligence chief Dai.

Before Stilwell's office arranged the mission, the OSS in China had secret plans in the works to somehow send their own officials to Yan'an. Capt. Joseph Spencer, based in Chongqing, named the plan "Palisade," based on the name of his hometown, Palisades, New Jersey. Stilwell, Davies, Service, and Ludden had so effectively influenced the White House that when approval came in for the observer group during Wallace's visit to China, the White House and Stilwell naturally put it under Army G-2 auspices. Spencer's July 8 memo to Washington illuminates how Stilwell's aides and the OSS negotiated the selection of personnel. Spencer reported to R&A director Langer and R&A Far East Section head Burton Fahs in Washington that Stilwell's men had approached Stelle and invited him to join the Dixie Mission. OSS supervisors in the region, including Spencer, met and "after much pro and con, agreed that Stelle was the best man available for such an assignment and in some ways a natural for the job."[66] Spencer reported that he had conferred with Col. Joseph Dickey, head of the CBI G-2 in July 1944, and that Dickey was satisfied with the selection of Stelle. The memo emphasized that the observer group was an interagency mission under army lead, and that the G-2 interest in Stelle is what pushed his selection, even though sending him to Yan'an would disrupt AGFRTS plans in the works in Chongqing. Spencer did not take the invitation for OSS inclusion at

Yan'an lightly: "This opportunity is really a tremendous one in many respects," he replied, and "I believe you can rest assured that OSS will come out very nicely and that, in OSS, R&A will come out nicely too."

Stilwell's inclusion of the OSS in the interagency Dixie Mission made the Palisade Mission moot, which was somewhat disappointing to Spencer. "My term Palisade was coined long before I knew of the Dixie Mission," Spencer wrote his superiors in Washington. "The latter term is the one most people are using, and the one Col. Hall [OSS China deputy director] used to Washington. He knew of mine but had forgotten. Best to replace mine with the other, for simplicity's sake."[67] Spencer and others would have preferred that the OSS lead the Yan'an mission, but in summer 1944 they were satisfied that it was moving forward and that they were included.

As in other military outposts, particularly those in remote areas such as Yan'an, Dixie's American personnel answered to a US Army officer who served as head of the mission. The Dixie Mission's commanding officer was typically a colonel with a career background in the G-2 or elsewhere in the Army General Staff. The commanding officer set the tone for the unit. He held responsibility for approving all major operational plans that affected Dixie personnel and the overall objectives of the mission. He also was responsible for implementing the standard operating procedures and basic rules of the unit as well as assigning certain basic responsibilities and dispersing certain resources among the personnel (e.g., housing assignments, budget for the mess hall, and distribution of office space and operational equipment).

Stilwell chose his old colleague Barrett as the Dixie Mission's first commander. Army colonel Barrett had the right combination of language ability, credibility with Chinese counterparts, and connections and credentials within army intelligence channels, particularly with Stilwell. Barrett was fifty-two years old when he arrived in Yan'an to head the observer group in 1944, and the majority of his twenty-seven-year career in the US Army up to that point had been spent in China.[68] Barrett had served in the attaché's office in the US embassy in China throughout the 1930s. He had first served under Stilwell in Tianjin at the headquarters of the Fifteenth Infantry Regiment, where George Marshall, then a lieutenant colonel, was the executive officer.[69] After officer training in Georgia, Barrett served in Tianjin as the regimental intelligence staff officer for the Fifteenth from 1931 to 1934.[70] He officially became US attaché to China in 1942 and served in that capacity until fall 1943. By then Barrett's former boss, Stilwell, had been promoted to a much more important role as head of the American military command in China.

Consistent with the G-2's basic initial criteria for Dixie Mission personnel, Barrett was fluent in Chinese. He started studying in Beijing in 1924, so he had accrued two decades of experience and practice with the language by the time he relocated to Yan'an to head the Dixie Mission.[71] When asked about the value of learning Chinese for his career, Barrett once said, "No man can study the Chinese language and learn it . . . without at the same time coming to understand the Chinese."[72] Throughout his career in China, Barrett's ability to comprehend these classical Chinese materials and recall them in appropriate settings during conversations and correspondence in China earned him credibility with and respect from his Chinese counterparts, who recognized him as a well-educated intellectual. According to John Hart, who wrote a biography of Barrett based on extensive interviews and correspondence with his subject, "Many years later Chinese who had known Barrett would still instantly identify him as that foreigner who could quote from the Chinese classics."[73] Journalist Theodore White, who traveled extensively in China in the 1930s and 1940s and who was loyal to Stilwell's approach to China, described Barrett's rapport with the CCP leaders as one reason he was so valuable for Stilwell to have on the Yan'an mission. White wrote: "The Communists loved him; his round jokes in flawless and fluent Chinese destroyed much of their imaginary picture of calculating American imperialism. Barrett's reports on the Communists were honest, hardheaded military assessments; a soldier himself, he recognized the Communists as effective fighting men; sound allies against a common enemy. They felt his respect and reciprocated it."[74] Barrett's deep understanding of the security issues and politics of China in the early decades of the twentieth century, cultivated while in frequent contact with warlords in northern China during his work in the attaché's office, added to his credibility with Chinese counterparts.[75]

Barrett is universally described as both jovial and practical. His own statements often mentioned that he felt a special personal connection to China. He talked about hoping that he could become a general and then retire from the army to spend the rest of his life in China.[76] Little in Barrett's life tied him to living in the United States. Barrett's American wife died in 1939 in Beijing where they were living, and he never remarried.[77] White once described Barrett as "the very prototype of a regular Army colonel whose personality was adorned by a warm humanity and an overwhelmingly infectious humor."[78]

As the commanding officer of a forward-deployed mission, Barrett was the Dixie Mission's ultimate authority in the field, but he answered to a variety of other managers and superiors beyond Yan'an. When the mission launched in July 1944, Barrett served under such officers as Col. Joseph Dickey, head of the army's G-2 contingent at CBI headquarters in Chongqing, and both Barrett and Dickey answered to General Stilwell.

The initial Dixie Mission roster contained a diverse collection of officials from numerous agencies of the American government, all subordinate to Barrett in Yan'an. Relevant agencies each sent their own representatives to help meet the heavy demands placed on the mission. Moreover, no intelligence organization wanted to miss out on the opportunity to have personnel at Yan'an or be forced to receive their intelligence secondhand from a rival organization. As of August 1944, the Dixie Mission included eighteen officials from five US government agencies.[79] Most of Dixie's initial personnel were military officers. Commanding officer Colonel Barrett represented the army and, more specifically, the G-2 Intelligence Division. Other army personnel included two officers and a noncommissioned officer (NCO) from the Army Air Corps (in this case two infantry officers and an officer from the Army Medical Corps). One navy intelligence officer was also part of Dixie's original contingent.

The OSS had a fairly significant presence among the initial Dixie Mission roster, with five of the first eighteen participants working for the OSS under various military covers, including from the Air and Ground Forces Resources and Technical Staff (AGFRTS) and the Army Signal Corps.[80] The OSS contingent included Stelle, from the R&A Branch, and Capt. John Colling, from the Secret Intelligence (SI) Branch, both of whom reportedly arrived "with a big package of R&D toys" to facilitate cutting-edge technical collection from the field locations.[81] The other three OSS officials on the first plane to Yan'an were radio operators sent to install and operate sensitive radio equipment and potentially help train their CCP counterparts on how to work the equipment themselves. OSS officer Maj. Ray Cromley, who specialized in collecting and analyzing enemy order of battle intelligence, also arrived on one of the first several planes to Dixie.

Civilians who were initially part of the Dixie Mission included Jack Service and Ray Ludden from the State Department and Japanese American George I. Nakamura, who was appointed by the G-2 to serve as a Japanese language officer, assisting in developing the Japanese order of battle, according to Stelle's detailed reports.[82] These men all served under Dixie's commanding officer, but they also answered to the various other organizations that had loaned them to the mission.

The Americans assembled to go to Yan'an and meet Mao indeed were the most qualified group that Stilwell and Davies could have conjured for the assignment. Characteristics that qualified them also gave the mission a certain ethos from its beginning. The Dixie Mission cohort was confident in their understanding of the Chinese context, whether or not this confidence was warranted. They were equally confident that they had knowledge about China that their audience of American leaders did not. They were committed to the mission of the war, and they were committed to helping China. They assumed that China wanted the kind of help they could give. Barrett gathered his men in Xi'an and awaited the American C-47 that would take them to Yan'an.

NOTES

Epigraph: "About Us," Fifteenth Infantry Regiment Association, accessed May 15, 2022, www.15thinfantry.org/aboutus.php.

1. Frank Dorn, *Walkout with Stilwell in Burma* (New York: Pyramid, 1973), 29.
2. Hans J. van de Ven, "Stilwell in the Stocks: The Chinese Nationalists and the Allied Powers in the Second World War," *Asian Affairs* 34, no. 3 (2003): 248.
3. The air route, known as "the Hump," brought almost 740,000 tons of cargo into China during World War II. For further on the logistics of the Hump's flights and how the airlifts fit into the broader American strategy, see John D. Plating, *The Hump: America's Strategy for Keeping China in World War II* (College Station: Texas A&M University Press, 2011).
4. Van de Ven, "Stilwell in the Stocks," 248.
5. Hans J. van de Ven, *War and Nationalism in China, 1925–1945* (London: Routledge Curzon, 2003), 8–9.
6. Jack Snyder, *The Ideology of the Offensive: Military Decision Making and the Disasters of 1914* (Ithaca, NY: Cornell University Press, 1984).
7. Van de Ven, *War and Nationalism*, 10.
8. Mark Stoler, *Allies and Adversaries: The Joint Chiefs of Staff, the Grand Alliance, and US Strategy during World War II* (Chapel Hill: University of North Carolina Press, 2000), 79–84.
9. Maochun Yu, *The Dragon's War: Allied Operations and the Fate of China, 1937–1947* (Annapolis, MD: Naval Institute Press, 2006), chap. 5.
10. Herbert Feis, *The China Tangle: The American Effort in China from Pearl Harbor to the Marshall Mission* (Princeton, NJ: Princeton University Press, 1953), 14.
11. Rana Mitter, *Forgotten Ally: China's World War II, 1937–1944* (Boston: Houghton Mifflin Harcourt, 2013), 244.
12. For examples, see Lloyd Eastman et al., eds., *The Nationalist Era in China, 1927–1949* (Cambridge: Cambridge University Press, 1991); van de Ven, *War and Nationalism in China;* and Mitter, *Forgotten Ally.*
13. For further on Chiang, see Jay Taylor, *The Generalissimo: Chiang Kai-shek and the Struggle for Modern China* (Cambridge, MA: Belknap Press of Harvard University Press, 2009); Grace C. Huang, *Chiang Kai-shek's Politics of Shame* (Cambridge, MA: Harvard University Asia Center, 2021); and Alexander V. Pantsov, *Victorious in Defeat: The Life and Times of Chiang Kai-shek, China, 1887–1975* (New Haven, CT: Yale University Press, 2023).
14. Mitter, *Forgotten Ally,* 250–51.
15. US Department of State, Correspondence between President Roosevelt and Chiang Kai-shek, January 1942, *Foreign Relations of the United States* (hereafter *FRUS*), *Diplomatic Papers 1942: China*, 1–10.
16. Memo, George C. Marshall to John Magruder, February 6, 1942, quoted in Mitter, *Forgotten Ally,* 250.
17. Mitter, 256.
18. John Paton Davies Jr., *China Hand: An Autobiography* (Philadelphia: University of Pennsylvania Press, 2012), 100.
19. Hsi-sheng Ch'i, *The Much Troubled Alliance: U.S.-China Military Cooperation during the Pacific War, 1914–1945* (Singapore: World Scientific, 2015), 322.

20. Hans J. van de Ven, *China at War: Triumph and Tragedy in the Emergence of the New China* (Cambridge, MA: Harvard University Press, 2018), 169.
21. Henry Stimson to President Franklin Roosevelt, May 3, 1943, FDRL, President's Secretaries' Files, Confidential File, box 10, folder: War Dept. Jan–June 1943.
22. Tuchman, *Stilwell and the American Experience in China,* 123–43.
23. Davies, *China Hand,* 99.
24. Tuchman, *Stilwell and the American Experience in China,* 4.
25. Van de Ven, "Stilwell in the Stocks," 248.
26. Tuchman, *Stilwell and the American Experience in China,* 3. Tuchman quoted from Darrell Kerrigan, "Uncle Joe Pays Off," *Saturday Evening Post,* June 17, 1944.
27. John N. Hart, *The Making of an Army "Old China Hand": A Memoir of Colonel David D. Barrett* (Berkeley: University of California, Center for China Studies, 1985), 32.
28. For further details on Stilwell's campaign setbacks, see van de Ven's "Stilwell in the Stocks" and *War and Nationalism in China,* introduction and chap. 1.
29. Davies, *China Hand,* 104.
30. Davies, *China Hand,* 105.
31. Davies, *China Hand,* 105.
32. A brief version of Gale's career biography can be found in his obituary: "Esson M. Gale, Expert on Far East," *New York Times,* May 16, 1964.
33. Yu, *OSS in China,* 18.
34. For more on the problems of the links between the COI/OSS and British intelligence, see Richard Harris Smith, *OSS: The Secret History of America's First Central Intelligence Agency* (Berkeley: University of California Press, 1972), 250.
35. For a comprehensive assessment of the Gale mission and its repercussions, see Yu, *OSS in China,* 14–22.
36. R. Smith, *OSS: The Secret History,* 252. Miles documented his memories of the war in China in his book, *A Different Kind of War: The Little-Known Story of the Combined Guerrilla Forces Created in China by the U.S. Navy and the Chinese during World War II* (Garden City, NY: Doubleday, 1967).
37. Miles, *A Different Kind of War,* 119.
38. Yu, *OSS in China,* 98.
39. Mitter, *Forgotten Allies,* 325–34.
40. US Department of State, "Memorandum by the Second Secretary of Embassy in China (Davies) regarding Observers' Mission to North China," January 15, 1944, *FRUS, Diplomatic Papers 1944: China,* 308.
41. US Department of State, Ambassador in China (Gauss) to the Secretary of State, January 18, 1944, *FRUS, Diplomatic Papers 1944: China,* 6–7. "North China" was a term the Japanese military used for the region between the Great Wall and the Yellow River during the Japanese occupation of China.
42. David D. Barrett, *Dixie Mission: The United States Army Observer Group in Yenan, 1944* (Berkeley: University of California, Center for China Studies, 1970), 19.
43. Kenneth E. Shewmaker, *Americans and Chinese Communists, 1927–1945: A Persuading Encounter* (Ithaca, NY: Cornell University Press, 1971), 1–4. See also Feis, *The China Tangle,* 157–65.
44. Shewmaker, *Americans and Chinese Communists,* 6.

45. Letter from John Davies to Harry Hopkins, quoted in E. J. Kahn, *The China Hands: America's Foreign Service Officers and What Befell Them* (New York: Viking, 1976), 102.
46. Edgar Snow, "First Pictures of China's Roving Communists," *Life* magazine 2 (January 25, 1937): 9–15, and "An Army of Fighting Chinese Communists Takes Possession of China's Northwest," *Life* magazine 2 (February 1, 1937): 42–45.
47. Edgar Snow, *Red Star over China* (New York: Garden City, 1938), 455.
48. Hart, *The Making of an Army "Old China Hand,"* 25.
49. Evans Fordyce Carlson, *Twin Stars of China* (New York: Dodd, Mead, 1940), 33–58; and Michael Blankfort, *The Big Yankee: The Life of Carlson of the Raiders* (Boston: Little, Brown, 1947), 188–94. Blankfort served under Carlson in the Marines and his biography of his former commander is somewhat hagiographic in tone but useful for its well-sourced details.
50. Shewmaker, *Americans and Chinese Communists,* 102; and "Carlson on Himself," notes from Helen Foster Snow's interviews of Carlson for a potential biography, in Hugh Deane, ed., *Evans F. Carlson on China at War, 1937–1941* (New York: China and Us, 1993), 7.
51. Shewmaker, *Americans and Chinese Communists,* 102–3nn53–56. Much of the correspondence between Roosevelt and Carlson has been preserved in Roosevelt's presidential library. Selections have also been duplicated in Deane, *Evans F. Carlson on China at War.*
52. The president discussed reading the letters with then–secretary of the Interior Harold L. Ickes. See Harold L. Ickes, *The Secret Diary of Harold L. Ickes,* vol. 2, *The Inside Struggle, 1936–1939* (New York: Simon & Schuster, 1954), 327–28.
53. Yu, *OSS in China,* 159.
54. Yu, 159.
55. Carl Hoffman to Richard Heppner, August 25, 1943, NARA, RG 226, entry 146, box 192, folder 2723. For more on the Army-OSS conversation about sending Americans to Yan'an, see Yu, *OSS in China,* 119.
56. Barrett, *Dixie Mission,* 22.
57. Barrett, 23–24.
58. Kahn, *The China Hands,* 88.
59. Many of these memos are reproduced in US Department of State, "Political Conditions in China; United States Army Observer Section Sent to Communist Territory; United States Interest and Concern Regarding Kuomintang-Communist Relations and Negotiations," January 5, 1944, *FRUS, Diplomatic Papers 1944: China,* 299–400.
60. US Department of State, "Memorandum by the Second Secretary of Embassy in China (Davies) regarding Observers' Mission to North China," *FRUS, Diplomatic Papers 1944: China,* 308.
61. US Department of State, "Memorandum by the Second Secretary," 305–6.
62. Davies, *China Hand,* 214.
63. Davies, 214.
64. Charles Stelle to Joseph Spencer, "Interim Report on Mission to Yenan," October 27, 1944, NARA, RG 226, entry NM-54 53, box 4: OSS Correspondence with Outposts, 1942–1946.
65. Stilwell demanded that the Dixie Mission be staffed by American personnel "whom the Communists would respect and who could speak Chinese well," according to Hart, *The Making of an Army "Old China Hand,"* 37.

66. J. E. Spencer to William Langer and Burton Fahs re Palisade Situation, July 8, 1944, NARA, RG 226, entry NM-54 53, box 4, folder: Dixie.
67. Spencer to Langer and Fahs re Palisade, August 1, 1944.
68. John K. Fairbank, preface to Barrett, *Dixie Mission*, 8.
69. Hart, *The Making of an Army "Old China Hand,"* 9.
70. Hart, 13.
71. Hart, 2–3.
72. Hart, 6.
73. Hart, 8.
74. Hart, 43–44. For further, see Theodore H. White and Annalee Jacoby, *Thunder Out of China* (New York: William Slone, 1946).
75. Hart, *The Making of an Army "Old China Hand,"* 10. For further on Barrett's experience meeting with warlords, see David D. Barrett, "Solders of Misfortune," *Society of American Military Engineers* 357 (January–February 1962): 357.
76. Kahn, *The China Hands*, 75.
77. Hart, *The Making of an Army "Old China Hand,"* 28.
78. Hart, 43–44.
79. Additional planes carrying personnel and supplies sporadically traveled from Xi'an to Yan'an when weather and logistics permitted in 1944.
80. Joseph Spencer to William Langer, August 1, 1944, NARA, RG 226, entry NM-54 53, box 4.
81. Spencer to Langer, August 1, 1944.
82. Stelle to Spencer, "Interim Report on Mission to Yenan," October 27, 1944.

3

THE SPELL OF THE CHINESE COMMUNISTS

Is it true what they say about Dixie?
Does the sun really shine all the time?
Do the sweet magnolias blossom at ev'rybody's door?
Do folks keep eating possum
Till they can't eat no more?
—Lyrics of song that inspired Yan'an mission nickname

It was a short and tense flight from the US airbase in Xi'an to Yan'an, the town in Shaanxi province's dusty loess hills where the CCP leaders had established their headquarters. Commercial airlines today make the trip in under an hour, but no US military plane had ever traveled this route prior to the afternoon of July 22, 1944. The trip put the Army Air Force C-47 and its escort of three smaller fighter planes at risk of attack by Japanese enemies.[1] Pilot Jack Champion had directed his passengers to don parachutes in case the Japanese shot down the plane. Yan'an had no airport, paved runway, or air tower, so the Dixie Mission planned to land on the rudimentary airstrip the Standard Oil Company had left behind decades earlier. The oil company had abandoned the site by the time the CCP had adopted the Yan'an area as its base in the 1930s. As the plane approached its destination, Champion carefully scanned the arid landscape for the landmarks he had heard would guide him to land the plane in the right place.

Champion soon caught a clear view of the prominent pagoda that stood at the top of a hill near the airfield. Far below, a crowd had gathered to welcome the plane. In lieu of a control tower to assist the plane in landing, bystanders on the ground signaled where to land. All ten passengers aboard the C-47 braced for landing on the precarious dirt.

The C-47's landing gear touched down in the dust. A perfect landing. A collective sigh of relief emerged from the passengers and crew as the plane taxied toward the greeting party and rolled to a stop. Suddenly, boom! The plane lurched sharply to the left. An extremely loud blow, like a sledgehammer, sounded just outside the cockpit.

The CCP's Honor Guard, assembled to greet the American guests, stared in stunned silence as the first members of the controversial US Army Observer

Group scrambled out of the plane and surveyed the damage to their only means of return transportation. The landing gear on the plane's left side had fallen into a cavity in the ground, which ultimately was revealed to be an old grave. Champion had never expected to find such an obstacle located on a space used as an airfield, and it was hidden from view before impact. The wheel's collapse into the hollow cavity had caused a propeller to hit the ground hard then bend back, knocking off the plane's nosecone and slicing up through the skin of the plane's fuselage. The propeller had gashed the pilot's arm. It narrowly missed injuring the pilot more seriously, potentially fatally. No one else was hurt. The stunned Americans awkwardly stared at the equally stunned Chinese Communists.

US Army colonel David D. Barrett, commanding officer of the American group, was first to recover his composure. He summoned the grace he had gained from his previous decade of experience working in the US embassy, stood up straight, and loudly declared, "We are mighty glad to be here, at last."[2]

Under other circumstances, landing with one wheel stuck in a grave might have appeared inauspicious—a bad omen for the start of a diplomatic relationship. However, the permutations of war and politics that had led these Americans and their Chinese hosts to meet had evidently hardened them to being sidetracked by such trivial impressions. According to Barrett, once all parties were declared safe and relatively uninjured, the incident caused only mild embarrassment and a collective shrug on both sides. Recognizing obstacles and then shaking them off to move forward became a recurring theme of relations between this first group of American observers and their CCP hosts.

From its first moments, the presence of the Dixie Mission in Yan'an required resilience and authenticity from its American and Chinese participants alike. The American observers attempted to approach the CCP leaders with open minds, despite the cynicism and caution they had absorbed working in the CBI Theater during Japanese occupation. The CCP leaders approached the Americans with similar apprehension. Nonetheless, CCP leaders were aware that the visitors might help them fight enemies and boost their legitimacy if they handled the relationship well. Despite the mutual prejudices and expectations, authentic human relationships developed at Yan'an between this first crew of American officials and their Chinese hosts.

The army's official name for the mission—the US Army Observer Section—was a thin disguise for the group's real objective: intelligence work. Lacking a centralized organization for intelligence activities before and during the war, the US government pushed the tasks of intelligence onto its agencies and military forces, which responded in organizationally specific ways. On top of this lack of norms governing US intelligence collection, US officials operating in China were subject to the rules of the SACO agreement and the actions that their ally—Chiang Kai-shek—would allow. Stilwell's staff designed the Dixie Mission to vault across all these hurdles and serve as an interorganizational field intelligence team. Putting the group under Army G-2 leadership slightly insulated it from intrusion by SACO. Collaborating with the OSS bolstered the Dixie Mission's roster and gave it political ballast. Everyone in Chongqing knew the mission for what it was, and the CCP leaders in Yan'an were soon to find out.

MAKING SENSE OF AMBIGUOUS ORDERS

After surviving the landing in Yan'an, Colonel Barrett faced the daunting task of managing an interagency team of Americans to work in an extremely remote area with hosts they were just getting to know. Leaders at CBI headquarters had armed him for the task with official orders that read like a laundry list, both vague and broad. Dated one day before the plane arrived, Dixie's orders directed Barrett and his subordinates to work with the CCP on what observers today would recognize as intelligence collection while also collecting intelligence about the CCP for the US government. Barrett was to report back to headquarters on two main topics: how successful the CCP troops were at fighting the Japanese and their assessment of the CCP itself.[3]

Specifically, the orders expected Barrett and his team to gather standard military intelligence such as Japan's order of battle, locations of Japanese airfields and air defenses, and already existing bomb damage in northern China. ("Order of battle" refers to the organization, structure, and strength of a military force and may include information such as leadership hierarchies, troop counts, base locations, and details about the quantity and capability of weapons.) The US officials were also asked to collaborate with CCP guerrillas to establish collection protocols for target and weather information, which affected bombing and logistics for both the US forces and the Japanese Army. Those who conceptualized the Dixie Mission expected Yan'an to become an important outpost for gathering and disseminating weather information including cloud cover, temperatures, and barometer readings, which influenced the planning of military operations in China, from aerial scouting of bombing targets in areas occupied by the Japanese to logistical missions designed to move personnel, supplies, and communications throughout the theater of battle.[4] To facilitate communications about the sensitive information they collected, the Dixie crew was asked to assess existing CCP radio capabilities, determine what equipment was needed, procure and install that equipment, and then train American or Chinese personnel (or both) to operate the new equipment.

Information about the Chinese Communists themselves would be considered strategic foreign intelligence reporting to those who comprised the Dixie

Mission's audience within the US bureaucracy, such as General Stilwell. Few US officials had interacted with Chinese Communist leaders. The team's orders required them to gather information on the "strength, composition, disposition, equipment, training and combat efficiency of the Communist forces," including their intelligence capabilities. Barrett would need to assess how the CCP could assist the war effort and encourage the Communists to do that. The orders anticipated that Barrett and his team would overtly gather the information through meetings and observation, as Barrett was accustomed to doing during his previous attaché work. Dixie Mission members lived in the Communist headquarters area, traveled to CCP base areas, interviewed CCP leaders, and observed CCP missions. Asking them to write up what they noticed was natural for this kind of military operation, but it would also be quite useful, given Chiang Kai-shek's unwillingness to even discuss the CCP.

Barrett and others deployed to Yan'an would have also known about US government goals that for political reasons could not be spelled out in the mission's official orders. Tapping into the CCP's internal intelligence on Chiang Kai-shek's forces was one such objective, which went unmentioned in the official orders. Information on troop strength of the Nationalist Chinese forces had been difficult for Stilwell to obtain, but he wanted to fully understand the capabilities of China's forces. The OSS similarly sought contact with the CCP in hope of negotiating some intelligence-sharing opportunities. They wanted to provide US generals with the information on Chiang's troops that the Generalissimo himself would not give. OSS China also felt hamstrung by the SACO agreement.[5]

Early Dixie Mission participants pursued various activities that diplomats and attachés still use to overtly elicit intelligence (i.e., gather information of interest to the government without using clandestine methods). They observed and talked with CCP leaders. Some meetings were formal and focused on military matters or speeches, but many more were casual interactions. Social gatherings occurred regularly. The CCP leaders frequently would invite the Americans to dances held outdoors when the weather was warm.[6] Whenever the C-47 pilots could make it to Yan'an, Dixie officials asked them to bring the latest American movies, which they would project on the Yan'an cave walls to enjoy with the CCP leaders and their families. In turn they would then send the planes back to Xi'an loaded up with their mail and reports as well as local Chinese language newspapers, pamphlets, and propaganda to ferry back to CBI headquarters.

Other kinds of overt information collection occurred as well. Several Dixie members were responsible for debriefing Japanese POWs captured by the CCP and held at Yan'an. OSS officers detailed to Yan'an also spent hours examining and copying documentary materials that the CCP had seized from the Japanese.

POSITIVE FIRST IMPRESSIONS

Reports of the first interactions between the first Dixie Mission personnel and the CCP leadership at Yan'an unanimously describe warm interactions and some surprise on the part of the Americans at the cordial reception they received. Barrett and Jack Service met directly with the top CCP political leaders; Chairman Mao Zedong was a main point of contact. They also met regularly with Zhou Enlai, a founding member of the CCP who served as Mao's partner and deputy for years following the founding of the People's Republic of China in 1949. In 1944 Zhou's official title was vice chairman of the Central Revolutionary Military Council, a tongue-twisting Marxist-Leninist designation that obscures his importance to the CCP's strategic and diplomatic planning.[7] The CCP's top military leaders also welcomed the Dixie Mission. Although they outranked him, Barrett regularly conferred with Gen. Zhu De, commander, and Gen. Ye Jianying, chief of staff, both of the Eighth Route Army. By 1949 troops of the Eighth Route Army had been reorganized into a single force, the Red Army, with Zhu at the helm as its commander.

US officials and CCP leaders developed a plan for working together to accomplish the Dixie Mission orders. In exchange for CCP cooperation with their efforts, the Americans promised training in military intelligence practices and the use of sophisticated radio and weather equipment. There was also the potential for expanded military support. Their first task was to become acquainted with the CCP leaders, who appeared to relish assisting. On the evening of Dixie's arrival, the CCP leaders hosted the delegation at a dinner and social gathering whose guests included their wives and children as well as foreign journalists and experts who were visiting Yan'an. Following standard CCP protocol for hosting such dignitaries, the hosts seated Barrett between Mao and Zhu.[8] As the highest-ranking representative of the US diplomatic mission to China, Service was seated on Mao's other side. These honors did not pass unnoticed by the Americans, who had attended many Chinese banquets in their careers in China and understood the gravity of the seating arrangement.

Service described Mao's sense of humor being on display during various personal remarks the CCP leader made over dinner. Service was quite taken in by Mao and interpreted Mao's attitude toward the Americans as one of genuine enthusiasm. He recorded Mao's questions about the relationship of the US State Department with the Yan'an mission, specifically inquiring if the United States might consider establishing a consulate at Yan'an. Mao also presciently expressed concern that American engagement with the CCP would end as soon as Japan was defeated, leaving the CCP vulnerable to Guomindang attacks and civil war.[9] Service did not record what he told Mao in response to that seemingly valid concern.

The dinner party was the first of many instances when the CCP showed the Americans typical Chinese hospitality. The CCP also insisted on providing the food for the American delegation. Dixie had its own mess hall and a budget for food. However, Mao and Zhou refused to take the funds from Barrett, despite several offers. The food was the simple rice-based and mostly vegetarian fare typical of Chinese cuisine, served in ample amounts. Several Dixie Mission members also recalled the ubiquitous presence of watermelon as a treat or dessert when it was in season.

The first day of the mission did not exclusively consist of social calls. It also included more serious meetings. In sessions that day the CCP leaders told Barrett they were learning for the first time of the Dixie Mission's intention to "investigate the needs of the Communist forces in arms and equipment."[10] Prior correspondence between CCP leaders and their Chinese Army (Nationalist Party) contacts had led them to believe the purposes of the mission were exclusively "air-ground aid and the collection of enemy intelligence." Barrett emphasized to Zhou and Ye that he could make no definite commitments that the United States would ever supply them materiel aid. Nevertheless, the CCP leaders were reportedly delighted to discover that the American observers intended to submit recommendations to their superiors on the CCP's needs.

The CCP leaders' positive response to Dixie's arrival was reflected in a written memorandum to Barrett from CCP general Zhu De on July 25, 1944, advising the US government (via Barrett) of the CCP's intention to fully cooperate with the American intelligence efforts in Yan'an. Zhu described his orders to subordinates: brief their American counterparts on the relevant subjects on which they were already well informed and begin working together to learn about additional areas of strategic interest.[11] The CCP leaders specifically agreed to work with the Americans on the following topics: weather; target analysis; orders of battle for Japan and the Manchuguo puppet state; air intelligence; communications; medical needs; use and expansion of the Communist Intelligence Net; Air Ground Aid Service; naval intelligence; and the organization, training, and procurement of equipment of Communist Chinese forces. Yan'an was far from the ocean, so in this case naval intelligence probably referred to signals intelligence and weather information along with any other strategic information that could benefit the ONI personnel in the CBI Theater. No end date for the Dixie Mission had been set. Based on his cordial meetings in the first week, Barrett recommended that the delegation remain in Yan'an at least through August 1944. The US government ultimately continued to operate the mission to Yan'an in some form until 1947.

OSS's Charles Stelle confirmed Barrett's assessment that the CCP leaders appeared eager to answer the Americans' questions. In communications exclusive to OSS channels, Stelle reported that the CCP leaders' "efforts to put their best foot forward, and our desire to avoid the duplications inherent in numerous individual interviews resulted in a somewhat formal and time consuming 'indoctrination.' For a period of several weeks, the major part of our time was taken up by what amounted to a series of lectures, with interpreters, by a succession of Communist leaders."[12] The Americans heard from CCP dignitaries Gen. Ye Jianying and Gen. Peng Dehuai, then the vice commander of CCP troops. Representative leaders from various CCP base areas located behind Japanese lines each described the history of their area as well as the political, economic, and military challenges each base faced.

Separate reports from the Dixie crew reveal a broad consensus about the CCP's capabilities and challenges. Notably, the reports universally express a charitable view of CCP activities in the fight against the Japanese and reveal respect—if begrudging—for the CCP's unique guerrilla capabilities. Barrett's first report, submitted a few days after the team's arrival in Yan'an, reflects cautious optimism for the mission, based on his favorable impression of their Chinese hosts: "To sum up, both military and civil officials are apparently doing everything in their power to cooperate with and assist the section. In this they are displaying a degree of initiative and planning ability which I have never before encountered in China. From present indications, the Section should be able to accomplish results commensurate with the effort which has been expended in getting it despatched to Yenan."[13] Stelle declared the CCP leaders to be "convincing" and emphasized that "according to all the independent checks we have been able to secure, they avoided exaggeration of their capabilities and accomplishments."[14] Positive initial impressions set a productive tone for the Dixie Mission's first few months.

INITIAL OSS REACTIONS

Ray Cromley, the OSS officer assigned the task of creating orders of battle, began the work with optimism in July 1944. In his first report to OSS China headquarters in Chongqing, Cromley described access to Japanese and Chinese publications; prisoners of war who could be debriefed; and captured documents, weapons, and equipment. He claimed that the CCP guerrillas had access to all Japan-occupied areas, which is significant because these places had been impossible for OSS officers to explore (Nationalist guerrillas did not always share their experiences in the occupied areas back to OSS). Of the CCP guerrillas, Cromley reported, "Because of their continual skirmishing with the Japanese, they are an excellent source of prisoners of war and captured documents. All they need is training in what Order of Battle information to collect and how to collect it."[15]

Cromley remarked on the eagerness of CCP guerrillas to obtain training in intelligence methods and their willingness to help collect the information that Cromley requested. He reported that the CCP officers based at Yan'an had forwarded via radio his intelligence requirements to guerrillas at the front lines. Records indicate they were already collecting captured documents and using Cromley's questions in debriefing POWs as of late July 1944, mere weeks after Dixie's arrival. Cromley's CCP contacts in Yan'an had also sifted through their files to provide him with useful materials they had already collected. They led him to a cave full of captured Japanese weapons, and they helped him copy the guns' markings.[16] Cromley reported that he had secured information from the guerrillas that was "so secret that even the G-2 in Chungking had previously gotten it neither from the Chinese nor from Washington (because top secret)."[17]

Cromley was adamant that it was necessary to collect order-of-battle intelligence in the field, as he was doing, rather than from a headquarters office located safely away from conflict areas, as was the custom. Cromley wrote, "After three months in China, I am convinced that work can be accomplished only in the field and only by continuous work in the field."[18] To this end, he recommended that the United States form small teams, mostly staffed by trained Chinese guerrillas, that could travel around China to perform the necessary intelligence duties.

OSS officers used the opinions of several independent foreign observers to corroborate the intelligence received from CCP leaders and counterparts. These observers included an American pilot who had received aid from the CCP guerrillas after being shot down in Shanxi province. Because the pilot had traveled through several base areas, he was able to verify the details provided to the Dixie Mission by the CCP regarding base area staff organization and basic positions in the countryside. Two other groups of American airmen who were rescued by the CCP in other areas were able to confirm, and even extend, the mapped territories held by the CCP guerrillas. Mission members also conferred regularly with Michael Lindsay, a British scholar who had moved to Yan'an in 1944 to learn about the CCP and help with China's war efforts against the Japanese.[19] Stelle described Lindsay as a "relatively objective observer" despite "his long connection with the Communists."[20] Dixie Mission members' observations were also generally consistent with information obtained from the few other Americans who had been operating in rural areas of northern China in 1944 and those who had been in any position to observe CCP actions, usually reporting on them to the OSS and G-2 in Chongqing. Stelle and the mission's OSS officers were sufficiently confident in their corroboration of CCP information to recommend that the mission to Yan'an be made a permanent outpost for intelligence collection in China.

JAPANESE POWS AND AMERICAN PSYCHOLOGICAL WARFARE

Americans in Yan'an in late 1944 found it extremely valuable to meet the Japanese POWs that the CCP guerrillas had captured. Observing the Chinese Communists' treatment of and attitudes about the captured Japanese soldiers yielded valuable intelligence about the practices and style of the Communists themselves. Debriefs with the Japanese POWs also helped shape US Office of War Information psychological operations that encouraged Japanese individuals to surrender.

OWI, an agency formed around the same time as the OSS and tasked with performing so-called white intelligence operations, including overt psychological operations, propaganda, and activities that today would be called public diplomacy, did not assign any personnel to the first cohort of the Dixie Mission.[21] The OSS handled the opposite of the "white" operations assigned to OWI: "black" operations, including covert plans of subversion, assassination, and the development of secret foreign agents. Upon learning of the presence of Japanese POWs at Yan'an and the potential ability to interview them, the OWI dispatched officer F. McCracken Fisher on a two-week trip to Yan'an in September 1944 to study the psychological warfare efforts of the CCP's Eighth Route Army. Fisher's task was "to determine what could be learned from their experience and methods that could be used in our American psychological warfare effort against the Japanese and to establish a source and channels for information about the Japanese army and conditions within Japan."[22]

Fisher reported that the CCP had achieved considerable successes in psychological warfare, which he attributed to several characteristics of the Communists' approach and methods. The CCP leaders had a clear understanding of the nature and goals of the war and were proficient at imparting this understanding to their troops, educating them thoroughly and "instilling the proper attitude toward the enemy."[23] Moreover, they had enlisted the help of captured or surrendered Japanese troops at Yan'an in developing their psychological operations, federating the prisoners into an organization they called the Japanese People's Emancipation League. Fisher noted that the location of the Japanese garrisons were easy targets for highly mobile CCP guerrillas to target with psychological warfare or propaganda missions. The garrisons were populated by puppet Chinese troops and Chinese peasants, making it easy for Communist guerrillas to blend in with the townsfolk. Fisher's reports emphasized the willingness of the CCP counterparts at Yan'an to share information with the Americans. In fact, they had important information to share about the "internal conditions of the Japanese Army in North China, especially as they affect the life and thinking of the ordinary soldier." CCP guerrillas also shared various captured Japanese documents, ranging from Japanese publications to actual Japanese military intelligence reports.

Based on Fisher's reports, the OWI dispatched officer John K. Emmerson to become a part of the Dixie Mission in late October 1944. Originally from Colorado like Barrett, Emmerson had joined the Foreign Service after earning a master's degree at New York University. The State Department assigned him to Japan in September 1935, where he served until October 1941.[24] His experience in Japan had allowed him to learn Japanese, which helped him communicate with the Japanese troops at Yan'an. After leaving Japan, Emmerson had been detailed to General Stilwell and worked with an OWI team in northern Burma. Emmerson arrived at Yan'an on October 22, 1944, bringing along Koji Ariyoshi, a Japanese American working with the OWI to assist with psychological warfare efforts.[25]

Reports by Fisher and Emmerson reflected unexpected positive impressions of CCP activities. Both men expressed surprise at the cordial treatment the CCP guerrillas afforded to captured Japanese troops and believed their approach aided the Communist psychological operations and propaganda efforts directed at the Japanese. For example, in memos describing his observations at Yan'an, Fisher explained that "every Japanese prisoner is regarded, first, as a potential worker or medium for psychological warfare, and second, as a potential instrument for the overthrow of the militarist government of Japan and the establishment of a people's government on democratic lines."[26] Fisher assessed the CCP approach to captured enemy soldiers to be unorthodox but highly effective. He encountered one American fighter pilot to whom the CCP had provided aid. Being shot down afforded the pilot a chance to see the CCP guerrillas work with the POWs outside Yan'an. From the pilot, Fisher learned that CCP guerrillas treated the Japanese troops "as if they loved them. I can't understand it—but it certainly does work." Fisher and Emmerson both expressed the view that the United States could learn about effective psychological warfare from the CCP. The work begun at Yan'an early in the Dixie Mission continued for the rest of the war with Japan.

CCP WINS OVER FOREIGN SERVICE OFFICERS

FSOs Service and Ludden reported their surprise and positive reaction to the CCP leaders and the Communist modes of operation on display in Yan'an. They delivered their most candid assessments of the Communist activities in China within their first few weeks at Yan'an. They trusted, perhaps somewhat naively, that the American recipients of their reports—in Kunming, in Chongqing, in

Delhi, and back home in Washington, DC—would be won over to their charitable view. Regrettably, their audience was not the open-minded observers they anticipated.

Initial reports from Service described his determination not to fall under what he refers to as "the spell of the Chinese Communists," which he had heard about from numerous American and European visitors to Yan'an before arriving there himself. Service reported that even the American observers who were most dubious of the Communists and their intentions shared a similar feeling, "that we have come into a different country and are meeting a different people [compared to the Nationalist Party members]."[27] Numerous ways that the CCP members in Yan'an seemed different to Service from the Chinese Army personnel in Chongqing included their simple clothing and lifestyle; their lack of bodyguards, fancy uniforms, or badges; and the overall "absence of show and formality, both in speech and action."

He described CCP efforts at Yan'an as "a well-integrated movement, with a political and economic program, which it is successfully carrying out under competent leaders" and noted that the CCP had not completely lost its "revolutionary character" due to its continual fight for survival against the Guomindang and the Japanese. But he assessed this character to have "grown to a healthy moderate maturity." Notwithstanding his early resistance to liking the CCP, Service clearly conveyed a charitable view in his July 1944 reporting: "One cannot help coming to feel that this movement is strong and successful, and that it has such drive behind it and has tied itself so closely to the people that it will not easily be killed."[28]

The positive tone of Service's initial reports is apparent throughout his official correspondence dispatched in August and September 1944. In one report from September 4 Service wrote, "The general impression one gets of the Chinese Communist leaders is that they are a unified group of vigorous, mature, and practical men, unselfishly devoted to high principles, and having great ability and strong qualities of leadership."[29] A different stream of Service's reporting that later generated significant controversy appeared in late August. One such report documented a six-hour personal meeting he had with Mao at the CCP leader's invitation. Service described Mao's concerns about the vulnerability of Chinese democracy if a civil war should follow the defeat of Japan. Service conveyed Mao's request that the US government support the creation of "a new national government" in China by "calling a conference of all leading political groups in China."[30] Service sent his report to the State Department through CBI headquarters and the embassy in China. In his posthumously published memoir of his time working in Asia, John Davies succinctly summarized the report's initial effect: "Washington did not deign to respond to Mao."[31]

The candor in Service's reports from Yan'an reflects pre–World War II institutional norms within the State Department that gave Foreign Service Officers considerable leeway in expressing their opinions and fulfilling their duties. Davies's memoir describes an atmosphere in which the Foreign Service Officer was seen as "a man of honor and that in his relations with the public and his colleagues he would so conduct himself."[32] Accordingly, the Foreign Service operations were "untormented by anxious preoccupation with security and discipline"—a state of affairs that featured "tolerance of considerable nonconformity and even eccentricity." The Foreign Service in the 1940s was a small and personalized organization. Foreign Service Officers likely did not anticipate the unique political challenges of interagency wartime work and the expansion of their intelligence-collection duties during the war. Although Service conveyed what he thought was a candid and true view of Mao, Zhou, and the CCP, the charitable nature of his remarks brought personal political repercussions for him by the end of the 1940s.

ARMY G-2 INTELLIGENCE PACE AT YAN'AN

The army personnel posted to Yan'an demonstrated their expertise in performing the collection of logistical military intelligence in China. Between July and October 1944 their work included installing equipment and establishing protocols to gather weather intelligence from Yan'an and the surrounding areas. They also worked with the Communist guerrillas to aid and rescue Allied airmen whom the Japanese had shot down in or near Communist-held areas.

Weather Intelligence

The Dixie Mission's determination to successfully establish new protocols for the collection of weather information from Yan'an was consistent with the broad demand for weather intelligence from Allied military officers operating in East Asia during World War II. Weather information was useful to military officers attempting to plan aerial bombings, troop deployments, and logistical transport during the war. Weather data also helped the Allies anticipate Japanese movements. Both extreme weather events and simple cloud cover could significantly affect military operations. Before the Japanese occupation in 1937, Americans and Europeans living in China had collected most of the weather data—a limited enterprise. After the war began, many of these expatriates fled south or left China altogether, sharply reducing the weather intelligence about northern and central China available to Allied military planners.[33]

Weather information from Yan'an specifically was useful to the US Army Twentieth Bomber Command once its pilots began long-distance bombing runs from Chengdu (in the southwest) all the way to Japan in 1944.[34] The Twentieth Bomber Command also frequently ferried fuel from the CBI base in India that served as its headquarters to Chengdu to support the bombing missions. In June 1944 the OSS staff in China even recommended Gen. William Donovan use the issue of providing weather intelligence support for the Twentieth Bomber Command to help lobby the White House and cabinet-level leaders for the creation of the Dixie Mission, with the assumption that "secondary opportunities" for intelligence collection would exist for the OSS once the outpost in Yan'an was established.[35]

The US Army Tenth Weather Squadron was responsible for collecting and disseminating all relevant weather information throughout the CBI Theater. The squadron posted a steady stream of personnel to Dixie, including Maj. Charles Dole, who was dispatched with the first group of American officials to Yan'an and served there throughout the second half of 1944. Prior to the arrival of the Dixie Mission, the CCP had not organized a systematic program for acquiring and transmitting weather information, but the CCP fighters were eager to be trained and contribute information.[36] Dole and several other Army Air Corps personnel included in the initial Dixie Mission roster began working with CCP counterparts to boost weather intelligence soon after the team's arrival. Personnel from the Tenth Weather Squadron spent much of their time in Yan'an assessing the equipment needed for collecting the necessary data, installing equipment, and taking measurements and readings. A significant part of their job evolved into training Communist guerrillas who operated behind the Japanese front lines to record weather assessments and transmit their observations via radio at designated times.

Air Ground Aid Service

In addition to building systems for collecting weather data, Dixie Mission members worked with their CCP hosts during their first few months in Yan'an to rescue, assist, and debrief Allied airmen who had been shot down or captured by the Japanese in northern and central China. The necessity of this mission intensified when the American long-distance bombing runs over China to Japanese-held areas increased in 1944 and 1945. The army introduced the B-29 aircraft for these missions because they carried very large bomb loads, but the planes had serious problems that made them particularly susceptible to accidents and crashes.[37] The Air Ground Aid Service (AGAS), the army organization responsible for the rescue of downed American airmen, had assigned Lt. Henry C. Whittlesey to the initial crew of Dixie. Whittlesey, in cooperation with the mission's medical officer, Maj. Melvin Casberg, was among the first of the initial Dixie contingent to venture into CCP guerrilla base areas outside Yan'an. When the weather cleared sufficiently in fall 1944 for safe travel, Whittlesey moved out with the guerrilla teams to provide aid to Americans whose parachutes dropped them behind the Japanese lines.

AGAS had personnel posted in locations throughout China, and they had already been working with Chinese Nationalist guerrilla troops when the Dixie Mission began. The CCP guerrillas were reportedly eager for information on how they could best support Americans in distress with whom they had come into contact.[38] AGAS officers posted to Yan'an sought information from the CCP guerrillas about the potential for escape from and evasion of Japanese troops so that they could inform the US Army Air Corps fliers who were engaged in the bombing runs. The army began instructing those involved in missions over North China to seek help from the CCP guerrillas if they found themselves in distress. On the CCP side, Gen. Ye Jianying appointed a special committee of CCP members to cooperate with the AGAS mission to determine how the CCP and Dixie Mission members could best cooperate to facilitate rescue missions.

Americans who had escaped or evaded Japanese capture in China served as an important source of intelligence for the Americans and the CCP alike. Once rescued, American evacuees that the CCP had helped went first to Yan'an, where they were debriefed, then were arranged safe passage back to a rear base area. As intelligence officers, the Dixie Mission members were in a good position to gain valuable information from these individuals because they already had some idea of the gaps in American intelligence knowledge about Japan's capabilities. They also had the means of communicating information gathered back to their CBI headquarters colleagues, who applied it in planning and preparing American personnel for future long-range bombing missions. The G-2 made efficient use of AGAS information to protect American personnel as much as possible. AGAS efforts at Yan'an were among the biggest successes of the observer group.

Debriefing the escapees also yielded interesting candid intelligence about life in the CCP guerrilla areas. In one fascinating example, the initial Dixie participants interviewed 1st Lt. J. P. Baglio, who was rescued by CCP guerrillas in June 1944 and handed over to American counterparts at Yan'an for evacuation in July. Jack Service drilled Baglio for examples of the extent of banditry in the areas controlled by the CCP People's Militia, so the Americans could compare the bandit situation in North China with the rife and serious banditry problems they had observed in areas held by Nationalist guerrillas elsewhere in China. To the great surprise of the Dixie members, Baglio had not observed or heard about any examples of bandits. Moreover, he reported that all the guerrillas he encountered appeared so dedicated to participating in war efforts that he could not imagine them having the time to participate in nefarious activities.

Baglio's report fed the favorable initial impressions that Dixie's political officers had formed of the CCP members, particularly compared to their experiences observing Guomindang troops.[39]

All parties recognized the great danger of the AGAS work. Indeed, Whittlesey became the only member of the Dixie Mission killed in action when Japanese snipers shot him in early 1945. Whittlesey posthumously received the Distinguished Service Cross for his valor in assisting fellow soldiers in distress and the American mess hall at Yan'an was named after him.[40] Given the dangers of the rescue work, Whittlesey (and his AGAS replacements), Casberg, and OSS officer Cromley repeatedly requested medical supplies and gifts for the CCP guerrillas to continue building their goodwill and eagerness to participate.[41] Unfortunately, these supplies were not forthcoming.

YAN'AN RADIO CAPABILITIES: A JOINT YENSIG EFFORT

American personnel posted to Yan'an cooperated as well as they could in developing radio capabilities to support their intelligence-collection activities. By the end of their first two weeks in Yan'an, most of the initial Dixie members had noted the deficiency of the CCP's radio equipment and procedures. Their initial reports unanimously emphasized the importance of developing a sophisticated and powerful radio network at Yan'an.[42] In most cases, the success of other operations coming out of Yan'an hinged upon Dixie's radio capabilities. The remoteness of Yan'an heightened the need for a radio system that could speed communication over long distances and minimize the need for personnel to travel through dangerous enemy areas. CCP guerrillas operating close to or behind Japanese lines could then utilize the radio network to report information from their respective positions. OSS plans also intended to rely on guerrillas using the radio network from remote areas to help administer programs of human intelligence agents throughout the region and to report updates to the order of battle for Japanese troops based on their observations from positions near Japanese troops.

OSS officers in Yan'an initially took the lead on acquiring the right equipment and training local personnel to use it. The OSS enjoyed access to some of the most notoriously substantial and forthcoming budgetary resources, secured by Donovan's force of personality and his personal relationship with Roosevelt. Throughout the mission, OSS personnel used the codename YENSIG to refer to the entire radio operation in Yan'an. The first American plane to Yan'an included OSS personnel trained in radio operations and carrying equipment the unit needed to begin establishing communications.[43] OSS officer Charles Stelle traveled to Kunming in October 1944 with the overt purpose of retrieving additional radio equipment designated for Dixie and cooperating with personnel from the Chengdu-based Tenth Weather Squadron to transport it to Yan'an.[44] Stelle successfully ferried some of the necessary components to Yan'an, but as of November the mission was still waiting on hand-powered generators that could adapt the radio units to the lack of infrastructure in and around Yan'an, according to Stelle's correspondence with his OSS managers.[45] This detail might seem minor—a single line in a memo in a stack of other memos on the desk of a busy OSS bureaucrat—but without these generator units, any information that the CCP guerrillas and Americans in the field were risking their lives to collect could not be reported in a timely manner to the central leadership of the CCP, Chinese, or American militaries. In effect, the lack of a functional radio network rendered much of the urgent intelligence-collection activities from Yan'an irrelevant or obsolete before it could be reported. Worse yet, communication challenges could force people into risky travel around hostile areas.

Acquiring the initial equipment for the radio base was only the beginning of the project. Establishing communications that could facilitate the Dixie Mission's intelligence goals also required distributing basic radio and weather equipment throughout the CCP guerrillas' area of operations and training them on how to use it. Within days of Stelle's departure for Kunming in October 1944, a party of American observers and CCP guides, led on the American side by Foreign Service Officer Raymond Ludden, set out on a study tour of North China. The trip aimed to assess CCP military and intelligence capabilities and to equip guerrillas operating at and behind the Japanese lines to collect and report weather information. The Americans also brought along basic medical supplies to encourage goodwill and support the CCP guerrillas' ability to provide aid to downed American soldiers.[46] The most vital and timely tasks the Americans asked the CCP guerrillas to perform all required radio. Unfortunately, guerrillas in remote areas would not immediately benefit from the additional equipment that Stelle acquired: the study tour did not return to Yan'an until February 1945.

The radio training programs also encountered unexpected obstacles. In addition to the technical training on how to operate the radio equipment and weather-monitoring instruments, Dixie Mission personnel had to explain the context of how the information would be used. Although the CCP had advanced intelligence capabilities to protect its domestic interests and physical security, the collection of meteorological intelligence was new. In his memoir, Barrett recalled one amusing miscommunication during a trial run soon after the first radios and other equipment had been installed at a CCP base area outside Yan'an. Barrett wrote, "Along with radios, there had been sent out forms to be followed in submitting weather reports. Under one heading, types of clouds, such as 'cumulus,' 'cirrus,' and so on, were to be noted. In describing the clouds, this particular message read, "不多不少 [Not many, and yet not few]."[47]

Although the Americans assisted the CCP personnel in substantially improving access to radio communications in 1944, the capabilities lagged far behind the needs. Desperation and frustration feature strongly in a memo that the OSS radio technician sent his managers in Chongqing in late November when requesting additional radio resources. The technician, Anton Remenih, noted that communicating via radio with Chongqing was becoming more difficult and only about half of scheduled radio contacts were able to be performed as planned. Even when Yan'an could make contact, "efficient and rapid transfer of traffic" was nearly impossible due to the "heavy interference and high noise level in Chongqing"—a situation that was likely to be resolved only by using more powerful radio equipment.[48] According to Remenih, the situation meant that some communications, including messages containing important weather intelligence, stalled for as long as thirty-six hours before personnel at Yan'an could send them.

The challenge of developing sufficient radio capabilities to accomplish Dixie's mission illustrates how basic administrative and logistical issues had a drastic effect on the intelligence capabilities of the United States in field conditions during World War II. Factors that previous historians have used to explain the failure of the Dixie Mission to achieve its purposes, such as ideological differences between the American personnel and their CCP counterparts, or diplomatic and strategic disagreements between Chiang and Stilwell, had comparatively little influence on the procurement, distribution, and operation of appropriate radio equipment for the American outpost at Yan'an. Moreover, US military leaders and policymakers could not even blame other agencies for the problem—all organizations participating in Dixie agreed on the need for advanced radio capabilities and developing the radio capacity was one issue on which the Dixie personnel continuously cooperated. Rather, the failure of the initial Dixie Mission personnel to quickly establish the radio capabilities necessary to achieve their intelligence mission reflects administrative and physical conditions that the US government simply was not yet prepared to handle.

RAISING CCP EXPECTATIONS

The disorganized and competitive nature of US intelligence practices in 1944 and the presence of the Dixie Mission at Yan'an had an important side effect that American strategic planners had not anticipated: raising the expectations of the CCP leaders regarding what their party might gain from a productive working relationship with the United States. FDR—rather naively—envisioned a US policy stance that would make the CCP leaders feel that cooperation with the Chiang-led Nationalist government was their best chance for obtaining continued US support and both preserve the CCP in some form in China's postwar republic and allow the CCP guerrilla fighters to continue fighting the Japanese. In fact, although they made clear that they welcomed any help the United States offered, the CCP leaders never viewed US support as vital to their cause or their survival.[49] Furthermore, as events unfolded in 1944, the presence of the American delegation at Yan'an and the intense commitment to defeating Japan that the United States and China shared may have given CCP leaders reason to hope that they could gain US aid and support regardless of the status of negotiations.

The CCP leaders, seasoned political and military operators with relatively limited experience interacting with senior US officials, viewed the effort that the United States expended in sponsoring the delegation in Yan'an as a sign of serious American interest in improving the Communists' military capabilities. Historian Niu Jun, who has analyzed early Chinese Communist foreign policy behavior, has closely reviewed Mao's speeches and writings in the 1940s in his analysis of early Chinese Communist foreign policy. He convincingly argues that the diplomatic and military actions of the United States in China in 1944 encouraged optimism among the CCP leadership sufficient to "change their tactics in dealing with the Guomindang from self-defense to taking the offensive, and from seeking a partial solution to the problems to demanding the reorganization of the Nationalist government."[50] Although CCP leaders sought opportunities to collaborate with the United States, they also repeatedly affirmed their lack of dependence on American aid. Soon after the US Observer Group arrived in Yan'an, the CCP leaders began expressing their interest in training, equipment, and funding from the United States to continue their efforts to wage guerrilla warfare at and behind the Japanese front lines in North China. The Dixie Mission members considered these requests carefully.

The Dixie Mission enjoyed its best possible chances for laying the groundwork to fulfill its intelligence collection requirements in the period from its arrival in July to around the time that Gen. Joseph Stilwell was recalled from China in October 1944. During this initial period, the mission enjoyed several advantages that did not last through the three years that the US government maintained a presence in Yan'an. Despite the cordial reception the observer group received from CCP leaders and despite both sides' commitment to the goals of the assignment, from the outset the Dixie Mission faced formidable challenges that it was ultimately unable to overcome. The results of observer group activities in this opening period reveal that even the best efforts of the highly qualified original participants were insufficient to achieve their broad and ambiguous goals. Extremely difficult operating conditions in the Yan'an area coupled with the immaturity of the US intelligence collection program impeded the collection and dissemination of timely intelligence information from Yan'an.

Upon their arrival in July 1944, participants in the observer group in Yan'an and their managers exhibited considerable confidence regarding the potential for unique and useful intelligence collection. These initial assessments relied on the continuation of several key conditions facilitating the group's activities, including the presence of a powerful network of like-minded expert personnel that spanned several government organizations; a broad interagency commitment to the success of the intelligence collection mission for the sake of the war; initial receptivity of the CCP leaders, who had little experience with Americans and were eager to reap recognition and tangible rewards from the relationship; the broad commitment of President Roosevelt to support the Chinese fight against Japan; and the nominal stated commitment of both CCP and Nationalist Chinese leaders to cooperate, presenting an ersatz united front in the fight against the Japanese. Inefficiency and rivalry within the US government bureaucracy compounded the challenges the mission faced. By the end of 1944 these conditions had deteriorated significantly, and the observer group experienced a rapid major shift in circumstances underpinning its early progress.

NOTES

Epigraph: "Is It True What They Say about Dixie?" lyrics by Gerald Marks, Irving Caesar, and Samuel Lerner, accessed March 17, 2022, https://www.lyricsmode.com/lyrics/m/mills_brothers/is_it_true_what_they_say_about_dixie.html. Several popular artists covered the song in the 1930s and 1940s, including the Mills Brothers, Dean Martin, and Al Jolson.

1. David D. Barrett, *Dixie Mission: The United States Army Observer Group in Yenan, 1944* (Berkeley: University of California, Berkeley, 1970), 13–14; and Memo, "Transmitting General Report on US Army Observer Section at Yenan," August 25, 1944, National Archives and Records Administration (hereafter NARA), RG 319, box 717, folder: Reports and Messages, 1918–51.
2. Israel Epstein, *Unfinished Revolution in China* (Boston: Little, Brown, 2013), 406–7. The narrative of the Dixie Mission's landing in Yan'an is reconstructed and paraphrased here from the recollections of participants recorded in Barrett, *Dixie Mission*; Carolle J. Carter, *Mission to Yenan: American Liaison with the Chinese Communists, 1944–1947* (Lexington: University Press of Kentucky, 1997), 28–30; and Memo, "Transmitting General Report," August 25, 1944.
3. Barrett, *Dixie Mission*, 27–28.
4. For further details on the strategic significance of weather information in China for the long-term planning of attacks during World War II, see Maochun Yu, *OSS in China: China: Prelude to Cold War* (Annapolis, MD: Naval Institute Press, 1996), 53.
5. Yu, 158.
6. See the chapter titled "Life at Yenan" in Carter, *Mission to Yenan*, 37–45.

7. Wolfgang Bartke, *Biographical Dictionary and Analysis of China's Party Leadership, 1922–1988* (Munich: K. G. Saur, 1990).
8. John N. Hart, *The Making of an Army "Old China Hand": A Memoir of Colonel David D. Barrett* (Berkeley: University of California, Center for China Studies, 1985), 44–45. See also John Service, "Memo of Conversation with Mao Tse-tung," July 27, 1944, Bancroft Library, University of California, Berkeley, Papers of John S. Service, carton 2, folder 3.
9. Service, "Memo of Conversation with Mao Tse-tung, July 27, 1944."
10. Report, "Transmitting General Report on US Army Observer Section at Yenan," August 24, 1944, NARA, RG 319, box 717.
11. Letter, Gen. Zhu De to Col. David D. Barrett," July 25, 1944, reproduced in Memo, "Transmitting General Report on US Army Observer Section at Yenan," August 25, 1944, NARA, RG 319, box 717.
12. Report, Charles Stelle to Joseph Spencer, "Interim Report on Mission to Yenan," October 27, 1944, NARA, RG 226, entry NM-54 53, box 4: OSS Correspondence with Outposts, 1942–1946.
13. Memo, "Transmitting General Report," August 25, 1944.
14. Stelle to Spencer, "Interim Report," October 27, 1944.
15. Ray Cromley, "Yenan as the Major Order of Battle China Base of Operations," July 30, 1944, NARA, RG 226, entry 148, box 7, folder 103: Dixie.
16. Cromley, "Yenan as the Major Order of Battle."
17. Ray Cromley, "Personnel Needed for China Order of Battle Work," July 31, 1944, RG 226, entry 148: OSS Field Station Files, Chungking, box 7, folder 103: Dixie.
18. Cromley "Personnel Needed," July 31, 1944.
19. Lindsay had helped the CCP design and construct its first radio capabilities at Yan'an, which the Dixie Mission observers were very curious about. For further about Lindsay and his Chinese wife, Hsiao Li, see Kenneth E. Shewmaker, *Americans and Chinese Communists, 1927–1945: A Persuading Encounter* (Ithaca, NY: Cornell University Press, 1971), 130.
20. Stelle to Spencer, "Interim Report," October 27, 1944.
21. For further, see Bradley F. Smith, *The Shadow Warriors: O.S.S. and the Origins of the CIA* (New York: Basic, 1983), 117–21.
22. F. McCracken Fisher, "Memo on Yenan Reports Series," October 16, 1944, NARA, RG 165, entry 79, box 2602: Reports 4–18. For more on Fisher's background, see Stephen R. MacKinnon and Oris Friesen, *China Reporting: An Oral History of American Journalism in the 1930s and 1940s* (Berkeley: University of California Press, 1987).
23. Fisher, "Memo on Yenan Reports Series," October 16, 1944.
24. E. J. Kahn, *The China Hands: America's Foreign Service Officers and What Befell Them* (New York: Viking, 1976), 42.
25. Carter, *Mission to Yenan,* 65. According to Carter, Emmerson and Koji Ariyoshi traveled on the same plane as John Davies and Theodore H. White, the famous *Time* magazine correspondent.
26. Report, "Yenan Report #11: Treatment of Prisoners of War by Eighth Route Army," October 23, 1944, NARA, RG 165, entry NM-84, box 2602, 79.
27. John S. Service, "First Information Impressions of the North Shensi Communist Base," July 28, 1944, reproduced in *Lost Chance in China: The World War II Despatches of John S. Service,* ed. Joseph W. Esherick (New York: Random House, 1974), 178–82.

28. Service, "First Information Impressions."
29. John S. Service, "General Impression of the Chinese Communist Leaders," September 4, 1944, reproduced in *Lost Chance in China: The World War II Despatches of John S. Service*, ed. Joseph W. Esherick (New York: Random House, 1974), 198.
30. John S. Service, "Interview with Mao Tse-tung," August 27, 1944, reproduced in *Lost Chance in China: The World War II Despatches of John S. Service*, ed. Joseph W. Esherick (New York: Random House, 1974), 292–94.
31. John Paton Davies Jr., *China Hand: An Autobiography* (Philadelphia: University of Pennsylvania Press, 2012), 217.
32. Davies, 19–20.
33. Yu, *OSS in China*, 53.
34. Carter, *Mission to Yenan*, 83–85.
35. Memo, Joseph Spencer to William Langer, "Re: Dixie Mission," June 4, 1944, NARA, RG 226, entry NM-54 53, box 4.
36. Carter, *Mission to Yenan*, 82–83.
37. Carter explains that when the B-29 planes took off fully loaded, the pilots said they "considered taking off to be more dangerous than facing flak or enemy fighters" (Carter, *Mission to Yenan*, 74).
38. Carter, 75.
39. Baglio's report and Service's comments appear in full in US Senate, Report No. 23, September 6, 1944, *The Amerasia Papers: A Clue to the Catastrophe of China* (Washington, DC: Government Printing Office, 1970), 1:842–44.
40. For further on Whittlesey's death, see Barrett, *Dixie Mission*, 81. Information on Whittlesey's service medal is available via *Military Times* at http://valor.military times.com/recipient.php?recipientid=33262 (last accessed June 12, 2015).
41. For example, see Cromley's memo, "Small Medical Kits Designed as Gifts for Chinese Army Units," August 1, 1944, NARA, RG 226, entry 148, box 7, folder 103: Dixie.
42. Cromley, "Yenan as the Major Order of Battle."
43. Memo, Joseph Spencer to William Langer and Burton Fahs, August 1, 1944, NARA, RG 226, entry NM-54 53, box 4.
44. Stelle to Spencer, "Interim Report," October 27, 1944.
45. Charles Stelle to John Coughlin, "Re: Affairs in Dixie," November 22, 1944, NARA, RG 226, entry 148, box 7, folder 104: Dixie Intel Reports.
46. Kahn, *China Hands*, 127.
47. Barrett, *Dixie Mission*, 35.
48. Anton Remenih to Chongqing, "Need for Increased Radio Power at Yenan," November 28, 1944, NARA, RG 226, entry 148, box 7, folder 103: Dixie.
49. The US government's declassification of the OSS papers and the first materials about the Dixie Mission in the 1970s precipitated a vitriolic and deeply politicized debate over the origins and effects of US anti-Communism in China. For further on the historiography of the "Lost Chance" argument and the CCP leaders' attitudes about foreign policy in the 1940s, see Chen Jian, "The Myth of America's 'Lost Chance' in China: A Chinese Perspective in Light of New Evidence," *Diplomatic History* 21, no. 1 (Winter 1997): 77–86; and Niu Jun, *From Yan'an to the World: The Origin and Development of Chinese Communist Foreign Policy*, trans. Stephen I. Levine (Norwalk, CT: Eastbridge, 2005).
50. Niu, *From Yan'an to the World*, 160.

4

CHANNELS, STOVEPIPES, AND GATEKEEPERS

We, the unwilling, led by the unknowing,
are doing the impossible for the ungrateful.
We have done so much for so long with so little,
we are now qualified to do anything with nothing.
—Poem in the papers of Forrest McCluney,
US Army intelligence courier

The members of the US Observer Mission to Yan'an were hardly the only US officials who would have appreciated the poem collected by Forrest McCluney during the war. But the verse was apt for the Dixie Mission, especially from its start in July 1944 to February 1945. The mission was a perfect example of the kind of improvised intelligence activities the United States sponsored in remote but strategic foreign areas at the time. The height of World War II created a demand for intelligence from multiple US agencies and organizations, some of which were new. However, the US executive branch lacked a functional prewar administrative system for coordinating efforts across agencies. No clear norms or precedents governed the collection or dissemination of foreign intelligence at the scale the war required. US agencies charged with intelligence duties thus developed their own ad hoc methods. Competition between agencies for budgetary resources and influence compounded the pressure on personnel to perform and achieve measurable results on behalf of their organizations. Consequently, organizations often duplicated efforts. The individuals involved with Dixie—mish kids and Army G-2 types who were used to operating far from home—had previous experience with being resourceful in China. Yan'an was deep in the so-called "forward echelon" of the war, close to enemy troops and far from Allied or Chinese Nationalist headquarters areas that could quickly offer guidance. Applying whatever means were available locally to meet their intelligence ends was a more natural response for them than asking for help from Chongqing or Washington, DC, which ultimately caused them trouble.

The lack of an established system for oversight of field intelligence operations further increased the risk that individual intelligence officers in the field, such as those embedded at Yan'an, would act independently, employing what they interpreted to be the best means for defeating the Japanese. Being far from headquarters, they were not necessarily aware of the full political and diplomatic ramifications of their actions. Expansive and vague operational directives for the Yan'an mission blurred the lines between intelligence collection and direct intervention in unconventional warfare. Elsewhere in China, US military advisers were directly assisting with guerrilla forces, but in those cases the collaborating forces were Chinese Nationalist Army troops. They had the approval of Chiang Kai-shek. In Yan'an, US officials had opportunities to plan, fund, and potentially even partner with CCP guerrillas in sabotage, demolition, and disinformation campaigns. In remote conditions they frequently had to make their own judgment calls on what was appropriate to do. They based these decisions on guidance from Gen. Joseph Stilwell or their own intuition, frequently subject to the paternalistic attitudes about China that they had either absorbed from Stilwell or that they already had in common with him. The Dixie Mission was in the crosshairs of systemic bureaucratic problems and institutional rivalries within the US government.

ROUGH CONDITIONS

The first few months of the Dixie Mission demonstrate an aspect of intelligence operations that is easy to overlook: mundane logistical challenges in the field can significantly inhibit progress. Conditions in rural northern China in 1944 often required personnel to spend considerable time solving physical problems, from banal matters such as acquiring typewriters to requisitioning carbon paper and envelopes. To save cargo weight, Dixie produced their reports on thin onion-skin paper. This paper generally had to be flown by the Fourteenth Air Force, from India over the Himalayan "Hump" to Xi'an and then to Yan'an. Claire Chennault, friend of Chiang Kai-shek and nemesis of Joseph Stilwell, led the Fourteenth Air Force. He and his subordinates controlled when pilots flew to Yan'an. The decision to fly was not strictly an emotional one. The CCP-held areas bordered Japanese-occupied areas, where Japanese troops had anti-aircraft artillery. Flying to Yan'an was quite dangerous on a clear day. Inclement weather made it more dangerous. Emergency landings due to weather put planes far from refueling posts and supplies, when they were lucky enough not to end up in enemy hands.

CCP leaders and Americans at Yan'an generally agreed that Yan'an was not a particularly pleasant place to live compared to other parts of China. Yan'an's climate seemed miserable most of the time: hot in the summer, snowy in the winter, and subject to high winds and drenching rain throughout much of the year. In a letter to John Paton Davies, who was planning a trip to Yan'an in October 1944, Jack Service cautioned that he should "bring bedding and plenty of warm clothes—it is cold as hell!"[1] Roads connecting the city to other places were mostly unpaved in the mid-1940s, which made traveling them difficult and slow. Most guerrilla convoys in the region proceeded on horseback or on foot.

Living conditions at Yan'an were challenging and put the Americans in close quarters with one another. The Dixie Mission established living quarters approximately a half mile from the city in caves dug out of a mud hillside. Caves were the most common type of housing in the area, where wood and other construction materials were scarce.[2] The caves lacked indoor plumbing and mechanical heat. The Americans at Yan'an also lacked central bathing facilities of any kind, and toilets were latrines dug into the ground. Stewards made daily rounds to provide thermal bottles filled with potable boiled water for washing and tea. Inside one of hundreds of letters and packages of ephemera he mailed home to his wife, Wilbur Peterkin, David Barrett's executive officer, saved a sample of the toilet paper from Yan'an—mercifully unused—that is now part of the Peterkin Papers at the Hoover Institution archives. Peterkin explained to his wife that workers at Yan'an soaked down old newspapers and reconstituted them into the rough loo paper.[3]

Each cave room at Yan'an had an iron brazier to hold hot coals for heating, which emitted dangerous carbon monoxide fumes. Medic Melvin Casberg reportedly had to rescue Barrett, Service, and Davies from the breathing conditions in their quarters more than once. To keep warm, Dixie Mission members wore thick layers of clothing. Peterkin was also photographed regularly in the winters of 1944 and 1945 wearing a Russian-style fur hat with earflaps.

There were some comforts. CCP canteens were communal chow halls that provided simple Chinese fare at mealtimes. Dinners were followed by tea, cigarettes, and watermelon when in season. Care packages from rear areas arrived sometimes, but other cargo often trumped them on the limited C-47s that came from Xi'an. American personnel posted to the mission regularly complained about their conditions in their personal correspondence.

Due to the nature of its forward-deployed field position in a remote area, personnel posted to the Dixie Mission also assumed a wide variety of responsibilities, including secretarial and administrative work. Many of the men serving in the Dixie Mission held officer ranks in the army or equivalencies in the OSS. Although they were capable of doing their own clerical work, they were not used to it. Civilian and military officers alike who worked on intelligence tasks depended on expert clerks to assist with managing the extensive paperwork and specialized filing systems required in intelligence collection. Clerks who were known for their expertise at this job were usually women. In the interwar period the US executive branch agencies had hired increasing numbers of women. Within the OSS, a few of these women were involved in intelligence operations, but many more handled various forms of administrative work in headquarters and field offices.

The Dixie Mission never included women, much to the frustration of its personnel. OSS operations officer Ray Cromley sent several impassioned memos to his superiors in 1944 specifically requesting the assistance of his favorite secretary. Cromley's memo in late July noted that both the Red Cross and the British Army had female staff in the field. He emphasized that the British secretaries were "of the clinging vine type who are not used to roughing it," implying that because American women were more adventurous and robust, they would find the conditions in Yan'an tolerable.[4] Cromley declared the lack of female secretaries to be "a matter of saving men's lives and winning the war more quickly." Cromley's request reflects sentiments shared by several other Dixie participants, but their CBI and OSS superiors rejected all the requests out of a theaterwide rule that forbade women from being posted to areas deemed to be dangerous combat zones, which included all of mainland China.[5]

OSS officers based at China Theater headquarters in Chongqing echoed the concerns of Dixie Mission members about the absence of file clerks and secretaries. Joseph Spencer, who in 1944 served as the main representative for OSS R&A at CBI headquarters in New Delhi, expressed these sentiments in a cable he sent to William Langer, OSS R&A Branch chief in Washington. Spencer explained for the record that the "clerk problem here in China is very bad."[6] He wrote that R&A personnel in the field were being pressed into service to perform administrative jobs with intelligence processing that were not typically included in their job responsibilities. According to Spencer, the extra work kept those officers from focusing on their actual duties, such as developing and training human assets in the field, debriefing field contacts, and writing reports based on raw intelligence information that the field base had collected through various means. Although Spencer was known by colleagues to be a pessimist, in the cable his outlook for the arrival of the mostly female administrative workforce was particularly grim: "I do not look for a full clearance on the problem of women coming to China in the very near future, so long as the Japanese land drive in Kwangsi keeps moving along. There is still too much uncertainty in the whole thing."[7] CBI Theater records offer no specific explanation for why the OSS and the G-2 did not simply hire or appoint more male clerks. The services may have found it challenging to convince men to perform what was usually seen as "women's work." However, soldiers at war can be ordered to do whatever tasks are required, even the undesirable ones, so this explanation is insufficient.

Spencer's predictions proved accurate: no female employees of any branch of the US government were ever deployed to Yan'an as part of the Dixie Mission, even after the Japanese surrender. Numerous female foreign press correspondents, including American journalists Agnes Smedley and Anna Louise Strong, lived in Yan'an for long periods, as did the wives and families of the CCP leaders. Not even the steady presence of nonmilitary, nongovernment women at the CCP base made any difference in the superiors' decision. It is impossible to tell for certain how requiring Dixie personnel, who had no clerical expertise, to serve as their own secretaries and clerks for the entire three years the mission was operating may have affected the amount of information the unit could collect, record, and disseminate, but it is easy to imagine that the situation had a negative effect on the mission's productivity.

Dixie's remote location had consequences far beyond the availability of clerical personnel. The schedule called for weekly planes flying in and out, ferrying personnel, mail, and supplies, but weather and other hazards (some of them bureaucratic) often prevented the planes' arrival in Yan'an. Delayed or canceled flights meant the lack of much-needed supplies and personnel as well as significant interruptions in communications and the flow of intelligence. US personnel based at Yan'an could send brief, urgent messages via encoded radio transmissions once they had the equipment set up. Most sensitive correspondence, intelligence reports, and material that Dixie participants collected went in physical copy to CBI rear base areas in Chongqing, Kandy, or Delhi. From there the information would slowly wend its way to Washington via plane or ship. Even after the mission improved radio capabilities from Yan'an, US intelligence officials favored hard-copy materials. It was easier to protect sensitive information in physical form and a much greater volume of intelligence material could be conveyed via paper documents or microfilm.

The US government agencies represented at Yan'an supposedly were working toward the same goals. However, the steady struggle to efficiently perform intelligence work in often spartan and remote field conditions provoked the personnel to establish procedural norms that favored their individual agencies. For example, the US Army, US Navy, and US State Department had formed the Joint Army-Navy Intelligence Collection Agency (JICA) as early as 1941 to resolve duplication of efforts in the dissemination of military intelligence from the field. Military officials serving JICA included staff officers in rear base areas and couriers, who physically transported sensitive government materials between war zones. Attempts by JICA personnel based in Chongqing to organize and centralize the flow of intelligence into and out of the city as well as into and out of China during World War II naturally attracted critiques and suspicion from OSS officials, who viewed the army intelligence procedures as the cumbersome status quo bureaucracy that the OSS had been founded to improve and replace.[8]

A SLOW START IN FALL 1944

The weather in northern China in 1944 also proved unsupportive of the Dixie Mission's early plans. Dixie personnel had sat through a series of "study sessions" put on by their CCP hosts in August. These were mostly lectures on the CCP military principles, plans, and successes. By September the Americans were eager to escape these sessions and see for themselves. However, wet and muddy weather conditions delayed American excursions into the remote areas where many CCP guerrillas were operating until late in the fall. The conditions frustrated the eager Dixie participants and stymied their efforts to observe CCP field intelligence practices or the Japanese front lines firsthand.[9]

While the group waited for the roads to become passable, the Dixie participants paired up with CCP counterparts to form small committees that could assist the Americans in learning more about the specific military and political intelligence capabilities at Yan'an. Committees formed on topics such as air intelligence, order of battle, communications, and pilot rescue. The progress during this phase was reportedly disappointingly slow to the Dixie personnel. However, Barrett and the CCP leaders had formed the committees deliberately to avoid duplication and encourage efficiency—legitimate concerns, given the interagency composition of the mission.[10] The committee work offered the American officials a warts-and-all understanding of the possibilities for meeting the goals of their mission. The observers found that the CCP guerrillas were not already collecting the kinds of intelligence that would be most useful for operations in CBI, but that they had the potential to do so. The Americans identified several challenges to intelligence collection in the region.

First, the CCP bases in Japan-occupied areas of northern China were geographically discontiguous and operated with autonomy, which made unifying the staff organization very difficult. CCP leaders in base areas operated on narrow and localized intelligence interests. American officials had comparatively broad intelligence requirements and sought to connect Japanese movements and capabilities in northern China with the broader Allied strategy. In describing this situation, Charles Stelle emphasized the Dixie Mission's ample evidence that the CCP headquarters at Yan'an administered the base areas through party ideology and through the army's organization, and "there is no question that its orders are obeyed" by the base areas.[11] However, the decentralized nature of the CCP's activities meant there were no staff officers with positions parallel to those of the US officials in Dixie. In fact, as Stelle noted, Yan'an's intelligence interests had been focused on political news and anecdotes that could either be used to plan CCP troop movements or in psychological operations of various types.

The Dixie members also assessed the CCP's intelligence capabilities to be focused on supporting specific Communist guerrilla operations rather than on any broader regional, global, or strategic political goals. OSS officers Stelle and John Colling noted the relative sophistication of the CCP's efforts to collect intelligence on the Japanese order of battle and capabilities, which directly affected how the guerrillas would design their operations. Stelle explained that "as guerrilla fighters, they have not had to concern themselves with air strength, airfields and their defenses, naval and shipping movements, production and movement of strategic materials, or the locations of military and industrial installations."[12] Although the CCP's focus on order of battle intelligence was a logical and strategic decision, given the CCP's overall situation and capabilities, it also meant that the CCP cadres were unfamiliar with many types of intelligence that were important to their Allied war planners, such as air, naval, strategic, and weather intelligence. The Dixie Mission sought to direct the guerrillas' attention to the importance of this intelligence and persuade them of the benefits of cooperation. For Yan'an to become a key intelligence-collection site, the Communist fighters would need training in collection methods.

A third initial limitation on the intelligence capabilities of the CCP at Yan'an was the Communists' weak communication system. Many reports from Dixie's members in the operation's first months describe the poor state of the CCP's radio equipment. The CCP had basic radios but lacked skilled operators, and the party had not implemented regularized schedules for radio operation. Increasing the flow of information over the existing radio network would have almost certainly overtaxed and collapsed the rudimentary system. Thus, replacing and augmenting the CCP's communication capabilities quickly became a top priority of the Dixie Mission, and the issue of providing the CCP with radio technology, equipment, and expertise became one of the most significant issues shaping the outcome of the mission throughout its existence.

GETTING ALONG IN REMOTE CONDITIONS

The heavy diplomatic lift required to get approval for American officials to go to Yan'an required the Army G-2 and OSS staffs in China to set aside their differences and collaborate as well as they could. Unfortunately, the arrangement left room for redundancy of efforts and occasional friction. On the surface their contemporaneous communications show a cohesive group of Americans in Yan'an who presented no divisions to their CCP hosts. A deeper look at the records, however, combined with a careful review of correspondence released after the mission tells a more nuanced story. Army G-2 and OSS officers at Yan'an could not completely set aside the turf war occurring between their superiors, and tensions trickled down to the interpersonal level, contributing to the events that ultimately reduced the utility of the mission.

The original Dixie Mission members had good reasons to bond with one another. They were posted together in a dangerous, underresourced, and remote part of China and depended on each other in virtually every way. Many of them had already worked together for years. Even the group members who barely knew each other before arriving, such as Service and Stelle, found common ground. No one in the group had just arrived in China. Most had been there for years, and some were born in China. Stilwell and Barrett had selected only personnel who could communicate in Chinese. The group members shared a general commitment to both the war effort and to being cultural brokers, translating political issues between the United States and China. A well-known columnist for the *New Yorker*, E. J. Kahn, noted in his 1972 book some of these traits among the Americans who were in Stilwell's network during the war. Dixie members bragged to Kahn in interviews that their group had a unique esprit de corps throughout the fall and winter of 1944. They viewed themselves as a "collective elite," Kahn claims, with a "shared pride comparable to that often found among United States Marines, and an elan stemming from their shared concern for intellectual inquiry, from their deep immersion into and understanding of Chinese ethnocentricity, and from the peculiar challenge of the problems that faced them in their work."[13]

Kahn's description echoes the "Can Do" motto of the army's Fifteenth Infantry, in which many of the Dixie Mission members had served. It also echoes the pride and paternalism that bonded some key members to Stilwell. To the extent that they took any side, State Department representatives in Yan'an moved toward the Army G-2 clique. The Observer Group itself was the brainchild of the three Foreign Service Officers detailed to Stilwell (Davies, Service, and Ludden), so this outcome is unsurprising. They helped Stilwell choose the non-OSS members of the mission, including Barrett, with whom they were all familiar because attachés work out of the embassy staff. Barrett was almost considered "one of them."

Long-term friendships developed among the original G-2 and State Department members of Dixie. David Barrett, John Davies, Jack Service, Frank Dorn, John Emmerson, Raymond Ludden, and Wilbur Peterkin regularly swapped written letters well into the 1970s. The personal papers of these men are a mix of serious correspondence regarding their memories of the mission and years of holiday cards, vacation postcards, and invitations for the weddings of children. They wrote each other long letters to make sense of the publications about the Dixie Mission that emerged in the 1960s and 1970s, when a large set of official records became declassified. In his meticulously kept personal papers, Service saved a program from the funeral of John Emmerson.[14] Folds in the program are the exact size of a man's suit jacket pocket, suggesting that Service filed it in his personal records after attending Emmerson's memorial service in 1993—nearly five decades after the two men served together in Yan'an. The fact that this core group of Dixie participants kept in touch over all the years lends some credence to Kahn's conclusions about the bond between the Foreign Service and G-2 members of the original Dixie crew. Kahn did not interview any of the OSS officers who served in Yan'an.

Dixie's OSS officers are a much quieter group in the records left behind. They did not attract the interest of Sen. Joseph McCarthy and the loyalty hearings of the 1950s. Many of them continued working in national security positions after the war. Stelle worked in the State Department's Policy Planning Office with George Kennan for a time and eventually became an influential figure in designing the US nuclear nonproliferation and disarmament policies during the Cold War.[15] Preserved records reveal only irregular contact over the years between the Army G-2 and State Department officials and those representing OSS. Davies, Service, and Peterkin sometimes refer offhandedly to OSS members of the crew in their voluminous papers, but they appear to have had little direct contact with them. The sparser files of Barrett and Dorn rarely mention OSS officers. The absence of such letters is not definitive proof of anything, but it does hint at the discord between the OSS and G-2 staffs that is mirrored in the contemporaneous government records left behind from the Dixie Mission in 1944.

THE PROBLEM OF CHANNELS

The commander of the Dixie Mission always came from the US Army, and communications from Yan'an followed army protocols. The army commanding officer held the ultimate responsibility for either avoiding or facing legal, diplomatic, or political debacles the mission's activities could create. Part of the job was attempting to eliminate the duplication of effort. As the first commander of the Yan'an Observer Group, Barrett also had a responsibility to attempt to resolve disputes over jurisdiction between various US officials in Yan'an. He imposed a chain of command like any other army unit of Dixie's size. The OSS officers at Yan'an sometimes bristled at the idea of army oversight, especially when the duties fell clearly in the emerging bailiwick of the OSS, such as sabotage missions or espionage.

OSS China managers recognized from the outset the implications of having their staff serve under an army command, but they had few other options. The situation had pros and cons for the OSS. Embassy and G-2 favors leveraged with the White House and the vice president had arranged the special situation in Yan'an; the OSS sought to take full advantage. On the other hand, army interests took top priority under Dixie's arrangement. In early August 1944 Spencer, OSS China officer based at CBI headquarters in New Delhi, explained to the head of the G-2 R&A Division in Washington that they would have to patiently wait to see reports from Dixie because communications all rested in Barrett's hands.[16] Barrett cared about the army's ability to pursue the war and he also presumably had a promotion at stake in the results of the Dixie Mission. Both factors might make him more inclined to run a tight ship at Yan'an, in Spencer's thinking. In fact, the outcome at Yan'an ended Barrett's upward mobility by 1945. OSS China had to wait for Stelle to work out the service's delicate relations with Barrett on his own in Yan'an.

Stelle reportedly experienced friction with the G-2 in the first few months in Yan'an. He perceived challenges with dispatching thorough reports out of Yan'an without first getting army approval. Stelle called this the problem of working through "channels," and it was a form of operational censorship between the field and headquarters.[17] He explained to OSS managers in October 1944 that the problems that he encountered encouraged him to travel to Kunming under the excuse of gathering radio equipment. He could have delegated such an errand to a colleague but went himself because he wanted a chance to dispatch his own candid report of the activity at Yan'an without the G-2's review. Stelle told Spencer that the regular channels of communication for Dixie went via Barrett through the G-2 and Col. Joseph Dickey, who was based at the CBI Theater's China headquarters in Chongqing. From there the G-2 would ferry information onward to the appropriate US government unit. Stelle reported that he had already irritated Barrett once by ignoring the proper channels when he sent a stack of Chinese Communist publications directly to OSS officers in Chongqing without running them through the G-2 system. The breech in protocol mattered enough to anger the normally jovial Barrett.

The incident ended up earning Stelle only a minor reprimand. However, it served as a warning to Stelle and his managers that "this mission is obviously an important one, and Theater HQ, as presently constituted at least, is going to hang onto direct control."[18] Stelle said that the OSS staff must respect the boundaries set forth by the G-2 until the OSS had a more established and secure presence in Yan'an. "It will probably pay for us to hew fairly close to this line until we have convinced G-2 that we are not going to run away with their baby."

From his temporary perch in Kunming, Stelle wrote a similar letter to John Coughlin, head of the OSS Special Intelligence Branch operations in China. He argued for biding time:

> It is my honest belief that we will get much further, much faster, not only in getting intelligence for war purposes, but also in promoting the interests of our own organization by a program of sincere collaboration in the Dixie

> Mission rather than by premature attempts to establish an independent operation. I believe that eventually the operation will be of such size that we will automatically be granted a considerable degree of autonomy—but I think we should let that take care of itself as the operation develops.[19]

If David Barrett was concerned about the turf war between the army and the OSS, he failed to mention it anywhere in records that are currently visible to historians. Instead, his comments to the OSS were focused on safety—an issue with which the OSS had encountered problems in China already. In August Barrett wrote to explain his concerns to Robert B. Hall, the deputy director of OSS China in Chongqing. Barrett expressed full support for training the CCP cadre in sabotage, unconventional war tactics, and espionage, as Stelle and Colling had planned. Barrett wanted to ensure that the training program did not endanger the tenuous political agreement that had enabled the Dixie Mission to stand up. He thus asked the OSS to seek specific approval from CBI headquarters for the training plans. He also warned that increasing the presence of US personnel behind the lines in North China would alert the Japanese and bring trouble, likely in the form of "active offensive operations."[20] Despite these caveats, Barrett's tone was friendly and upbeat: "There are many other questions to be considered," he wrote, "but it is perfectly clear that opportunities for your work in North China with the cooperation and assistance of the Communists are almost unlimited."

Evidence of personality clashes among American personnel at Yan'an in 1944 is rare in the historical records. One example that stands out is Service's comments about Stelle. Service regularly sent Davies personal letters updating him on events at Yan'an. Although the mission was Davies's brainchild and he made several long visits to Yan'an, he was not an official member. Service kept him updated. Planes brought personal letters to and from Yan'an when they could, though personal letters were barred from containing sensitive information or specific details about locations or operations. The content of personal letters was not subject to the army protocols for official documents. In one such personal letter in early October 1944, Service described Stelle as the "most useless and lazy bastard that God ever created."[21] Stelle's reports offered no commentary on Service, and there is no way of knowing if the animosity was reciprocal. Moreover, Stelle may have intentionally avoided conveying such feelings in official records due to Barrett's censorship of the reports. Stelle's behavior in late September may have fed Service's prejudice about OSS personnel. Conversely, Stelle's reports describe his frustration at trying to work within the strict pecking order of an army-run mission, and communications between Stelle and his OSS superiors in rear areas allude to—but never specify—a domestic personal problem of Stelle's that affected his work.[22] In a way, Service and Stelle personified the ongoing interagency arguments between the State Department and the OSS, their respective employers.

FIELD-VERSUS-HEADQUARTERS ISSUES

Headquarters offices in Allied base areas for the organizations represented at Yan'an regularly encountered bureaucratic challenges in the first six months of the mission, within and between their representative structures. These problems are particularly evident in OSS correspondence. The OSS was the newest organization with a presence at Yan'an, and some controversy surrounded it among intelligence operators from other agencies. The OSS was taking over some of the intelligence responsibilities that other groups had previously handled, and when responsibilities were transferred, budget allocations usually followed. Managers in OSS China field offices served multiple audiences, communicating intelligence requirements to remote field offices and advising operations in the field. They also faced the burden of managing the expectations of those in Washington, including lateral colleagues as well as more senior intelligence officials and policymakers.

Correspondence between OSS order of battle expert Cromley and his SI Branch handlers Hall and Coughlin displays the challenges. Cromley described feeling "baffled" at the conflicting orders he received, which he claimed were deliberately vague to hide OSS priorities from competing US organizations. Cromley faults the ambiguous orders for not providing specific guidance on actions or behaviors expected in the field. Cromley wrote, "I am anxious to do the right thing, but I can only do the right thing if I have the situation explained to me."[23] OSS China directors Coughlin and Hall likely found it extremely difficult to explain to their colleagues at Yan'an all the sensitive bureaucratic politics and diplomatic negotiations influencing OSS activities. Trying to accomplish this task in the brief (and G-2 monitored) communications going into Yan'an would have been a fool's errand.

Just as Yan'an-based OSS officials did not always receive a complete picture of political conditions in Chongqing, New Delhi, and Washington, OSS audiences in those areas did not always understand what intelligence operations in remote China entailed. OSS R&A Branch director William Langer sent a message to OSS China officers in October 1944 in which he wondered why SI Branch was "both slow and not too successful at setting up agent nets throughout the whole of the Far East."[24] Joseph Spencer, then the CBI acting chief for SI Branch in China, veered into a somewhat flippant response when responding to Langer's query: "SI does not have scads of agents at every crossroad to secure 'information on specific economic questions for R&A Washington.'" Spencer cautioned Langer that intelligence collection on demand is never easy or fast.

Instead, it is all quite uncertain, and "not like putting a nickel in a jukebox." As Spencer wrote at length, "You make elaborate preparations for an agent net, you provide radios, special equipment, special training (and R&A provides some briefing), the agent goes out and you do not hear from him. Was he caught? Was he watched so closely he had to lie still? Is his radio broken? How long do you wait before you start again?" Spencer explained to Langer, who had never been a field intelligence collector, that "a conservative guess" for turnaround reporting once an agent was dispatched was four months. In the very best-case scenario, where a qualified agent was already operating, the soonest turnaround would be three weeks. In other words, in very rare and lucky cases OSS Washington could ask CBI China a question and receive a brief answer via radio within three weeks. In 1944 three weeks might have seemed like eternity for anyone working in Washington, but for those operating in China, this would have been their fastest pace.

Spencer explained the steps to the intelligence dissemination process for information collected in China. Upon receiving a question from OSS in Washington, OSS R&A officers in China would first draft a short memo to an OSS SI officer in China, who would review materials available and task out the question to SI colleagues. But he cautioned that "under SACO it is doubtful whether we will get much of an answer." The R&A officer could use other spokes of his network in the field, but these typically resulted in the request passing through multiple time-consuming relays, such as a delay in the mail plane or the review process of Barrett and the G-2 in Yan'an, before reaching a destination where the information might reside. In many cases, after all that, the requested information was still unavailable or unknown. He ended the description saying, "OSS is a bit undeveloped yet throughout the whole of the Far East. It will both take more time and more personnel for us to achieve a smooth efficient organization. We are still trying."

Communication problems between those requesting intelligence from headquarters offices and those providing it from the field were not at all exclusive to the OSS. In his October 5 personal letter to Davies, Service apologized for an intelligence mix-up over a typographical error that in hindsight is borderline comical. According to Service, Davies requested information on "factions" (as in political factions) of the CCP Army, which reached Yan'an as "functions," presumably "after 16 paraphrasings" as it passed through the various channels of communications.[25] Because the request seemed military in nature, Service passed it to Barrett, who reportedly "hit the roof" at receipt of such a broad request, and queried Chongqing to determine its meaning. They told Barrett to complete the request, which resulted in both a largely unnecessary extensive report on CCP Army functions and a severe delay in providing Davies the intelligence on factions that he had requested.

ORGANIZATIONAL STOVEPIPES

Intelligence from Dixie was not necessarily circulating between agencies either. According to Stelle's description of dissemination practices, Service's political reports—which addressed some of the most important political questions Dixie had been created to answer—experienced a slow, narrow, and dysfunctional distribution process within the US government's China experts.[26] Stelle noted that due to the G-2 channel structure, only Stilwell's office received Service's Dixie reports. From there, the army was supposed to forward them on. Temporarily free of army oversight on his communications while on his short trip to Kunming, Stelle complained to his superiors that "there is no point in Jack continuing his former practice of giving me unofficial copies [to send separately], since in the first place the general community style of living we enjoy at Yenan isn't too conducive to doing things unbeknownst to the powers that be, and in the second place there is no way for me to get them out without their going through G-2."[27] To circumvent the problems, Stelle suggested that OSS officials in CBI offices access Service's reports via Davies, and then disseminate them secretly through OSS channels back to the OSS officers serving in Kunming who needed the information. The OSS ultimately accepted this recommendation, based on the copies of documents preserved in OSS files. According to Stelle, the G-2 had also failed to deliver copies of Cromley's initial order of battle reports to OSS officials in Kunming, who obviously had an immediate need and use for them. In both cases Stelle specified that he doubted the slights were deliberate or political but rather were due to the volume of Dixie's reporting coupled with the "limitations of staff and inefficiency in the G-2" that created "a first-class bottleneck" in G-2 offices in Chongqing.[28]

RISK AVERSION IN OSS HEADQUARTERS

OSS officials assigned to Yan'an and their managers recognized the potential for important intelligence collection from the Yan'an base, but they found that capitalizing on this potential was extremely difficult and time-consuming. Reports from Dixie's initial five OSS officers follow a general pattern: an enthusiastic officer in the field attempts to wade through the various turf wars to design and propose a bold plan for an intelligence operation; the plan inadvertently conflicts with US military or diplomatic interests in the area; first-line managers respond to the plan with optimism and support, but that soon gives way to some mix of risk-aversion, simple bureaucratic inertia, and disagreements in headquarters offices over jurisdiction, scope, and vision. The problems at the management level were sufficiently serious to prevent the release of resources and necessary approvals to the officers in Yan'an. During long communication delays, field officers were often moving forward on plans without permission while they waited to hear back, including operations involving CCP cadre. When headquarters finally weighed in, killing the operation or scaling it back, those in Yan'an experienced disappointment and frustration. This pattern was on display in the first few months of the Dixie Mission for projects designed to respond to some of the OSS's top priorities for their work in China: developing a network of human intelligence assets in North China and gathering the intelligence necessary to produce and maintain a complete order of battle on Japanese troops.

A Rotten APPLE

OSS officers in Yan'an were under some pressure from managers to establish a Yan'an-based network of Chinese and Korean intelligence assets and operators in North China and beyond. In the European Theater, recruited OSS assets often participated in clandestine war efforts beyond the simple collection and reporting of intelligence. OSS handlers tasked assets to engage in sabotage and demolition operations, capture enemy documents, and conduct other similarly dangerous activities behind enemy lines. Stelle and Colling sought to develop such teams of agents behind the Japanese lines in North China; they code-named the operation APPLE.

OSS had attempted to start such operations much earlier, but ineptitude in the Chinese environment stymied their first efforts. The SACO agreement prevented the rest. OSS directors initially thought that running the operations out of Yan'an would insulate them from SACO agreement repercussions. This was a poor assumption. If such an OSS operation were successful enough to evade Japan's detection and be wiped out, Chongqing was sure to learn of it either through Dai's network or via CCP leaders' taunts of the Guomindang. The operation never achieved sufficient momentum to encounter any of these problems.

The APPLE operation presented an extreme challenge for Stelle and Colling. Circumstances were stacked against them at nearly every turn. Stelle, the senior of the two at thirty-four years old, had been serving primarily in R&A Division positions related to psychological warfare. He had participated in a year of OSS training, but he was new to operational work. Like many officials who were recruited into the R&A Division, Stelle was highly educated. He earned a PhD in East Asian history from the University of Chicago. He spoke Chinese, Japanese, French, and German. Prior to serving in China, Stelle had served as one of three deputy heads of the OSS R&A Branch's Far East Division in Washington, DC.[29] In early 1944 Stelle had moved from that job to chief representative of the OSS's R&A Division in Chongqing. His experience working closely with the Air and Ground Resources Technical Staff at that time had secured his selection to join the Dixie Mission in July 1944.[30] Stelle had impressed Davies, and Dixie sought capable linguists who were comfortable operating in China. Stelle participated in the Dixie Mission in the capacity of what would today be called a targeting analyst.[31] He investigated and analyzed potential intelligence opportunities in the field and reported back to headquarters about them. Stelle had the expertise to support the research and cultural planning aspects of APPLE, and others collaborated with him to ensure operational security and support of the intelligence conclusions. Stelle regularly reminded Coughlin and Hall in Chongqing that he was more analyst than operative.[32]

Though the more junior officer of the two, Colling had some training and experience participating in intelligence collection operations. This experience was not quite the same as designing and executing operations. Colling's communication style came off arrogant, which made it difficult for him to curry favor with colleagues when he required help. Colling was the son of US Army captain William Colling, who had served in the Fifteenth Infantry Division in Tianjin in the 1920s. Colling Sr. and his wife had remained in Tianjin after his retirement in 1929 and raised their three sons there.[33] John Colling had joined the army after Pearl Harbor. Having requested assignment in the CBI, he ended up supporting guerrilla operations in Burma under General Stilwell before his assignment to Dixie.

The first reports by Stelle and Colling from Yan'an to OSS managers in Chongqing regarding the APPLE program recommended collaborating with CCP guerrillas and some Japanese Communist POWs to begin collecting intelligence in North China. Under the SACO agreement the United States was allowed to team up with guerrilla groups loyal to Chiang Kai-shek.[34] These groups were different from what APPLE proposed in two important ways. First, the troops were loyal to Chiang Kai-shek and the project had the blessing of the SACO implementation team. Dixie Mission projects enjoyed nothing like this top cover. Second, the Nationalist guerrillas had some operations in North China, but not in the same areas where the CCP operated. The CCP area was strategically located near Japanese troops. It had previously been completely inaccessible to American intelligence collectors. Some Japanese POWs being held at Yan'an were members of the Japanese Communist Party. A few had chosen to defect from Japan and serve the CCP instead. Okano Susumu, head of the Japanese Communist Party, expressed a willingness to help send US agents to Manchuria, Korea, and Japan to assist in psychological warfare efforts and sabotage, similar to OSS foreign asset operations occurring in Europe.[35]

Colling and Stelle reportedly found Okano's offer both credible and exciting. The operation to train and dispatch Chinese agents in North China and beyond became a significant source of communication and debate between

OSS headquarters, various field-based OSS branch offices, and the OSS officers based at the Yan'an outpost. In an August 1944 report addressed to OSS managers serving in New Delhi, Chongqing, and Kunming, Colling enthusiastically claimed, "We are sure that the only limits on the cooperation we can secure from the local Chinese authorities and on the results that can be attained will be the amount of personnel and equipment that we are prepared to invest and able to transport."[36] Stelle and Colling requested radio equipment to use in the initial training of Chinese agents, as well as additional personnel who could train Chinese agents in demolitions, radio, and general intelligence techniques.[37] They planned a trip with their Chinese counterparts deep into the northern Chinese countryside in early September 1944.

Robert Hall, deputy director of OSS China and immediate supervisor of Stelle and Colling, initially reacted to the APPLE plan with optimism but also with some ambiguity. His response was to "neither approve nor disapprove" the project. Hall wrote, "The idea is magnificent, and we will go all the way as soon as the road is clear. It is the greatest idea in Cathay, if the necessary courage and imagination can be mustered to put it through."[38] He also noted that he needed more details on financial and equipment requirements. Hall recognized that launching the operation might cause political problems for the United States. However, he was hopeful. He argued that "this is just the kind of project Oboe Sugar Sugar was created to do," invoking the internal nickname for the OSS. "I am hoping we will be allowed to undertake it, even if it means a slight exposure of the neck."

Hall's measured enthusiasm may have simply been his way of managing morale for the Dixie officers. His communications with other managers reflect less optimism. Hall forwarded the details of the APPLE project as outlined by Stelle and Colling as well as Cromley's order of battle plans to the chief of the Secret Intelligence Branch at the OSS's Far East Desk in Washington, DC. Hall's cover letter explained the potential of the projects and their consistency with the overall mission of the OSS. However, he also expressed numerous qualms: "These projects will not develop as rapidly as our young men imagine."[39] The majority of Hall's memo explained political problems that the mission could raise, chief among them ruffling the feathers of Chiang Kai-shek and Dai Li. Hall questioned how far both the Guomindang and the army officers at CBI headquarters were willing to go in cooperating with the CCP, particularly given the sensitivities of the SACO agreement.

By the time Hall sent Yan'an a follow-up message on August 27, his enthusiastic tone toward the Dixie officers had shifted to one of greater risk aversion and less support. Hall first told Cromley, "Probably because you have been so constantly on the go since your arrival in China, it has been impossible for you to get the overall picture and the many patches of thin ice upon which you are compelled to operate."[40] Hall warned that taking autonomous actions that OSS headquarters had not approved could land him in serious trouble, noting, "I realize that I probably sound overly cautious and conservative to you, but if so, I have come to be that way by the hard school. We are getting forward, and I am not anxious to lose our gains."[41] With this response Stelle and Colling had their first glimpse of the struggle they would encounter in obtaining headquarters' support for their plans. Discussion over if, how, and under what conditions APPLE could proceed continued to occur well into 1945. The operation never occurred.

OSS officer Ray Cromley had slightly better success launching his plan for collecting intelligence for the OSS order of battle on the Japanese military—a project that required overt, rather than clandestine, collection methods. At the same time, he created a similar order of battle for the CCP forces. He believed the CCP leaders were unaware that the project was unfolding. It is unlikely that the Dixie Mission members were able to keep any secrets from the CCP, but records the CCP might have kept about it are not currently available to researchers. The OSS had also asked Cromley to develop a training program for Chinese intelligence officers and POW interrogators.[42] Cromley was chosen for the Dixie Mission due to his expertise in order-of-battle work and his excellent reputation within the G-2. Prior to World War II, Cromley had been a journalist, working for several years as the *Wall Street Journal*'s Tokyo correspondent. When war broke out, the Japanese arrested and convicted him for distributing information "detrimental to the national defense of Japan." He was imprisoned in Japan for several months before being repatriated in a prisoner exchange. Upon his return to the United States, he joined the army and was assigned to work in the G-2.[43]

Cromley's experience moving between army and OSS posts was typical. When posted to Dixie, Cromley was technically an officer of the OSS, but he served under AGFRTS and G-2 covers. Stelle also had a military cover, with respective ranks of first lieutenant and captain, which irked Gen. William Donovan, who thought Stelle should be ranked at least a major based on his experience and what the OSS was asking him to do.[44] Cromley was sent to the OSS post from his previous position in the G-2 specifically to work in the China Theater on order-of-battle intelligence.[45] When he arrived in Chongqing in May 1944, OSS China officials assigned him to the AGFRTS personnel.[46] He was under that cover for his first few weeks in Yan'an before plans changed when AGFRTS decided it was not interested in the intelligence he produced and was nervous about potential political blowback from American operations in forward areas deep in China.[47] Cromley's cover then shifted back to the G-2.

Cromley learned from his CCP counterparts that intelligence was typically passing across Japanese lines via guerrillas riding horses or mules. He thus requested specific radio technology and staff who could help support the installation of the equipment from the base in Yan'an. Cromley also sought to establish a well-equipped microfilm station to facilitate the work of guerrillas who continued to carry items into Japanese areas. These men had to be selective about paper copies of publications and reports they carried, which were conspicuous for their bulk, but they could easily carry hundreds of microfilmed documents in a small space without detection.[48] Documents on microfilm were also significantly easier to transport back to OSS field offices away from the front lines and to counterparts in Washington, DC, particularly because most communication emerging from Yan'an traveled via airplane. Once Cromley received information from the CCP guerrillas moving through the countryside, he sent it all to Chongqing, where OSS's Joseph Spencer had to weed through it and match it with questions CBI headquarters and Washington had asked.

CBI GATEKEEPERS

Spencer ran into obstacles in the task of matching intelligence collected with intelligence requested. In December 1944 Spencer, the OSS official at CBI headquarters who served as direct supervisor for OSS personnel stationed in Yan'an, wrote to OSS R&A Branch Chief William Langer complaining that OSS intelligence requirements sent from Washington for Yan'an officials were not reaching his office. Lists of questions and requirements OSS headquarters sent to the field through military channels were languishing at the JICA offices. Spencer noted that none of the requirements that Langer claimed to have sent to the unit through the JICA had arrived. He speculated that the failed deliveries were deliberate and related to competition between military intelligence and OSS in Chongqing. "Frankly, JICA has been looking for opportunities to get into research for some time, and this is just one of the ways," Spencer wrote.[49] With liberal use of all capital letters—the most expressive formatting available in diplomatic cable communications at the time—Spencer implored Langer and his subordinates to bypass military communication channels and send their questions directly to OSS R&A officials in China. JICA records fail to reveal if the delay in delivery of OSS correspondence in China was indeed intentional, as Spencer suggested, or simply a side effect of the fabled inefficiency of that short-lived organization. Spencer's perception of the situation is instructive, regardless of the reality.

Spencer's memo also highlights a separate problem associated with the coordination of intelligence collection that emerged as operations at Yan'an limped along before the Japanese surrender: intra-agency rivalry. US intelligence officials felt pride toward their agencies and loyalty to their own divisions within agencies. Divisions were often responsible for different portions of what intelligence officers today would recognize as the standard cycle of intelligence collection: collection, processing, analysis, dissemination, and tasking.[50] The cycle is meant to be collaborative and iterative rather than competitive. However, the US intelligence regime then was not sufficiently developed to smoothly collaborate (and it has never completely resolved this tension). Two examples of the effects of such competitive attitudes surface in Spencer's December 5 memo alone. First, Spencer responded to Langer's concern that OSS intelligence analysts in Washington were not receiving sufficient answers to their questions by reminding Langer that the collectors in the field needed to receive more timely and specific requests for information. Spencer wrote, "Give us as much of a detailed statement as you can—please do not just say 'any new material on . . .' since we do that automatically when we get anything—and give us something realistic on what your deadline may be so that we know how to plan our programs."[51]

Spencer's remarks note an important gap in awareness and communication between the OSS R&A headquarters officers and those working in the field in remote parts of China. His next comments also reveal how he prioritized his loyalty to the various groups he was serving. He detailed how one visiting OSS R&A officer in China was "seeing the evidence that R&A is the best damned branch in the whole shop." Obviously taking considerable pride in his affiliation with the OSS R&A, he continued, "It's that way because we worked hard at it, because with all our heckling back and forth, R&A at home and in the field is in closer touch, is better organized, and doing a more effective job than any other branch. On that we stand. We are all zealous to keep it that way, to improve our production, to serve you better, and to get on with both the war and the chances of the peace."

These examples highlight one of the most obvious problems that surfaced during World War II as US leaders expected a prewar national security bureaucracy to adapt itself and assume demanding new strategic responsibilities. The establishment of the OSS moved the US government toward a capacity to collect and absorb strategic foreign intelligence. However, at least within China, expecting the individuals within older organizations to simply put their expertise and autonomy aside to make way for the OSS proved naive.

The experiences of the first crew of American officials in Yan'an opened a rift within the US government between those who supported the Dixie Mission and those firmly in Chiang Kai-shek's camp. US officials took sides. Stilwell's network tended to be more excited about the potential of Yan'an and more dismissive of Chiang's leadership. For all the claims by the US government and FDR that the United States would not take a side in China's domestic political disputes, it began to look as though American officials indeed had their favorites. Importantly, they were not of one mind. The lack of internal processes for collaboration and coordination between US agencies and organizations did not help matters.

NOTES

Epigraph: Harry S. Truman Presidential Library, Papers of Forrest McCluney, box 8: Printed Materials, folder 7. The folder holding the poem is labeled "Army Chair Force song," applying a facetious term to the US officials who served as intelligence officers for the Army Air Force during World War II.

1. Letter, Jack Service to John Paton Davies, October 5, 1944, Bancroft Library, University of California, Berkeley, Papers of John S. Service, carton 2, folder 51.
2. Carolle J. Carter, *Mission to Yenan: American Liaison with the Chinese Communists, 1944–1947* (Lexington: University Press of Kentucky, 1997), 36–38; and author in-person interview of Sidney Rittenberg, Scottsdale, Arizona, February 2013.
3. Visitors to the archives of the Hoover Institution at Stanford University can commune with this sample and Peterkin's other curated artifacts of the Dixie Mission in the Personal Papers of Wilbur J. Peterkin.
4. Report by Ray Cromley, "Personnel Needed for China Order of Battle Work," July 31, 1944, NARA, RG 226, entry 148, box 7, folder 103: Dixie.
5. According to Maochun Yu, Stilwell and Ambassador Clarence E. Gauss vehemently opposed the use of American female secretaries and clerks in China during World War II. Maochun Yu, *OSS in China: Prelude to Cold War* (Annapolis, MD: Naval Institute Press, 1996), 170.
6. Memo, Joseph Spencer to William Langer, "RE: OSS China," November 19, 1944, NARA RG 226, entry NM-54 53, box 4.
7. Spencer's pessimism is mentioned in Memo, William Langer to Burton Fahs, November 21, 1944, NARA RG 226, entry NM-54 53, box 4.
8. For more on the JICA and military intelligence bureaucratic procedures during the war, see Bruce W. Bidwell, *History of the Military Intelligence Division, Department of the Army General Staff: 1775–1941* (Frederick, MD: University Publications of America, 1986), 401.
9. Memo, "Transmitting General Report on US Army Observer Section at Yenan," August 24, 1944, NARA, RG 319, box 717.
10. Report, Charles Stelle to John S. Spencer, "Interim Report on Mission to Yenan," October 27, 1944, NARA, RG 226, entry NM-54 53, box 4.
11. Stelle to Spencer, October 27, 1944.
12. Stelle to Spencer, October 27, 1944.
13. E. J. Kahn, *The China Hands: America's Foreign Service Officers and What Befell Them* (New York: Viking, 1976), 35.
14. Found in Papers of John S. Service, box 1.
15. US Department of State Policy Planning Staff/Council, Member Chronological Files 1947–1962, NARA, RG 59, entry A1–558F, boxes 13, 16, 18, and 35.
16. Memo, Charles Spencer to William Langer, August 1, 1944, NARA RG 226, entry NM-54 53, box 4.
17. Stelle to Spencer, October 27, 1944.
18. Stelle to Spencer, October 27, 1944.

19. Memo, Stelle to John Coughlin, "Re: The Dixie Mission, October 1944" (Stelle's record copy, specific date not given), NARA, RG 226, entry 148, box 7, folder 103: Dixie.
20. Memo, David Barrett to Robert B. Hall, Chunking, August 7, 1944, RG 226, entry 148, box 7, folder 103: NND 857148.
21. Service to Davies, October 5, 1944.
22. Spencer to Langer, November 19, 1944.
23. Memo, Ray Cromley to Robert B. Hall with John Coughlin's response to Hall's August 27 letter, September 18, 1944, NARA, RG 226, entry 148, box 7, folder 103: Dixie.
24. Memo, Joseph Spencer to William Langer, October 31, 1944, NARA, RG 226, 1944.10.31; and Langer to Spencer, RG 226, box 4, entry NM-54 53.
25. Service to Davies, October 5, 1944.
26. Stelle to Spencer, October 27, 1944.
27. Stelle to Spencer, October 27, 1944.
28. Stelle to Spencer, October 27, 1944.
29. Barry Katz, *Foreign Intelligence: Research and Analysis in the Office of Strategic Services, 1942–1945* (Cambridge, MA: Harvard University Press, 1989), 23.
30. Memo, Joseph Spencer to William Langer, Burton Fahs regarding Dixie Mission (codenamed PALISADE), July 7, 1944, NARA, RG 226, entry NM-54 53, box 4; and Memo, John Coughlin to Joseph Dickey, May 18, 1944, NARA, RG 226, entry 148, box 7, folder 103.
31. Stelle to Spencer, October 27, 1944.
32. Report, John C. Colling and Charles Stelle, "Re: Details of APPLE Project," August 7, 1944, NARA, RG 226, entry 148, box 7, folder 103.
33. John C. Colling, *The Spirit of Yanan: A Wartime Chapter of Sino-American Friendship* (Beijing: Foreign Languages Press, 2004), xxvii.
34. Milton Miles, *A Different Kind of War* (New York: Doubleday, 1967), chap. 16.
35. For more on Okano Susumu, see Yu, *OSS in China*, 168.
36. Memo, Charles Stelle and John C. Colling to Robert Hall and Peers, "RE: Possible OSS Operations from Yenan as a Base," August 7, 1944, NARA, RG 226, entry 148, box 7, folder 103: Dixie.
37. Stelle and Colling to Hall and Peers, August 7, 1944.
38. Report, Robert Hall to David D. Barrett for John C. Colling and Charles Stelle, August 24, 1944, NARA, RG 226, entry 148, box 7, folder 103: Dixie.
39. Memo, Robert Hall to OSS, "Re: Dixie Mission and Two Proposed Projects," August 26, 1944, NARA, RG 226, entry 148, box 7, folder 103: Dixie.
40. Memo, Robert Hall to Ray Cromley, "Re: Matters OB, China," August 27, 1944, NARA, RG 226, entry 148, box 7, folder 103: Dixie.
41. Hall to Cromley, August 27, 1944.
42. Ray Cromley, "Yenan as the Major Order of Battle China Base of Operations," July 30, 1944, NARA, RG 226, entry 148, box 7, folder 103: Dixie.
43. Memo for John Coughlin, "Re: Cromley Order of Battle Expertise," April 1, 1944, RG 226, OSS Field Station Files, Chungking, entry 148, box 7, folder 103: Dixie.
44. Personnel file of Charles Stelle, NARA, RG 226, entry 224, box 743.
45. Memo for Coughlin, April 1, 1944.
46. Letter, John Coughlin to Joseph Dickey, May 18, 1944, NARA, RG 226, entry 148: Chungking, box 7, folder 103: Dixie.

47. Memo, Robert Hall to David Barrett for Ray Cromley, August 26, 1944, NARA RG 226, entry 148: Chungking, box 7, folder 103: Dixie.
48. Cromley, "Yenan as the Major Order of Battle China Base."
49. Joseph Spencer to William Langer, December 5, 1945, NARA, RG 226, entry NM-54 53, box 4.
50. For more on the intelligence cycle, see Mark M. Lowenthal, *Intelligence: From Secrets to Policy*, 2nd ed. (Washington, DC: CQ, 2003), 41–51.
51. Spencer to Langer, December 5, 1945.

5

ZAIJIAN, STILWELL

And as the soldiers are dead bodies by,
He called them untaught knaves, unmannerly,
To bring a slovenly unhandsome corse,
Betwixt the wind and his nobility.

—Joseph Stilwell's favorite Shakespeare passage, from *Henry IV*

When Army major Wilbur "Pete" Peterkin returned to Yan'an in January 1945 from a four-month inspection tour behind Japanese lines in northern China, he found that both the CBI Theater and the Dixie Mission had experienced significant personnel changes. Roosevelt had replaced Joseph Stilwell; Ambassador Clarence Gauss had resigned in frustration; and Stilwell's replacement, Gen. Albert Wedemeyer, had moved David Barrett from Yan'an to a different position in Chongqing in December 1944.[1] Instead of assisting his mentor and patron, Peterkin would now serve as executive officer to Col. Morris DePass, who had been hastily appointed to take charge of American affairs in Yan'an in January 1945 (and who lasted less than a month). Meanwhile, the entire future of the American presence at Yan'an was under discussion. The pace of intelligence collection in the countryside surrounding Yan'an compared to the pace of communications and decisions by American leaders was a startling contrast. Peterkin had some catching up to do.

INTELLIGENCE MISSION TO JIN-CHA-JI

Having to cope with all the issues at Yan'an did not dissuade Dixie Mission members from investigating more remote and more dangerous areas with their CCP hosts in the final months of 1944. Initial discussions with Communist military leaders and cadre about their activities stoked American interest in getting out and into the countryside to see for themselves how the CCP guerrillas were faring. In September Barrett had put Peterkin in charge of a small group of American personnel assembled to make a thorough inspection tour of the main CCP guerrilla base area, Jin-Cha-Ji (陕-甘-宁边区). The name was an abbreviation derived from the area's location at the intersection of three provinces:

Shanxi, Chahar, and Hebei.[2] CCP guerrillas referred to the headquarters of the area as Fuping; Dixie Mission records often refer to the base by this name or the older spelling, Fouping. The group embarked by mule on October 6, 1944, and did not return to Yan'an until January 23, 1945—effectively missing the time of greatest transition and upheaval for the rest of the Dixie Mission.

Barrett's orders to members of the field inspection team had focused mainly on verifying the stories about CCP successes that Mao and the other party leaders had been telling. The inspection crew was to "gather intelligence on the Japanese and set up weather stations and air rescue bases for downed American airmen."[3] In addition to reports about the Communists' organization, equipment, and troop physical conditions, Barrett's orders directly asked, "Are the Communists fighting the Japanese?" The orders also directed the crew to gather information about the self-sufficiency of the CCP guerrillas and their relations with civilians in the towns where they were operating.[4]

Peterkin had a capable group of Americans and CCP guides on his crew. His own Yan'an roommate (or cavemate, as it were) Ray Ludden served as Peterkin's second in command. Capt. Brooke Dolan and Capt. Paul Domke, from the army, joined the group. Dolan had traveled on several other remote treks in China and Tibet. In 1942 the OSS had sent him and Ilya Tolstoy to Tibet as Roosevelt's envoys. In Lhasa they were the first American officials to meet the Dalai Lama, who was then nine years old.[5] The next entourage member was Sgt. Walter Gress. He was an OSS radio tech under Signal Corps cover. Lt. Henry Whittlesey represented the Air Ground Aid Service. Lt. Simon H. Hitch, the Dixie Mission's sole representative from the US Navy, also made the trek.[6] Yan'an was far from the ocean, but the ONI was interested in the locale for gathering signals intelligence collection and weather information that could affect navy operations. Charles Stelle, John Colling, and Ray Cromley—Dixie's OSS officers who represented the R&A and SI Divisions—were not part of the entourage. Records make no mention of this omission being a deliberate or consequential decision, but it is interesting considering the correspondence about OSS plans and Barrett's concerns about increasing the American footprint in the area around Yan'an. CCP military officers and troops traveled with the American entourage for protection. A small cohort of CCP guerrillas always stayed with the Americans as guides, but other CCP members, including some high-ranking military officers, met up with the expedition in the countryside.

PETERKIN LEADING THE CHARGE

Prior to the war Pete Peterkin lacked the depth of experience in military or diplomatic service in China that other Americans in Yan'an had. However, he spoke Chinese well, and Barrett trusted him. Like Barrett, Peterkin had come from an ordinary, working-class background in rural America. Born in 1904, Peterkin was forty-one years old when he joined the Dixie Mission, close in age to Service and Davies, who were both in their late thirties. All were younger than Barrett, who was fifty-two in 1944. Peterkin grew up in Clinton, Iowa, and he had put himself through college at the University of Oregon by working odd jobs to pay for tuition. He had graduated and started his teaching career in 1931 at age twenty-seven, and before the war he worked as a high school teacher and principal in a Seattle suburb.[7] Peterkin was called into active duty in the summer of 1941. He entered the Fifteenth Infantry Regiment, where he soon learned of his regiment's deep connections to China. He was in infantry school at Fort Benning, Georgia (now Fort Moore), when the Japanese attacked Pearl Harbor. Given his background in education, Peterkin spent the first part of the war as an infantry school trainer before being sent to officer school in April 1943.[8]

Peterkin shipped out to China in the fall of 1943 and was helping train Chinese troops in the large American-run base area in Guilin when he first met Barrett. At the time, Barrett oversaw the G-2 at the Guilin base. In spring 1944 Barrett chose Peterkin to be his executive officer (a sort of military clerk and secretary for a ranking officer). Stilwell organized a program at Guilin to train Chinese Nationalist military officers how to protect airbases against Japanese attack. It was from this location that Stilwell summoned Barrett in March 1944 for help in leading the Dixie Mission. Recognizing Peterkin's abilities as a trainer and aware that part of the Dixie Mission duties might be to train CCP troops, Barrett tapped Peterkin to join him on the trip to Yan'an. Both Barrett and Peterkin had already rotated to Chongqing in preparation for the Yan'an mission when Guilin fell to the Japanese in late June 1944.[9]

Peterkin's experiences working closely with the CCP generals and the successful completion of several observation missions may have bolstered Barrett's confidence in sending him on the Fuping trip. Peterkin arrived in Yan'an on the second Dixie flight on August 7, and his duties included the day-to-day staff administrative work for the mission as well as various training and observation duties Barrett assigned to him. Before the trip to the Jin-Cha-Ji border region, Peterkin frequently gave talks and lectures to the CCP military leaders at Yan'an to compare notes on how they were fighting the Japanese. His audiences often included such influential generals as Zhu De, Peng Dehuai, Ye Jianying, He Long, and Chen Yi. Before the big inspection trip, he also made frequent shorter excursions into the countryside around the Yan'an base area. The CCP guides escorted the American team to Naniwan, forty miles from Yan'an, where they watched a brigade of CCP soldiers building a new base.[10]

IN DISGUISE IN FUPING

The trip to Fuping afforded Peterkin's entourage an unprecedented view of the activities in Communist-held North China. Their travels were neither quick nor comfortable. Peterkin and his group ultimately traveled around twelve hundred miles "entirely by mule or on foot."[11] Between October 6 and November 10 they hopscotched from one guerrilla hamlet to another, slowly making their way to Fuping. On arrival they were issued the "blue gray insulated pants and jacket, as well as a goatskin coat" that the guerrillas typically wore.[12] Their Chinese guides also gave them Chinese-style haircuts as disguise. The Americans slept and ate alongside CCP hosts, experiencing the basic living conditions of people in the Chinese countryside at the time, which typically included no plumbing, heating, or home electricity and a diet of rice with the occasional vegetable. Along the entire route, CCP guerrillas escorted the American delegation in groups that Peterkin said numbered anywhere between small squads of six or seven troops to an entire fifteen-hundred-man brigade at one point.[13]

Several remarkable intelligence accomplishments emerged from the Fuping mission. The Americans happened to be at Fuping in November 1944 when CCP guerrilla troops brought from the field a six-man American flight crew from a B-29 that the Japanese had shot down over North China. The presence of Dixie Mission personnel at Fuping facilitated the rapid debriefing of these American airmen, which Peterkin claimed yielded extremely rare and valuable intelligence on Japanese capabilities and positions in Manchuria.[14] In addition, Peterkin and his American crew cooperated with their CCP hosts to collect intelligence on Japanese positions in the vicinity. The information that the CCP guerrillas provided enabled the Americans to produce highly detailed maps of the respective areas held by the Japanese and the guerrillas.

The maps were a completely unique intelligence source for the United States at the time. Contacts between the US military and Guomindang guerrilla troops had charted out some other areas in eastern and northern China that happened to be under Nationalist control, but Peterkin's Fuping delegation yielded the first tangible cartographic material to document CCP and Japanese positions in terrain that US troops might have to briefly help control or occupy if North China needed to later serve as a launching position for a final assault on the Japanese islands themselves at the end of the war.

The Fuping trip also allowed Peterkin and his team to investigate the potential capabilities of the CCP troops for supporting a US military presence in North China on the chance it might be warranted later in the war. Peterkin agreed with the CCP leadership's assessment that with even a minimal amount of US aid in the form of explosives, Communist troops "could effectively tie up all [Japanese] railroad traffic for two or three weeks," which would help provide cover for American forces who might be planning an attack on the Japanese islands.[15] Inspection of the railroads and tunnels near the Japanese military bases in the Jin-Cha-Ji base area bolstered Peterkin's confidence in the assessments of CCP capabilities. Peterkin discovered that the CCP guerrillas had built miles of tunnels secretly connecting buildings and villages where CCP troops could move or hide without detection. The tunnel system undoubtedly helped the CCP troops in the civil war.

However, these inspections of the Japanese areas proved to be quite dangerous work. Barrett's fears that American presence in the region might attract negative attention from the Japanese came true. Peterkin's group ultimately had to retreat from the countryside back to Fuping after December 12, when they learned the Japanese knew of their presence in the region. Japanese posters began offering a reward of $5,000 in gold for the capture of Peterkin, dead or alive. According to Peterkin, the group waited at Fuping until late December for the return of Whittlesey. As he remembered it, Whittlesey had teamed up with some CCP contacts and ventured out on an independent mission while Peterkin was away from Fuping inspecting the Japanese-held Beijing-Hankow Railroad. The lack of direct communication between the two made it impossible for Peterkin to learn of Whittlesey's complete plans, leaving Peterkin with a very unclear picture of where Whittlesey might be.

Peterkin and the rest of the entourage were restless. The longer they waited, the more likely the Japanese would become aware of their presence, and they also risked the safety of their hosts. Cold temperatures and snow were threatening to severely compromise their planned land-based return to Yan'an. By December 29 Peterkin said the Americans "could wait no longer" and departed Fuping for Yan'an, which they reached on January 23, 1945. They trusted that the CCP guerrillas hosting their mission would facilitate Whittlesey's passage back to Yan'an once it became sufficiently safe and possible to do so.

Unfortunately, Whittlesey did not survive—the sole casualty of the Americans who served at Yan'an during the entire mission. Peterkin and his fellow Dixie participants learned of Whittlesey's death via a special message from an extremely apologetic Ye Jianying on February 4.[16] Ye conveyed that Whittlesey and a CCP guerrilla who was serving as his guide had been shot and killed by a Japanese sniper in a town where fighting had occurred, even though they had been told the area had been cleared of enemy fighters. Whittlesey and the CCP counterpart had gone into the town to attempt to collect intelligence. Whittlesey's death had a profound effect on the morale of the remaining Dixie participants. It was the first in a series of hits that unfolded by spring 1945.

VINEGAR JOE AND THE PEANUT

Far from Yan'an in Chongqing, disagreements and tension between Chiang Kai-shek and General Stilwell that had been brewing almost since their first meeting boiled over in September 1944, ending in the dramatic departure of Stilwell on October 20, 1944. Forced to choose between keeping Stilwell and potentially losing Chiang's cooperation with Allies, FDR reassigned Stilwell—a change that triggered a cascade of personnel shifts and policy revisions throughout the CBI Theater. The moves severely tested the resolve of the American officials serving at Yan'an, who were part of Stilwell's personal faction. When the dust settled, many of Stilwell's people in Yan'an had been redistributed in the theater or beyond. The overhaul hurt Dixie's momentum, leaving the Yan'an mission an empty G-2 shell of its early interagency reality. Beyond simply hampering the intelligence initiatives the Dixie Mission had started, the administrative chaos led to permanent negative career outcomes for several of the Dixie Mission participants.

Stilwell's basic approach to the war in China, which had been at the heart of a major disagreement between Stilwell and Chiang for months, involved training Chinese troops in American infantry methods and leading them to secure the main transportation routes from India to China—a dangerous and grueling project that was also unsuccessful. Instead of recognizing what historians have later assessed to be his own poor plans and strategies, Stilwell made erroneous assumptions about Chiang's willingness to fight and wrongly accused him of stockpiling US aid. Both Hans van de Ven and Hsi-sheng Ch'i have carefully reviewed historical records from China and the United States related to the Stilwell-Chiang confrontation, and their analyses vindicate Chiang Kai-shek and the Nationalists from the bulk of Stilwell's erroneous assessments.[17]

From their very first meetings, Stilwell had a negative view of Chiang, whom he privately nicknamed "the Peanut," against the expressed wishes of Roosevelt.[18] Personal diaries and letters found after Stilwell's death drip with criticism for Chiang, some of it using language sufficiently offensive that journalist Theodore White had to tone it down to include it in the publication of the documents in the late 1940s. Stilwell was personally contemptuous of Chiang, whom he saw as ungrateful and surrounded by yes men. Stilwell regularly predicted China would be a political mess after the war, with Chiang at the center. "Peanut knows only what goes on immediately around him, and the country is so big that he will not be able to control it. Obstinate, pigheaded, ignorant, intolerant, arbitrary, unreasonable, illogical, ungrateful, grasping," Stilwell wrote in his journal in 1943.[19]

Chiang's view of China's role in the war against Japan differed significantly from Stilwell's and caused the Chinese leader to repeatedly question Stilwell's strategies and motives. Chiang and his troops had been fighting one opponent or another for most of the twentieth century, and they had been fighting the Japanese specifically since the 1930s. Many times Chiang had been fighting domestic opponents. These decades of fighting, as well as the demoralizing occupation of China that forced Chiang to reconstitute his government in Chongqing, a furnace of a city in the rural backwater of southwest China, had left the Chinese leader and his troops depleted and jaded. In a highly effective summary of the Chinese government's perceptions during World War II, historian Rana Mitter describes Chiang's view of China "as the first and most consistent foe of Axis aggression."[20] According to Mitter, Chiang and many elites around him perceived that China's perseverance, even in the complete absence of foreign assistance, entitled it to Western support and treatment as an equal power.

Moreover, the high number of Chinese military casualties potentially required to pursue Stilwell's plans was concerning to Chiang, who remained distrustful of Stilwell and most other Western officials throughout the war. He suspected that Stilwell and other Western military commanders valued Chinese lives less than the lives of their own troops—a reasonably valid view, given some of the evidence Chinese leaders had of foreign behavior in China. Chiang doubted that Stilwell would pursue the same dangerous land-based strategy if he had been commanding US ground troops to participate in the battles. Chiang questioned why the United States, with all its resources and technology, would not make greater use of aerial campaigns in China, which he believed would achieve some of the same military purposes with a much lower cost of life.

Chiang saw the Pearl Harbor attack as an opportunity to finally entice the United States and other Western powers to provide the resources and capabilities he believed should have been shared with China much earlier, before the Japanese had become such a strong global threat.[21] Chiang's pleas for the United States to provide American ground troops, planes, heavy artillery, and training in air warfare that Stilwell deemed unnecessary for the strategy being applied fed Stilwell's perceptions that Chiang lacked seriousness about defeating the Japanese and was merely preparing for the coming domestic political showdown. Beyond their strategic disagreements, Chiang and Stilwell each had willful, stubborn personalities and frequently clashed over issues of personal pride, which probably contributed most to bringing the conflict between them to its finale when Roosevelt became frustrated with them both in October 1944.

The conflict had been brewing throughout the summer of 1944. When Vice President Wallace visited China in June 1944, Chiang repeatedly complained about Stilwell to the extent that Wallace's trip report alerted Roosevelt of the seriousness of the situation. Wallace suggested that Roosevelt make a personnel change. After his talks with Chiang, Wallace reported that "it appears impossible for General Stilwell to maintain the close and continuous contact with the Generalissimo which is a sine qua non, and the Generalissimo also informed me bluntly that General Stilwell does not enjoy his confidence because of his alleged inability to grasp overall political considerations."[22] Wallace reported that Wedemeyer "has been strongly recommended to me" for the job of being Chiang's counterpart. Wallace recognized the difficulty of finding the right person to fill the job. It required someone with the ability to command American forces in China, master the coordination of American and Chinese militaries there, and garner the confidence of Chiang.

Neither Wallace nor Roosevelt appear to have considered Stilwell's actual job performance in their assessments. The release of Stilwell's complete papers and records from China eroded the heroic view of Stilwell in contemporary mass media during World War II. In fact, Stilwell was hardly ever present in Chongqing and thus able to pay close enough attention to perform the actual duties of Chiang's chief of staff.[23] Instead, Stilwell spent most of his time in other parts of the CBI Theater, walking the jungles of Myanmar with individual Chinese troops or complaining to Roosevelt and other Americans about Chiang.

In August, Roosevelt sent special emissary Patrick Hurley to China as his personal representative to Chiang reporting directly to Roosevelt himself. Roosevelt said Hurley's mission was "to promote efficient and harmonious relations between the Generalissimo and General Stilwell to facilitate General Stilwell's exercise of command over the Chinese Armies placed under his direction."[24] The idea that Chiang would even consider handing over command of his armies or that the US president would be obnoxious enough to ask this is startling. Hurley came away from their first meeting charmed by Chiang and believing that Chiang had accepted the request. He reported back to Roosevelt that Chiang had agreed to put Stilwell in full charge of his troops.[25] This turned out to be all talk on Chiang's side, with no meaningful action to follow. It is almost impossible to believe that Chiang ever intended to yield control of his troops to any foreign power. Hurley's efforts had not been particularly helpful to Roosevelt or Chiang.

Roosevelt had heard—and shared—many of the misperceptions that Stilwell expressed about Chiang Kai-shek's practices. However, from the president's strategic perspective, Stilwell's behavior and attitude was also beginning to threaten American relations with Chiang's government, which Roosevelt believed would ultimately undermine US interests in Asia and the US war effort. Even if what Stilwell had been saying about Chiang were true, Roosevelt thought that Chiang's government still presented the most legitimate and capable ally for the United States in China. Roosevelt calculated that the United States could ill afford to alienate Chiang. Moreover, mediating bickering between Stilwell and Chiang had become a serious distraction, absorbing attention that the White House could not spare as the United States fought the war on two fronts and as Roosevelt approached the election for his fourth term in office. Over September 1944 Roosevelt became convinced that fundamental disagreements between Chiang and Stilwell over several key aspects of the strategy for fighting the Japanese had become irreconcilable.

By the end of the summer of 1944 the threat Japan presented to China had intensified. US-operated base areas at Kunming and Guilin, key elements in the Allied supply chain through China, became vulnerable. Appropriately sensing urgency, Stilwell's establishment in CBI began pressuring Roosevelt to intervene in his relationship with Chiang and his troops. After weeks of increasingly tense dialogue and correspondence between Stilwell, Chiang, officials in the Chinese government and diplomatic establishment, George Marshall, and Roosevelt, the situation came to a head on September 16, 1944. Marshall and his staff drafted a stern and condescending ultimatum to Chiang, which Roosevelt signed. The letter read, "Only drastic and immediate action on your part alone can be in time to preserve the fruits of your long years of struggle and the efforts we have been able to make to support you. . . . Otherwise political and military considerations alike are going to be swallowed in military disaster."[26] The letter requested that Chiang place Stilwell in full command of all China's troops or risk losing US support—a toothless threat because the US had no intention of abandoning China, which Chiang knew.

Stilwell insisted on delivering the letter to Chiang in person in a humiliating and spiteful move. Verses that Stilwell left in his diary on this day give a hint at the tone of the meeting and Stilwell's immature mindset:

> I've waited long for vengeance—
> At last I've had my chance.
> I've looked the Peanut in the eye
> And kicked him in the pants.[27]

Unsurprisingly, the Generalissimo responded with extreme outrage, requesting Stilwell's immediate removal. The incident, which highlights the willingness of both Chiang and Stilwell to become intractable to the point of childishness, served as the last straw for Roosevelt, who initiated Stilwell's recall without delay.[28]

FALLOUT IN YAN'AN FROM STILWELL'S EXIT

Stilwell reportedly left China in a hurry. Most journalists had not learned of his reassignment or reported his recall before he was already out of the country. Stilwell left China with bitterness, not staying to brief his successor, Albert Wedemeyer, or taking the time to leave any useful advice for filling his new role as Chiang's main counterpart in the US military. Stilwell and Chiang reportedly bid each other a shallow and cordial farewell. According to Barbara Tuchman, Stilwell's final words to the Generalissimo were a popular Chinese proverb: 最后胜利 (*Zuihou shengli*, often translated as "For the Final Victory!").[29]

Stilwell's abrupt removal precipitated numerous significant changes to the US war effort in the CBI Theater that were implemented starting in late October 1944. The theater command split into three distinct sections—instead of a China-Burma-India Theater with US troops under the command of one US general, the activities of US forces in East Asia divided into a China Theater, under the command of Wedemeyer; a Southeast Asia Theater, under command of Lt. Gen. Raymond Wheeler; and an India-Burma Theater under Lt. Gen. Daniel I. Sultan. The latter two sections both fell under the Southeast Asia Command (SEAC).[30] Many US military leaders had argued for this change throughout 1943 and early 1944, and it met with substantial support from Americans serving in China, particularly for the perception that it would streamline communication channels. Fighting the war and cooperating with China became significantly easier after Stilwell's departure.

WEDEMEYER ON THE SCENE

Albert Wedemeyer represented a consensus choice for Stilwell's replacement—an amiable and articulate officer who knew "how to work with everyone."[31] He was one of the people Chiang had suggested for the job.[32] Wedemeyer's salient characteristics when promoted to command the China Theater included youth—forty-seven years old, compared to Stilwell, who was sixty-one that year—ambition, and a confident persona. Youth and capability may have helped mitigate the effect of Wedemeyer's reputation for arrogance among both the Chinese leaders and the senior US diplomatic and military officials in China, all of whom supported his selection as Stilwell's replacement. Wedemeyer had some credibility with the army in China because he had served under Stilwell and Marshall in the Fifteenth Infantry in Tianjin from 1930 to 1932. However, it was a short stint and Wedemeyer was not considered part of the Stilwell network within the broader US Army organization.

Shortly after serving his time in Tianjin, Wedemeyer had pursued advanced officer training at Fort Leavenworth and had studied how the General Staff of the Nazi regime worked during time he spent at the German War College from 1936 to 1938.[33] He distanced himself from the regime's ideology. However, by his own account his experience studying the German military heavily influenced his rigid commitment to staff protocols and deep respect for the chain of command. This approach to staff work, rules, and normalization of procedures, combined with his outsider position to the clannish community of US China experts, helped him streamline wartime intelligence efforts in China during his time in command. After his return from Germany, Wedemeyer served in the War Department Planning Division until after the Pearl Harbor attack. He was then assigned to head American efforts in the SEAC Theater.

Wedemeyer's distance from Stilwell and lack of familiarity with Chinese domestic politics may have appealed to Chiang Kai-shek and his close advisers, who believed that Wedemeyer's naiveté could make him more malleable and accepting of their recommendations. Wedemeyer showed much greater personal deference to Chiang than Stilwell had, particularly on intelligence matters within China's territorial boundaries, but Chiang's optimism about a significant strategic shift once Stilwell was gone proved baseless. Wedemeyer's commitment to continue many of Stilwell's policies, particularly the tight control of US Lend-Lease supplies to China, angered the Chinese leader. Chiang accused the United States of using its aid to China's military to convince the soldiers to worship foreigners, undermining his leadership over his own troops.[34] Chiang also worried—appropriately—that the CCP was taking advantage of Stilwell's one-sided version of his departure from China, which was playing as Stilwell hero story in the US media.[35]

Wedemeyer despaired at the lack of coordination between the various US intelligence organizations vying for influence in China. To disentangle intelligence activities occurring in his theater of battle, Wedemeyer sought to consolidate control over all China intelligence in one officer. In early November Wedemeyer offered the position to Col. Richard Heppner, an OSS officer who had been serving in the China Theater since the beginning of the war. Heppner would not have been Gen. William Donovan's first choice for the position, but OSS China was reeling from a humiliating late October diplomatic incident when a senior OSS officer in Chongqing had gone on a drunken tirade at a party hosted by China's central government and publicly insulted Chiang Kai-shek and his wife.[36] The incident so angered the Chinese government that Dai Li considered refusing to allow any future OSS operations in the country. Wedemeyer intervened and suggested that Heppner could perform the OSS position in a way the Chinese would find acceptable and bring to heel the various American intelligence officers in the country.

Heppner agreed to take the position only on several significant conditions: he would answer directly to Wedemeyer, all OSS supplies would be routed through India and not China (that is, separated from other US military supplies and thus unknown to the Chinese government), and three hundred American "commando units" would be provisioned for China.[37] Furthermore, Heppner would staff his office in Chongqing with subordinates he trusted, which meant even more personnel shifts among the American government presence in

China. By late November the deputy officer in charge and every OSS branch officer serving OSS China in Chongqing was new to the job.

REORGANIZATION UNDERWAY IN WASHINGTON

As the members of the Dixie Mission attempted to weather the changes to their leadership structure in China, top civilian and military leaders in Washington began to propose their own plans for how the broader US government should manage the collection and dissemination of intelligence once World War II ended, given the changed global security environment. The State Department submitted to the White House the first proposals for intelligence organization in August 1944. Proposals recommending that the State Department serve as the central coordinator of postwar intelligence circulated in Washington throughout September and October.[38]

After the State Department initiated debate of the issue, the OSS began drafting proposals of its own. Donovan had argued for the creation of a standalone strategic intelligence agency for wartime and peacetime when the Coordinator of Information office had been established in 1941, and the proposals he made to the White House in late October and November 1944 simply extended and specified these plans. Donovan distinguished his proposals from those of the State Department by recommending the creation of an independent agency that put supervision of US intelligence activities directly under the president's authority rather than running them through the diplomatic and military executive branch departments.[39]

The flurry of debate and proposals for the reorganization of US intelligence duties reflected several priorities of the top US leaders at the time. Policymaker interest in postwar intelligence demonstrated an awareness among the American leadership both that the national security interests and obligations of the United States had changed and that prewar intelligence processes were inadequate for the tasks the United States now faced in the global security environment. The leaders of individual agencies also wanted a postwar intelligence plan that preserved resources and powers that they already considered to be their agencies' responsibilities, and in many cases they sought to expand the power and influence of their own agencies. In the face of disagreements over best practices in the intelligence process and having experienced frustration in acquiring helpful and timely foreign intelligence through the American government throughout the war, heads of the US civilian and military national security organizations displayed little faith that counterpart agencies elsewhere in the government could collect and disseminate foreign intelligence effectively.

Given these assumptions, competition for influence and resources seemed inevitable. The new intelligence agency that Donovan proposed would retain the functions that had become most positively identified with the OSS, including the branches of Special Operations (SO); Secret Intelligence; X-2, which handled covert action; Morale Operations (MO), which handled propaganda; and R&A. The proposed peacetime strategic intelligence agency would focus on the collection of sensitive strategic foreign intelligence information relevant to US national security and interests. A key component of Donovan's proposals included making the new agency the center hub within the US government for coordinating the intelligence activities of other US government agencies, exclusively retaining the right to perform intelligence analysis, "synthesis, and dissemination within the government."[40]

Unsurprisingly, the other agencies with vested budgetary and procedural interests in intelligence work perceived Donovan's proposal as an attack on their interests. Although the military leaders who comprised JICA agreed on their opposition to the proposals by both the State Department and Donovan, they struggled to form their own alternative plan (not a particularly unexpected outcome, given JICA's reputation for duplicating efforts, slowing the release of intelligence, and generally adding a layer of intractable bureaucracy on top of the archaic methods of military intelligence in operation in 1943 and 1944). Bradley Smith summarizes the overall effect of Donovan's proposals for achieving his goal of establishing a new peacetime intelligence agency, with himself as head, as "an unmitigated disaster." But Smith also argues persuasively that Donovan's proposals, along with those of the State Department, succeeded in accelerating the debate over the long-term future of intelligence activities within the US bureaucracy. As Smith explains, "Every agency of the regular government was compelled to clarify its position and confront more directly the shortcomings of the prevailing intelligence system."[41]

Roosevelt allowed the debate between his subordinate executives to unfold until he finally entered the fray in mid-January 1945 after recognizing that the war, and particularly the Pearl Harbor attack, had demonstrated the need for intelligence reform. Roosevelt argued for the consolidation of foreign intelligence duties between the State Department, the War Department, and the Department of the Navy, but rather than specifying how to resolve the conflict, he called on their leaders to negotiate a solution. Roosevelt's response placed the status quo national security organizations at the center, largely ignoring Donovan's plea for a new independent agency and dismissing outright the need to include the collection of commercial and economic intelligence along with the diplomatic, political, and military topics that formed the mainstay of traditional US strategic intelligence.

These debates occurred at a high level in Washington, and the written record does not appear to make specific reference to the intelligence activities that Americans at Yan'an were pursuing. However, missions such as Dixie had highlighted the need for postwar intelligence reform. Moreover, the leaders of the organizations involved had the interagency competition in mind as they made decisions regarding intelligence operations around the world—any example of which could help or hurt their organization's status in the struggle for influence. The Dixie Mission been a provocative project from the start. It was responsible for collecting and disseminating information that had the potential to stoke sensitive political controversies within the US government. It also had the potential to gather uniquely useful strategic information that could hasten the end of the war with Japan.

Bureaucratic growing pains within the nascent US intelligence community, just when the requirements of World War II had expanded its mandate, were beginning to have transformative effects on both the execution of intelligence operations in and around Yan'an and how Washington perceived reports that the Dixie Mission participants generated. In the 1930s and 1940s the ability to penetrate the foreign policy discourse occurring within the US government generally required at least one of the following forms of status: influence from personal rank or title; influence by virtue of a close personal connection to an influential top leader; or influence resulting from one's position within an accepted and respected bureaucratic process, such as the military, an executive branch organization, or Congress. Roosevelt demonstrated his preference for the first two forms of status and his begrudging acceptance of the last. The fact that low-level officials comprised the Dixie Mission throughout its tenure, combined with the ad hoc and unprecedented nature of the mission's administrative organization, placed American officials posted at Yan'an at a distinct disadvantage in terms of communicating their observations to the top leaders in Washington, particularly given Roosevelt's highly personalized foreign policy leadership style.

THE DIXIE MISSION IN EARLY 1945

As badly as Chiang Kai-shek might have desired it, Stilwell's departure did not lead to the discontinuation of intelligence activities in Yan'an. Instead, the mission limped along. The group continued to implement its vague operational orders despite dramatic personnel changes in the China Theater. By the beginning of November 1944, the relatively new US Army Observer Mission in Yan'an had transformed into a jaded unit of political survivors struggling to anticipate the next external shocks that might affect its future. Although the initial few months of the Dixie Mission's presence in Yan'an generated a spirit of cooperation and aura of optimism about the potential for an intelligence windfall, the fall of 1944 delivered an undeniable reality check for all mission participants and their supporting colleagues in Chongqing and Washington.

Amid so many obstacles, the individual American officials posted at Yan'an from October 1944 to March 1945 collected a surprising amount of important information about the CCP and about the Japanese, but it had little influence on policy at the time. Dixie Mission members who teamed with CCP counterparts to pursue field trips in the northern China countryside and develop radio capabilities in the Communist-held areas drafted a series of reports that are impressive in quality and quantity. Official communications of the Americans at Yan'an show a steady stream of intelligence reports ranging from topics such as the demolition capabilities of the CCP and the orders of battle of the Japanese troops operating in North China to political assessments of the CCP's plans and intentions. Jack Service alone filed fifty-one reports in the few months he was based at Yan'an in 1944.

Had these American officials served within an experienced and professionalized American intelligence community, the reports may have influenced US China policy. However, the immaturity of the dissemination channels for foreign intelligence within the US bureaucracy in World War II, coupled with the level of distraction caused by personnel changes and diplomatic negotiations among American officials in Chongqing and Washington, prevented the intelligence reports from influencing the policy discourse. Communications among managers within the OSS describe some of the turmoil inflicted on China operations by the leadership turnover in fall and winter 1944.

In late November 1944, Burton Fahs, the Far East section head for the OSS R&A Branch, traveled to Chongqing and made a brief visit to Yan'an. R&A Branch head William Langer had a letter waiting for him when he arrived providing some personnel context in preparation of his visit. Langer emphasized the issues OSS China was having and that "the upheaval in the Far East has reduced everything to a state of uncertainty."[42] He also noted that Joe Spencer was not getting along well with managers John Coughlin and Robert Hall, having outbursts of frustration about how things were working in OSS China. Given the situation and all the other personnel moves, Langer even asked Fahs to extend his trip and stay in the CBI Theater until Donovan's expected arrival, potentially as late as the very end of 1944. Langer reported that Heppner would take over as head of OSS China under Wedemeyer, with Coughlin heading to India-Burma. All other personnel moves were on hold until Donovan could gauge the situation in person, but Langer feared the results of leaving Spencer to handle things on his own while others were in transition.

Stilwell had played a major role in supporting Dixie Mission efforts and in resisting the bureaucratic forces in the United States and China that opposed the group's creation or, in Donovan's case, its army leadership. The network of people that Stilwell had developed from his protégés and carefully selected subordinates had been instrumental in launching the Dixie Mission and establishing constructive, cordial initial relations with the CCP between July and October 1944. Stilwell's removal from his position as the figurehead of these efforts presented a major blow to the momentum and morale in Yan'an and called into question the group's future. Subsequent leadership changes among the American contingent in China worsened the outlook for its continuation and productivity.

NOTES

1. In December 1944 Barrett was appointed chief of staff of the China Combat Command, a new army-run organization in Chongqing directed by Gen. Robert B. McClure.
2. Contemporary sources use the most common romanization system, but in the 1940s it was referred to as Chin-Ch'a-Chi.
3. Military historian William Head wrote a biography of Peterkin that relies on Peterkin's published memoirs and extensive interviews with Peterkin he conducted in June 1982. William P. Head, *Yenan! Colonel Wilbur Peterkin and the American Military Mission to the Chinese Communists, 1944–1945* (Chapel Hill, NC: Documentary Publications, 1987), 60.
4. Directive, Col. David D. Barrett to Maj. Wilbur J. Peterkin, "Subject: Objectives of Trip behind Japanese Lines by Peterkin's Group, October 6, 1944 to January 22, 1945," October 4, 1944, quoted in Head, *Yenan!*, 124–25.
5. For more on the Tolstoy-Dolan envoy trip, see Karl E. Meyer and Sharon Blair, *Tournament of Shadows* (Washington, DC: Counterpoint, 1999), 531–47.
6. Head, *Yenan!*, 60.
7. Head, 3.
8. Head, 37, 43.
9. Head, 42.
10. Head, 53.
11. Head, 60.
12. Head, 77.
13. Head, 74.
14. Head, 77.
15. Head, 77–78.
16. Head, 82–84.
17. Readers interested in the nuances of the confrontation between Chiang and Stilwell should consider reading Hsi-sheng Ch'i, *The Much Troubled Alliance: US-China Military Cooperation during the Pacific War, 1941–1945* (Singapore: World Scientific, 2016); and Hans J. van de Ven, *China at War: Triumph and Tragedy in the Emergence of the New China, 1937–1953* (Cambridge, MA:

Harvard University Press, 2018). Van de Ven also explores reasons behind Stilwell's own misperceptions and how and why his views convinced the US public in both *War and Nationalism in China, 1925–1945* (London: Routledge Curzon, 2003) and "Stilwell in the Stocks: The Chinese Nationalists and the Allied Powers in the Second World War," *Asian Affairs* 34, no. 3 (2003).

18. Stilwell, *The Stilwell Papers,* 245.
19. Stilwell, *The Stilwell Papers,* 215.
20. Rana Mitter, *Forgotten Ally: China's World War II, 1937–1944* (Boston: Houghton Mifflin Harcourt, 2013), 243–44.
21. Mitter, 242; Ch'i, *Much Troubled Alliance,* 489–91.
22. US Department of State, "Conversations between Vice President Wallace and Chiang Kai-shek," June 1944, *FRUS, Diplomatic Papers 1944: China,* 236–39.
23. Ch'i, *Much Troubled Alliance,* 495–500.
24. Memo, FDR to Patrick Hurley, August 18, 1944, FDRL, President's Secretary's Files, subject files, box 138: Harry Hopkins to Hyde Park, folder: Hurley, Patrick.
25. Memo, Patrick Hurley to President Roosevelt and George Marshall, September 7, 1944, US Department of State, *FRUS, Diplomatic Papers 1944: China,* 154.
26. Letter, FDR to Chiang Kai-shek, September 16, 1944, US Department of State, *FRUS, Diplomatic Papers 1944: China, 1944,* 157–58.
27. Stilwell, *The Stilwell Papers,* 334.
28. Diplomatic events in China in the days leading up to Stilwell's removal have been a subject of historical analysis for decades. For a succinct recent assessment, see Mitter, *Forgotten Ally,* 335–43. Jay Taylor offers a broader assessment of Chiang's perspective of events more than most other accounts in *The Generalissimo: Chiang Kai-shek and the Struggle for Modern China* (Cambridge, MA: Belknap Press of Harvard University Press, 2009), 270–95.
29. Barbara Tuchman, *Stilwell and the American Experience in China, 1911–1945* (New York: Macmillan, 1970), 5, 504.
30. Woodburn S. Kirby, *The War against Japan,* vol. 3, *The Decisive Battles* (London: H. M. Stationery Office, 1961), 117–19. See also Tuchman, *Stilwell and the American Experience in China,* 502.
31. Tuchman, *Stilwell and the American Experience,* 429, quoting Joseph Alsop, a famous American foreign journalist and newspaper correspondent who served in the US Navy during World War II. Alsop was posted to Kunming, China, where he worked as an assistant to General Chennault in 1944.
32. Taylor, *The Generalissimo,* 297.
33. Albert C. Wedemeyer, *Wedemeyer Reports!* (New York: Henry Holt, 1958), 50.
34. Mitter, *Forgotten Ally,* 346–47.
35. Taylor, *The Generalissimo,* 295.
36. Maochun Yu devoted a chapter of his comprehensive monograph to describing the full details and consequences of the so-called Miller incident. See Yu, *OSS in China: Prelude to Cold War* (Annapolis, MD: Naval Institute Press, 1996), 172–82.
37. For the full details of Heppner's conditions, see Memo, "Reorganization of OSS under Colonel Richard P. Heppner," [n.d.], NARA, RG 226, entry 154, box 170, folder 2941. Yu also describes the context of Heppner's promotion in *OSS in China,* 180–82.
38. Bradley F. Smith, *The Shadow Warriors: O.S.S. and the Origins of the C.I.A.* (New York: Basic, 1983), 396.

39. B. Smith, *The Shadow Warriors,* 396–97.
40. Memo, William Donovan to FDR, October 24, 1944, FDRL, President's Secretary's Files, Subject File, box 167.
41. B. Smith, *The Shadow Warriors,* 397.
42. Memo, William Langer to Burton Fahs via John Coughlin, November 21, 1944, NARA, RG 226, entry NM-54 53, box 4, folder: China July–December 1944.

6

THE HURLEY BURLEY

As far as documents, materials, and contents of conversations are concerned, things that we reveal should be true; things that cannot be revealed should be concealed.
—CCP internal directive, August 1944

On November 7, 1944, a small crowd gathered at the dusty airstrip in Yan'an, awaiting the arrival of the beat-up C-47 David Barrett often called the "Wounded Duck," after its mishap landing the previous July. The arrival of the plane was rare enough to be exciting. Barrett, Zhou Enlai, and a crowd of Yan'an residents had spontaneously come out to greet the plane and help gather the supplies and mail aboard. None in the crowd were expecting the tall, uniformed American who stepped out when the door opened. That American was Gen. Patrick Hurley, President Roosevelt's special representative to China, and the visit was a surprise.

Barrett noticed that Hurley was decked out in what he described as "one of the most beautifully tailored uniforms I have ever seen and with enough ribbons on his chest to represent every war, so it seemed to me, in which the United States had ever engaged except possibly Shay's Rebellion."[1] Hurley's emergence from the plane "visibly startled" Zhou Enlai, according to Barrett. "Please hold him here until I can bring Chairman Mao," Zhou told Barrett, as he disappeared in a cloud of dust, only to return "in a shorter time than I would have thought possible with the chairman." They pulled up in the "only piece of motor transport" that Barrett had ever seen at Yan'an, an overused truck with an enclosed cabin. A "hastily mustered" infantry company honor guard followed on foot close behind.

Mao and the honor guard lined up to welcome the general following the protocols he was due. Hurley walked down the line, closely inspecting the troops. He then returned the salute of the company commander, stood up to his full six-foot-two-inch height, and released a full Choctaw war whoop at his highest volume. Mao and Zhou stood speechless at this unusual but vintage Oklahoman display.

The stakes of the visit for Mao and Zhou were high. Meeting Roosevelt's personal emissary could offer them political legitimacy they sought, not necessarily in China but with other international actors, the Chinese diaspora, and elites. The CCP leaders had extended repeated invitations to Hurley beginning in September 1944. A few days after arriving on his first and only visit to Yan'an, John Paton Davies had also urged Hurley to tour Yan'an and meet the Communist leaders.[2] But Hurley had ignored all their requests lest his recognition of the CCP leaders be seen by the American public as undermining America's main ally in China, Chiang Kai-shek. This would have been particularly bad form so close to election day in the United States.[3]

Although initially impressed at Hurley's determination to visit Yan'an—a dangerous act, given the escalation of Japanese bombings—the CCP leaders reportedly were not amused at Hurley's bizarre debut appearance. Hurley's ostentatious display presented an awkward contrast to his battle-hardened CCP hosts. They had spent most of the previous decade living in caves and engaging in guerrilla warfare; Hurley was showing off his badges from a brief and nominal military career. Hurley's dramatic entrance gave the Americans living at Yan'an a small taste of the embarrassment they would regularly experience when observing Hurley's interactions with the Chinese Communists. The combination of Hurley's lack of respect for subordinate American officials in China, his apparent lack of understanding of the domestic conflict in China, and his slightly obnoxious personality ultimately did little to endear Hurley to the American officials at Yan'an. However, these traits were not on full display during Hurley's first visit to the CCP, which set a deceptively cordial tone that the CCP leaders later said they found confusing.

Once the CCP leadership recovered from Hurley's war whoop at the airfield, Mao, Hurley, and Barrett crushed into the Communists' dilapidated vehicle. Barrett nominated himself to translate Hurley's salty and rambling remarks, anecdotes, and jokes. And thus began the CCP's relationship with America's unusual new representative in China, with the Dixie Mission thrust directly into the middle of it.

"THE HURLEY BURLEY"

The arrival of Patrick Hurley in Yan'an changed the tone of relations between the United States and the Chinese leaders. Hurley did not completely dissolve the American mission to Yan'an, but the effects of his vision and personal style on the Americans' relationship with their Chinese Communist counterparts permanently altered it. He made an entrance on the delicate political landscape in China that Barrett's biographer, John Hart, likened to the level of "devastation of a tornado from his native Oklahoma."[4] Hurley's verbose and boisterous approach to diplomacy was about as foreign to Chinese diplomatic norms as possible, compared to the standard demure disposition exhibited by most Chinese statesmen at the time. Based on demeanor, Hurley stood in particularly sharp contrast to Zhou Enlai, who has gone down in history as one of the most sophisticated, urbane, and cosmopolitan diplomats of the twentieth century. Another biographer described Hurley as "mercurial-tempered," an apt assessment, given that the ambassador "roared commands; he hurled profane charges; and he threatened to fire his ablest people."[5] US officials who met with Hurley universally described his affinity for hearing himself talk and his tendency to monopolize meetings with rambling and disorganized monologues. Barrett noticed this tendency within the first few minutes after Hurley set foot in Yan'an. US embassy staff in China facetiously referred to Hurley's brash and garrulous style as the "Hurley Burley."[6]

To say that Hurley was unpopular among American officials in China in 1944 and 1945 profoundly understates the intensity of the contemporaneous accounts and remembrances of the officials involved, which contain a litany of derogatory comments on Hurley's behavior, remarks, and attitude. Hurley is a well-known and comprehensively documented figure in many histories of US-China relations and World War II. Despite the volume of reporting, positive impressions of President Roosevelt's chosen ambassador in this period are rare. One of the few people to make approving comments about Hurley in this period was Chiang Kai-shek, who wrote to Roosevelt that Hurley had Chiang's "complete confidence," praising Hurley's "rare knowledge of human nature."[7] Far more common are descriptions of Hurley similar to this one, from an OSS CBI manager based in India: "People are generally at a loss to discover those qualities which have made him such a great favorite with the president."[8]

Years later, negative perceptions of Hurley had intensified for those who had encountered him in China. For example, in a letter to Sen. J. William Fulbright in 1972, the normally amiable and genteel Jack Service wrote, "Hurley in my opinion was a stuffed shirt and phony, of limited mentality, and in some ways as vicious as a rattlesnake. At the time he came to Yenan, he had already begun to show symptoms of senility. Why President Roosevelt ever chose him for such an important mission, I have never been able to understand."[9] Hurley attracted even stronger disapproval from the CCP leaders he met in 1944 and 1945. Mao Zedong and Zhou Enlai were said to have privately referred to Hurley as "the clown" (丑角) beginning as early as their first meeting with him in November 1944.[10]

Hurley did not share the skepticism that Amb. Clarence Gauss and General Stilwell had expressed about Chiang Kai-shek's intentions and capabilities. Hurley, a complete newcomer to China with no previous knowledge of Chinese politics, developed admiration for Chiang. Hurley shared the paternalistic attitude of Gauss and Stilwell—that American goodwill and aid could "fix"

China—and Hurley thought this could happen through Stilwell. If he held any impressions of the CCP before his arrival in Yan'an, they are not recorded. Conversely, Gauss and Stilwell both had contemptuous views of Chiang, and they had determined the CCP to be serious challengers for political power in China.

In the days before his resignation, Gauss expressed pessimism about the future of negotiations between the Nationalists and Communists. He succinctly articulated his assessment of the situation in a cable to the secretary of state on November 4, 1944: "Almost all moves these days, political or military, of Chiang and his medievally minded cohorts revolve around the pressing problem of maintaining themselves in power, and under these circumstances there is little if any possibility of achieving a reasonable or realistic settlement of either the Communist or the other difficulties which are more and more besetting Chiang's regime as the weeks go by."[11] Numerous American officials who had served in China through the early 1940s agreed completely.

Hurley, however, viewed the Generalissimo with the highest possible respect and an uncritical eye. Hurley built a close personal relationship with Chiang, and the two spent time dining and conversing. Chiang's comments about the CCP made an impression on Hurley. Based on conversations Hurley had with then–Soviet Foreign Minister Vyacheslav Molotov during a brief trip to Moscow, Hurley believed the Soviets could (and would) pressure the CCP to accept a deal with Chiang.[12] In his attempts to reassure Chiang regarding CCP capabilities and intentions, Hurley frequently repeated Molotov's assurances that the CCP did not conform to the true definition of a Communist Party and therefore had little hope of bringing about a socialist revolution in China.[13] Molotov's comments about the CCP may have held a grain of truth, but they also conveyed a good dose of manipulation, to which Hurley appears to have been oblivious. It is worth noting that although Hurley later took a staunch anti-Communist ideological position, evidence hinting at this position is largely absent from contemporaneous reports of his actions and statements early in his time in China. Rather, Hurley's anti-Communist attitudes on display in the 1950s probably resulted from his disappointment and frustration after failing to sufficiently persuade the CCP leaders of his credibility as a mediator—more like a personal grudge than a deeply held conviction.

Hurley displayed little respect for American officials stationed in China, military and diplomatic alike. The latter were technically his embassy subordinates, and having their support would surely have made his life in China easier. However, Hurley rarely shared any information with his embassy staff about his negotiations with either the Chinese Communists or the Generalissimo, preferring to bypass State Department channels and communicate exclusively with President Roosevelt. His staff responded to this treatment by referring to Hurley behind his back as "Colonel Blimp" and other derogatory names. When

US diplomatic officials finally began to complain to the White House through back channels about Hurley's actions, Hurley in turn accused the embassy staff of disloyalty and ignorance regarding US interests in China.[14]

Hurley's behaviors and attitudes did not earn him the trust or support of diplomatic staff, who presumably could have been an asset in the negotiations between the Guomindang and Communists he attempted to undertake. In some cases, Hurley's disrespect for other Americans working in China degenerated into actual arguments. At one cocktail party in Chongqing, Hurley engaged General Wedemeyer's chief of staff, Robert McClure, in an argument so heated that Hurley ultimately challenged McClure to a fistfight in front of a group of Chinese counterparts. Other American officials interrupted the fight before it could escalate further, but the situation cast the American delegation in a bad light vis-à-vis their Chinese allies.[15]

HURLEY'S NEGOTIATIONS WITH THE CCP

The tumult that Hurley caused among American officials serving in Chongqing spread to Yan'an, beginning with Hurley's first visit to the CCP base. After surprising the CCP leaders with his arrival, he began negotiating their role in a new coalition government. Dixie Mission members, who served as Hurley's hosts, were still reeling from the sudden departure of Stilwell, about which they had just learned. Whatever they were expecting Hurley to be, they collectively ended up shocked and discouraged.

Hurley's opinions on China policy were congruent with the president's, and he had considerable influence in the Oval Office. As Roosevelt's friend and special appointee, Hurley traveled to Yan'an prepared to represent Roosevelt's specific interest in finding a way to maintain a stable China as a bulwark against the expansion of Japanese territory. Hurley, Roosevelt, and Stilwell did not share much, but they did all harbor a belief that a stable China was essential to winning the war and future global security. They also believed the United States could impel this stability.[16] Based on reports he had received from Stilwell and others during the first years of the war, Roosevelt had determined that a politically unified China could best achieve this goal.

Although the events of 1944 had clearly shaken Roosevelt's confidence in Chiang, he continued to argue that China's best chance of political unification involved forming some sort of democratic coalition government with Chiang at the helm. He assessed Chiang to be the most competent leader in China and the one most likely to be accepted by other world leaders. Roosevelt concluded that the greatest potential threat to a unified democratic government in China would be a civil war with a Communist victory, believing the Communists were not sufficiently strong to hold the country together. He also feared Soviet intervention and Asian expansion via China. From October 1944 until his death in April 1945 Roosevelt cooperated with Hurley in trying to prevent Soviet aid to the CCP. He and Hurley believed this would force the Communists into negotiations with the Nationalists. Historian Michael Schaller succinctly describes this approach as "flawed in both conception and execution."[17] In service of this policy, Hurley undertook the chore of mediating the conflict between Chiang Kai-shek and the CCP. The November visit to Yan'an was his first step.

NEGOTIATING THE FIVE POINTS AT MAO'S HOUSE

Hurley met with Mao Zedong at Mao's home for over an hour on the morning of November 9. Hurley presented a set of terms he had drafted for an agreement between the CCP and the Guomindang over the future of China's government. To support Mao, the CCP gathered an entourage that included Gen. Zhu De; Zhou Enlai; Zhou's secretary, Chen Jiakang; and another aide who gave his name as Yu Guansheng. Yu claimed to be a journalist, but it is more likely he was a CCP intelligence officer.[18] On the American side, David Barrett helped Hurley as well as a US Army lieutenant surnamed Eng, the interpreter, and a sergeant named Smith, who was temporarily serving as Barrett's aide. At any other time, John Service would have assisted in meetings between an American diplomatic visitor and the CCP, but Service was temporarily gone from Yan'an on a trip to Washington. The other Foreign Service Officer posted to Yan'an, Raymond Ludden, was traveling in the border area with Pete Peterkin and the CCP guerrillas. These absences put Barrett in what John Hart aptly described as the "untenable position of acting as a go-between for the emotional, egotistic, and, in this setting, inept and incompetent Hurley with the shrewd, calculating man who over the previous two decades had managed to overcome all his rivals within the Chinese Communist Party, as well as the opposition of Stalin and the Comintern, to emerge as the sole leader of the Chinese Communist movement. It was truly no contest."[19]

The official State Department account of the meeting lists a variety of comments Hurley made that surely were surprising to the Americans present but likely put the CCP leaders at ease. For example, Hurley said "he would like to have it understood that the United States does not desire to participate in the internal politics of China" and that he had come to "discuss how we can defeat the common enemy of democracy."[20] The focus of the meeting was on Hurley's interest in unifying Chinese military forces to defeat Japan. Hurley described a conversation he had with Chiang Kai-shek in which Chiang agreed to "legalize" the existence of the CCP under certain conditions.

Hurley asked Mao to agree to allow China's National Army, under the leadership of Chiang Kai-shek, to assume command over all Communist forces. In exchange the CCP would have a seat on the National Military Council, which Chiang chaired. The council, whose name is sometimes translated as "Military Affairs Commission," included civilian and military representatives of the various military and defense organizations operating in China.[21] Hurley presented the initial draft of what became known as the Five Points Proposal, repeatedly assuring Mao that Chiang had agreed to the draft as presented. The group then took a break so the CCP entourage could review the draft, then reconvened for almost four more hours later in the day.

Barrett's memoirs depart a bit from the State Department readout of the second meeting. Barrett remembered Hurley as bending over backward to appeal to Mao and find terms on which he could agree. In Barrett's memory, Mao rejected the terms of the first draft, full stop. Mao articulated in detail why the CCP did not trust Chiang, including that a seat on the National Military Council meant nothing to them because many of the council's current members "were denied all knowledge of its actions" and "the whole body had not met for some time."[22] Upon hearing Mao's reasons for rejecting Hurley's proposed terms, Barrett reported that Hurley surprised all other parties in the room by asking Mao to propose alternate terms that the CCP could find easier to accept. State Department records document Mao's attempts to educate Hurley about the political situation in China and his argument that ceding more political power to the Guomindang would ultimately fail because the Chinese people doubted Chiang.[23] Mao called for a reorganization of the Chinese government into a multiparty system.

Mao claimed it was the Nationalists' authority over the country that was causing instability: Chinese troops were underpaid and deserting, and warlords and bandits were eating away at governance in Nationalist-held cities. He explained that out of a force of 1.9 million Nationalist troops, 779,000 were focused on surrounding or attacking the CCP instead of fighting the Japanese. These numbers were exaggerated, but Nationalist troops were indeed attempting to encircle CCP-held areas.[24] Mao said Chinese elites and scholars were starting to doubt Chiang's leadership capability. He said new equipment and airplanes from the United States would not be enough to help China if the Chinese government itself suffered from corruption and organizational problems and Chinese troops could not or would not fight.[25]

After conferring overnight with his comrades, Mao presented the CCP proposals to Hurley. At this point Hurley reportedly further stunned Barrett by suggesting that he would review the terms with an eye toward making them even more favorable to the CCP. Describing the November meetings in his memoirs, Barrett wrote that at first he held a positive impression of Hurley's negotiating skills. "But when the General offered to amend the terms in a way to make them 'go farther'—in other words, to be more favorable to the Communists—I thought he had definitely got off the rails."[26] Other Dixie observers were incredulous too. Barrett said, "In truth, if I had not been present that day, I would have found it difficult to believe General Hurley would have acted the way he did."

Hurley augmented Mao's drafted terms and the new document became known as the Communist Five Points Proposal. Before departing for Chongqing, Hurley surprised Barrett a third time by suggesting that Hurley and Mao both sign the proposal to indicate that both parties considered the terms "fair and just." Both signed, and Mao retained the signed copy.

When he returned to Chongqing, Hurley brought the Five Points to Chiang Kai-shek, who flatly refused to entertain any form of agreement with the CCP unless the GMD gained full control of all Communist military forces. In mid-November the Chinese government produced a counterproposal that removed most of the concessions to the CCP. The new proposal added a concluding clause that gave the government full control of the military situation in China.[27] Ultimately, despite his many assurances to the CCP of his interest in serving as a neutral mediator, Hurley sided with the Nationalists and backed Chiang's demands.[28]

STUCK IN THE MIDDLE AGAIN

Hurley asked Barrett to take the revised terms back to Mao and do his best to persuade the CCP leaders to accept them. According to Barrett, "the session with the two Communist leaders was an experience I shall never forget."[29] Given his lack of authority for direct official communications with General Hurley, Barrett recorded his experience in an immediate note to Wedemeyer, his superior officer: "Chairman Mao's attitude throughout the interview was recalcitrant in the extreme. He was not discourteous to me, but several times he flew into a violent rage. He kept shouting, over and over again, 'We will not yield any further!' 'That turtle's egg, Chiang!' . . . I left the interview feeling that I had talked in vain to two clever, ruthless, and determined leaders who felt absolutely sure of the strength of their position."[30] (Turtle's egg is a Chinese expletive that loosely translates to "bastard.")

Mao and Zhou argued that the terms presented would mean submitting their troops completely to the control of Chiang Kai-shek and placing the CCP completely "at his mercy," which was unacceptable. The CCP leaders expressed confusion at the US position in the conflict, particularly at Hurley's behavior first in drafting the proposed agreement in Yan'an, then certifying his belief in its fairness and yet presenting a revised version that offered "absolutely no guarantee of our safety."[31] According to Barrett, the CCP leaders said, "We cannot trust the good faith of the Generalissimo, and no one who has studied impartially the history of the relations of the Kuomintang and the Chinese

Communist Party could reasonably expect us to have any confidence in him." Mao threatened to release to the press a copy of the Five Points that he and Hurley had signed. It appears he never did so.

Barrett deliberately omitted Mao's threat in his written report. Instead, he verbally explained the terms when he met with Hurley and Wedemeyer in Chongqing in late November.[32] Of Hurley's reaction to this point in their meeting, Barrett later wrote: "I was afraid for a moment he might burst a blood vessel. 'The mother——!' he yelled, using an expression now in rather common use but seldom heard at the time. 'He tricked meh!' At this point, I ventured to remind the general I was not Mao Tse-tung."[33] December 1944 marked both a low point in Hurley's effort to mediate a settlement in China's domestic conflict and a major transformation in the role of the Dixie Mission, toward US intelligence and US-China relations.

FAREWELL, HONEST BUDDHA

Meanwhile, within days of the Hurley visit, another major domino fell in the US diplomatic mission to China: Ambassador Gauss announced his retirement. A veteran diplomat who received his first diplomatic appointment in 1906, Clarence Gauss had spent most of his career representing the United States in China in various diplomatic positions. His calm and thoughtful demeanor and his frank assessments of foreign affairs earned him the nickname "the Honest Buddha." He lived up to the quiet, earnest reputation that the name implies to the very end of his tenure in China.[34] Roosevelt had appointed Gauss to be US ambassador to China in 1941, but Roosevelt's attitude toward Gauss vacillated between ambivalence and episodes of quietly looking for more politically favorable replacements.[35]

Ambivalence toward Gauss extended to most of his subordinates in China as well, most of whom neither loved nor hated him but felt something in between. Gauss lacked the depth of linguistic and cultural expertise on China that many of his subordinates had achieved. This fact made an impression on the close-knit group of professionals who staffed the embassy and the military attaché offices in the 1930s and 1940s. Barrett, who had served as attaché under Gauss, had a good impression of him as "scrupulously fair" in dealing with Chinese people and a considerate chief of mission. Barrett also noted that Gauss did not speak Chinese, which made him seem like a "treaty port businessman" who did not have what Barrett called "a missionary outlook."[36]

Gauss was no friend to the OSS. He had offered Gen. William Donovan little support and made no plans to expand US intelligence activities in China beyond the status quo activities of diplomats and attachés. Gauss had reportedly used back channels in the State Department in 1942 to protest the first awkward operations of the OSS in China. He also closely supervised John King Fairbank, one of Donovan's first and most capable intelligence officers focused on China, who was assigned to the US embassy undercover in 1942.[37] The tepid reaction of Gauss to the dispatch of the Yan'an Observer Group in 1944 did not present an obstacle for Dixie per se, but neither did it provide help. Despite his ambivalence about the mission to Yan'an, Gauss reportedly had great respect for and supported Jack Service, with whom he had cooperated in the Foreign Service in various capacities over several decades.

Both Gauss and Roosevelt had raised the possibility of Gauss resigning his position numerous times between 1941 and 1944. However, Roosevelt's interest in appointing a new ambassador failed to reach a boiling point until Stilwell's conflict with Chiang Kai-shek necessitated changes to US personnel in China. Even though Gauss and Stilwell regularly experienced professional disagreements and did not seem to particularly like each other, Gauss expressed grave concerns over the treatment of Stilwell and the direction of US-China relations in 1944 among his reasons for resigning.[38] On November 14, 1944, Gauss officially quit the position and requested reassignment elsewhere in the diplomatic service. Gauss resigned of his own volition, but Roosevelt did not protest.

HURLEY REPLACES GAUSS

Days after Gauss officially resigned, Roosevelt quickly filled the vacancy in the US embassy in Chongqing with his longtime friend and political crony Patrick Hurley. The White House announced Hurley's selection on November 17. Although the effects of this decision did not manifest until later, the choice of Hurley had an immediate and pronounced impact on the relationship between the US government and the CCP, a relationship that Dixie Mission officials had been working hard to foster. It did not make the work of the mission any easier. Compared to Gauss, Hurley was less ambivalent about the CCP but also less well informed—a difference that had significant repercussions for the Dixie Mission and for American foreign policy in China in 1945.

The transition from Gauss to Hurley is emblematic of a shift in emphasis of US policy in China that affected intelligence operations. Gauss symbolized the traditional cohort of well-educated and articulate but reserved and noninterventionist American public servants who joined the US Foreign Service in the 1920s and 1930s. While Open Door paternalism was endemic among Americans of Gauss's generation, Gauss did not stand out among them as a vocal proponent. Although Gauss maintained a distance from Chinese culture, he did attempt to serve as an objective observer of Chinese affairs and effective representative of US interests. Hurley brought to the position a much different background that directly reflected Roosevelt's leadership style and the expansion of

US strategic interests, including intervention into Chinese politics. Rather than perceiving himself as one part of a long-standing and elite network of public servants representing American interests abroad, Hurley's attitudes about his position in China were based on his personal history as a seasoned Washington insider and Roosevelt's appointed personal emissary to Chiang Kai-shek.

In stark contrast to Gauss, Hurley bonded with Roosevelt over their shared position that in diplomacy personal relationships often mattered more than ideology. For them diplomacy and foreign affairs required highly personalized engagement, private communication channels, and one-on-one relationships. Neither man exhibited much respect for the role of professionalized bureaucratic administrative processes in international relations. Hurley's biographer assesses him as having "believed that handshakes, smiles, anecdote swapping and other forms of personal camaraderie would sweep away divisive and long-standing issues; in this sense he resembled Franklin Roosevelt."[39] In service of this belief, Hurley could reportedly be extremely charming, possessing a tendency to communicate with a sense of familiarity that caused many to remark on his ability to make a good impression, at least with other Americans. Although several presidential administrations had dispatched Hurley as a negotiator on behalf of the US government in previous diplomatic engagements (e.g., in the Philippines and the Middle East), foreign travel and international exposure seemingly reinforced Hurley's narrow Western-centric worldview rather than expanding his ability to communicate across cultural boundaries. On behalf of Roosevelt, Hurley also traveled to New Zealand, the Soviet Union, Iran, and Afghanistan in 1942 and 1943. In one famous gaffe, Hurley publicly referred to Chiang Kai-shek's wife, whose full name was Soong Mei-ling Chiang, as "Madame Shek," never realizing or recognizing his mistaken assumption that Chinese names adhere to Western conventions.[40]

In his relations with China during World War II, Roosevelt frequently bypassed traditional diplomatic channels. He made no secret of his willingness to shut out the State Department, and Gauss in particular, in driving his China policy. In November 1942 Roosevelt's aides attempted to persuade State Department East Asia specialist Stanley Hornbeck to take over for Gauss. Hornbeck expressed reservations about undercutting his colleague Gauss, so Roosevelt moved on.[41]

Nearly a year later, in October 1943, Roosevelt continued to consider making a change. The president sent a memo asking trusted State Department under-secretary Ed Stettinius, whom Roosevelt later appointed secretary of state, to quietly research Gauss's standing in China and whether replacing him would be prudent. Regarding the US ambassador position in Chongqing, Roosevelt wrote, "I do not believe that it is necessary to send a career diplomat there."[42] Roosevelt himself corresponded directly with Chiang Kai-shek throughout the early 1940s, and throughout World War II the president bent the traditional rules of diplomatic representation by frequently relying on a combination of personal contacts with Chiang Kai-shek and with those in his immediate inner circle, often selecting special personal emissaries to meet with Chiang on his behalf.

ROOSEVELT AND HURLEY

Roosevelt did not add Hurley to his list of contenders to replace Gauss until late in the conflict between Stilwell and Chiang, but he felt he owed Hurley a bit of a favor for the sake of their friendship. Hurley had emerged from humble beginnings in a large Irish Catholic family in Oklahoma, supported by his father's work as a rancher and coal miner. He became an influential and wealthy attorney for the burgeoning oil industry in his home state. His successful legal career not only made Hurley a young millionaire but also launched him onto a political trajectory. He accepted an appointment as the federal legal representative to the Choctaw Tribe, which had been relocated to a reservation in Oklahoma. Hurley worked for the Taft and Wilson administrations in this capacity.[43] Hurley never held an elected political office, but his connections with the Republican Party in Oklahoma eventually led to his appointment to serve as undersecretary of war at the start of Herbert Hoover's presidential term. The death of Hoover's appointed war secretary only days later led to Hurley's sudden and unexpected promotion to secretary. That position opened the door to Hurley's lasting political presence, both in the Hoover administration and in Roosevelt's network.

A staunch Republican, Hurley might have seemed an unlikely friend for Roosevelt. However, Roosevelt is well known for collecting an eclectic network of supporters, and Hurley's ability to form personal relationships had superseded his commitment to partisan politics throughout his career. Hurley's deep admiration for Theodore Roosevelt and the era of progressive reform had shaped his views in a way that FDR apparently found palatable. Hurley's biographer, Russell Buhite, describes Hurley as "an opportunist" and "an accommodator of people in high position, especially of presidents."[44] Like Roosevelt, Hurley liked to "collect" people. According to Buhite, "while he served his country ably in various capacities, some of them requiring considerable sacrifice on his part, his life and work may best be understood in terms of the promotion, for some explicable and some inexplicable reasons, of Hurley—his wealth, influence, and prestige."

Hurley cultivated a special relationship with Roosevelt throughout the 1930s. By the 1940s their friendship was sufficiently intimate that when Hurley had prostate surgery in June 1943, Hurley's doctor called the White House to inform the president that Hurley's operation had successfully removed a benign enlargement the size of a tangerine. Hurley was reportedly "full of pep and ginger" and was expected to make a full recovery.[45] Hurley must have made a good recovery because no other references to his health appear in the historical records from 1943 on, when Roosevelt asked Hurley to serve as a "personal international emissary" to China.[46]

Throughout the war Roosevelt had been seeking openings where Hurley could serve. The Pearl Harbor attack had spurred Hurley to approach George Marshall about serving the war effort in a military capacity. Hurley had remained in the Army Reserves after a short military career in the US Army during World War I. Marshall was, unsurprisingly, less than excited about finding a position for an aging friend of the president with no particular military capabilities, and he rejected Hurley's appeal. When Hurley asked Roosevelt to intervene and overturn Marshall's decision, Roosevelt had vowed instead to find an appropriate alternate assignment for Hurley. Roosevelt first thought to send Hurley as a negotiator in war efforts with the Saudis, but advisers in the War Department saw too many potential conflicts of interest and suggested that Hurley instead be sent to China, where friction between Stilwell and Chiang threatened war efforts as early as 1942.[47]

When Patrick Hurley became Roosevelt's most important emissary in China, his arrival overshadowed Gauss. As a keen observer of matters of diplomatic protocol and administrative norms in both the US and Chinese governments, Barrett noted the breach in protocol and worried about its implications. He pointed to Roosevelt's decision not to invite Gauss to be present at the meetings between Chiang and Vice President Wallace in June 1944, when Wallace pushed for and ultimately obtained Chiang's acquiescence to American plans to send an observer delegation to the CCP base in Yan'an. According to Barrett, Gauss quietly endured this humiliating snub, although other American officials of "much less importance" did attend the meetings. Barrett described the situation as "an example of 'representation by special emissary' at its worst" and explained that because Gauss had a responsibility to maintain US relations with the Chinese government on a "continuous, not just a 'here today and gone tomorrow' basis," his absence from the meetings would "unavoidably operate to make his [own] task in China more difficult."[48]

In November 1943 Hurley was sent to China to meet with Chiang in advance of the Cairo Conference. The conference was important to China, and especially to Chiang, who met Roosevelt there.[49] Chiang hoped to persuade Roosevelt to arrange a private audience for him with Joseph Stalin in Tehran.[50] Chiang feared that Russia intended to "communize" all of China and annex portions of it.[51] Historians of the Cold War era, who ultimately viewed Hurley as one of the greatest American opponents of communism in China, might be surprised to realize that Hurley spent a significant portion of his first meeting with the Generalissimo trying to convince him that Stalin had renounced "world conquest as a fundamental policy of communism" and, in Hurley's opinion, "Russia was no longer subsidizing or directing communist activities in other nations."[52]

Although Hurley's commentary about Stalin proved unconvincing to the Chinese leader, Chiang perceived Hurley's arrival as an effort by Roosevelt to ensure that he fully understood the position Roosevelt intended to take in discussions with Churchill and Stalin. For Hurley's part, although he lacked specific expertise on Chinese politics, he emerged from meetings with Chiang in agreement with Stilwell and other American officials in China regarding the Chinese leader's motives. Hurley informed Roosevelt that "it is advisable to consider with some skepticism the Chinese capacity, or readiness, to contribute materially to offensive warfare" and similarly advisable to "give consideration to the relative importance placed by the Chinese Central Government upon conserving its strength for the maintenance of its postwar internal supremacy as against the more immediate objective of defeating Japan."[53]

While his relationship with Stilwell gradually became more strained in 1943 and early 1944, Chiang's willingness to work with Hurley increased.[54] Hurley enjoyed working with Chiang and formally asked to be appointed ambassador, a request that Roosevelt had probably decided to honor by August 1944.[55] Hurley's vantage point on the situation between Stilwell and Chiang hastened the end of Stilwell's career in China. In a memo to Roosevelt on October 9, 1944, only a few days before Stilwell's dismissal, Hurley described Stilwell and Chiang as "fundamentally incompatible."[56] Based on this assessment, Hurley advised Roosevelt, "Today you are confronted with a choice between Chiang Kai-shek and Stilwell."[57] Roosevelt, judging the Generalissimo to be the more vital to US interests in China, followed Hurley's recommendation and recalled Stilwell. FDR continued to follow most of Hurley's suggestions about China until his death in April 1945. Undoubtedly Roosevelt's appointment of Hurley had significant and lasting effects on the ability of the Dixie Mission to perform its intelligence duties.

A BOOST FOR OSS CHINA

OSS officers in China in late 1944 expressed enthusiasm about the combination of Wedemeyer and Hurley commanding US strategic actions. Hurley and Donovan had formed a lasting friendship when both served in the Hoover administration. They also shared the dubious distinction of being Irish Catholic Republicans serving Roosevelt. Under Donovan's leadership the OSS had developed a reputation as a "Republican establishment, filled with the upper crust of American society."[58] The OSS appealed to Hurley in part due to Donovan's leadership and because Hurley approved of the mission and approach adopted by the OSS. The top OSS official in China once quoted Hurley in a cable to Donovan just before Donovan's arrival on a visit to China: "OSS rates #1 in my opinion." Of Donovan, Hurley reportedly opined, "I am behind him from Hell to Harrisburg."[59] Hurley displayed no such affection for army intelligence, based on negative opinions the ambassador had formed during his term as war secretary, and believed the OSS would fully replace the G-2 once World War II ended.[60] Nevertheless, Hurley's affinity for the OSS did not liberate the organization from the challenges it faced in China in 1944 and 1945, particularly when it came to Yan'an.

OSS officials in China also initially had a positive view of Wedemeyer. The OSS had assessed that Stilwell's disagreements with ONI officials in Chongqing, who were responsible for the creation of the restrictive SACO agreement, had also consequently constrained the ability of OSS officers to operate in the China Theater.[61] More than Stilwell, Wedemeyer had been supportive of expanding US efforts to collect strategic intelligence in China throughout the war and particularly vocal in complaining to Donovan about the lack of "reliable information on the structure, conditions, and quality of the Chinese Army" in late 1943.[62] Joseph Spencer, the main official representing OSS R&A for CBI in theater headquarters in Delhi, doubted the army would plan any active operations during or immediately after the transition period, thus opening a gap in the field that the OSS could fill. Spencer speculated that this change could significantly increase the influence of the OSS in China, both in terms of operations run by the SI Branch and the role that the R&A Branch would have in supporting operations and processing the information that intelligence-collection activities produced.[63]

WHITHER DIXIE

In the period between General Stilwell's departure in October 1944 and the death of President Roosevelt in April 1945, Dixie Mission participants weathered shifts in their leadership and personnel that, combined with the ever-present bureaucratic and logistical constraints at Yan'an, significantly influenced both their effectiveness and morale. Dixie Mission participants had taken much of the blame when disagreements within the US government over the direction of America's policy toward the CCP devolved into a personalized power struggle between the US ambassador, career diplomats, and intelligence officials in the army and OSS. The 1945 departure of the Foreign Service Officers from Yan'an all but eliminated the dissemination of political assessments of the CCP from US government communication channels. Meanwhile, the army shifted gears and significantly amplified efforts to collect information on weather and monitor military activity in northern China. The latter was considered useful military intelligence work but broke no new ground in providing strategic intelligence support for the policy that the United States was struggling to implement in China.

Mao and the other CCP leaders regularly clarified to the Americans at Dixie what they were and were not willing to offer in return for US assistance. Dixie Mission participants dutifully recorded these comments and communicated them back to superiors in Chongqing, Delhi, and Washington. It appeared to the CCP leaders that the United States needed the CCP guerrillas at least as much if not more than the CCP needed help from the United States. Mao and Zhou delivered some of the clearest statements to this effect in their response to the National Government's proposal countering the Communists' Five Points in December 1944. They specifically told Barrett, "We have fought the Japanese for seven years without any outside help, and we will keep on fighting them no matter what happens" and "if the United States abandons us, we shall be very sorry, but it will make no difference in our good feeling toward you."[64] To further clarify their perspective, the leaders continued: "We have welcomed the United States Army Observer Section, and we have done our best to cooperate with it. If the Section stays, we shall be glad; if it goes, we shall be sorry. If it goes and later returns, we will welcome it back again. If the United States does not give us one rifle or one round of ammunition, we shall still continue to fight the Japanese and we shall still be friends of the United States." Mao's and Zhou's statements echoed the comments the CCP leaders had been making to the Dixie Mission participants since their arrival at Yan'an in July.

NOTES

Epigraph: Internal party statement drafted by CCP leaders after the arrival of the Dixie Mission, "Directive of the Central Committee on Diplomatic Work," August 18, 1944, quoted in Tony Saich, ed., *The Rise to Power of the Chinese Communist Party: Documents and Analysis* (Armonk, NY: M. E. Sharpe, 1996), 1211–14.

1. David D. Barrett, *Dixie Mission: The United States Army Observer Group in Yenan, 1944* (Berkeley: University of California Press, 1970), 56.
2. Telegram, John Paton Davies to Patrick Hurley, October 27, 1944, US Department of State, *Foreign Relations of the United States* (hereafter FRUS), *Diplomatic Papers, 1944: China*, 659.
3. Davies to Hurley, October 27, 1944.
4. John N. Hart, *The Making of an Army "Old China Hand": A Memoir of Colonel David D. Barrett* (Berkeley: University of California, Center for China Studies, 1985), 45.
5. Russell D. Buhite, *Patrick J. Hurley and American Foreign Policy* (Ithaca, NY: Cornell University Press, 1973), 191. Buhite wrote the first unauthorized scholarly biography of Hurley, which is still the most authoritative objective account of Hurley's life.

6. Hart, *The Making of an Army "Old China Hand,"* 45.
7. Memo, Patrick Hurley to FDR, October 10, 1944, *FRUS, Diplomatic Papers 1944: China*, 170. Memo includes Chiang Kai-shek's response to Roosevelt's requests.
8. Memo, OSS R&A Division head William Langer [in Washington] from Rosamond Frame, CBI OSS R&A Director [based in Delhi], December 29, 1944, NARA, RG 226, entry NM-54 53: Correspondence with Outposts, 1942–1946, box 4.
9. Letter [copy], John Service to Sen. J. William Fulbright forwarded to David Barrett, January 28, 1972, Bancroft Library, University of California Berkeley, Papers of John S. Service, carton 2, folder 35: David Barrett.
10. E. J. Kahn, *The China Hands: America's Foreign Service Officers and What Befell Them* (New York: Viking, 1976), 122.
11. Telegram, Clarence Gauss to Secretary of State, November 4, 1944, *FRUS, Diplomatic Papers 1944: China*, 665.
12. For more on Hurley's visit with Molotov, see Michael Schaller, *The U.S. Crusade in China, 1938–1945* (New York: Columbia University Press, 1979), 178–79.
13. For example, see Letter, Patrick Hurley to President Roosevelt and Chief of Staff George Marshall, September 7, 1944, *FRUS, Diplomatic Papers 1944: China*, 154.
14. Buhite, *Patrick J. Hurley*, 190.
15. Buhite, 190; Albert C. Wedemeyer, *Wedemeyer Reports!* (New York: Henry Holt, 1958), 318.
16. Since the 1970s, when many of the relevant official documents were declassified, historians have achieved a broad consensus on Roosevelt's views and interests at this point in the war. For example, see Warren I. Cohen, *America's Response to China: A History of Sino-American Relations*, 5th ed. (New York: Columbia University Press, 2010), 159–65; and Schaller, *The U.S. Crusade in China*, 177–78.
17. Schaller, *The U.S. Crusade in China*, 177.
18. The name "Yu Kwang-sen" appears in the official State Department of roster of Hurley's November 8 meeting in Yan'an, unsigned but likely written by Barrett (see *FRUS, Diplomatic Papers 1944: China*, accessed on May 15, 2022, https://history.state.gov/historicaldocuments/frus1944v06/d490). No CCP official with a name similar to this appears in records available about Yan'an. The name "Guan Sheng" is a famous character in the book *Water Margin* (水滸傳) by Shi Nai'an, one of the four great classical novels of Chinese literature. It seems possible that "Yu Kwang-sen" was a pseudonym.
19. Hart, *The Making of an Army "Old China Hand,"* 49. Other details of these meetings appear in Schaller, *The U.S. Crusade in China*, 177.
20. Memorandum of Conversation (Yenan), November 8, 1944, *FRUS, Diplomatic Papers 1944: China*, 674–87.
21. In Chinese, 國民政府軍事委員會 (Guómínzhèngfǔ Jūnshì Wěiyuánhuì). For more on the council, see https://art.archives.gov.tw/Theme.aspx?MenuID=355.
22. Barrett, *Dixie Mission*, 66.
23. Memorandum of Conversation (Yenan), November 8, 1944.
24. See Hsi-cheng Ch'i, *The Much Troubled Alliance: US-China Military Cooperation during the Pacific War, 1941–1945* (Singapore: World Scientific, 2016), chap. 11.
25. Memorandum of Conversation (Yenan), November 8, 1944.
26. Barrett, *Dixie Mission*, 62.
27. Barrett, 68.

28. For more on the negotiations that Hurley mediated, see Cohen, *America's Response to China*, 159–65; Schaller, *The U.S. Crusade in China*, 194–96; and Ch'i, *The Much Troubled Alliance*, chaps. 11–12.
29. For the full text of Barrett's memo to Wedemeyer, see *FRUS, Diplomatic Papers 1944: China*, 727.
30. Barrett, *Dixie Mission*, 74.
31. Barrett, 71.
32. Barrett, 75.
33. Barrett, 75.
34. US Department of State, Office of the Historian, "Clarence Edward Gauss (1186–1960)," accessed June 12, 2023, https://history.state.gov/departmenthistory/people/gauss-clarence-edward; Kahn, *The China Hands*, 64–65.
35. Maochun Yu, *OSS in China: Prelude to Cold War* (Annapolis, MD: Naval Institute Press, 1996), 64–65.
36. Barrett, *Dixie Mission*, 27.
37. Yu, *OSS in China*, 62.
38. Yu, 62.
39. Buhite, *Patrick J. Hurley*, 27.
40. Buhite, 148.
41. See Handwritten Notes, November 30, 1942, FDRL, President's Official Files, box 3: China, folder: China endorsements. The notes include lists of potential candidates.
42. Memo, FDR to Ed Stettinius regarding Gauss, October 22, 1943, FDRL, President's Secretary's File, departmental files, box 71: State Department, April–December 1941 through 1945, folder: July–December 1943.
43. Buhite, *Patrick J. Hurley*, 18.
44. Buhite, xi.
45. "Memo for the President," June 19, 1943, FDRL, President's Secretary's Files, subject files, box 138: Harry Hopkins to Hyde Park, folder: Hurley, Patrick.
46. Letter, FDR to Patrick Hurley, August 18, 1944, FDRL, President's Secretary's Files, subject files, box 138, folder: Hurley, Patrick. Includes official confirmation of Hurley as FDR's personal representative to Chiang Kai-shek.
47. Buhite, *Patrick J. Hurley*, 147–48.
48. Barrett, *Dixie Mission*, 27.
49. Barrett, 27.
50. Rana Mitter, *Forgotten Ally: China's World War II, 1937–1944* (Boston: Houghton Mifflin Harcourt, 2013), 306.
51. Memo, Patrick Hurley to FDR, November 20, 1943, FDRL, President's Secretary's Files, subject files, box 138, folder: Hurley, Patrick.
52. Hurley to FDR, November 20, 1943.
53. Hurley to FDR, November 20, 1943.
54. Mitter, *Forgotten Ally*, 335–45.
55. Memos, Maj. Gen. Patrick J. Hurley and Mr. Donald M. Nelson as Personal Representative of President Roosevelt, *FRUS, Diplomatic Papers 1944: China*, 247–48. Includes memos from the undersecretary of state (Stettinius) to the secretary.
56. Memo, Maj. Gen. Patrick J. Hurley to President Roosevelt, October 10, 1944, *FRUS, Diplomatic Papers 1944: China*, 170.

57. Hurley to Roosevelt, October 10, 1944, *FRUS,* 170.
58. Yu, *OSS in China*, 178.
59. Cable, John Coughlin to William Donovan, October 29, 1944, NARA, RG 226, Roll 127, M1642, microfilm, quoted in Yu, *OSS in China*, 178.
60. Yu, 194.
61. Yu, 172.
62. Memo, William Donovan to OSS Chiefs of CBI and SEAC Missions, December 16, 1943, NARA, RG 226, entry 110: Field Intelligence Reports, box 51, folder 510.
63. Memo, Joseph Spencer to William Langer, October 31, 1944, NARA, RG 226, entry NM-54 53, box 4. Includes description of the CBI and Stilwell's departure.
64. Memo, Col. David D. Barrett to Maj. Gen. Albert C. Wedemeyer, December 10, 1944, *FRUS, Diplomatic Papers 1944: China*, 730.

7

IN THE CANNON'S MOUTH

Then a soldier,
Full of strange oaths and bearded like the pard,
Jealous in honor, sudden and quick in quarrel,
Seeking the bubble reputation
Even in the cannon's mouth.
—Shakespeare, *As You Like It*, quoted by David Barrett
on his final departure from Dixie

The rough draft of the plan that became a key turning point in the fate of the Dixie Mission, and in the history of US relations with the CCP, was cooked up in the four-by-five-meter dirt-floored home office of Gen. Ye Jianying, while his three-year-old daughter, Niu, was playing just outside.

John Paton Davies had started the initial conversation on October 25 at Zhou Enlai's house, while Zhou and Mao Zedong riffed over what form US-CCP cooperation on operations might take. The next day Davies and David Barrett joined Ye to hash out more of the details for a potential US-led military operation against Japan in northeast China. CCP combat commanders Peng Dehuai, Lin Biao, and Nie Rongzhen were present, but Davies recalled that he asked most of the questions and Ye gave most of the answers.[1]

John Paton Davies was never a member of the Dixie Mission, although he was instrumental in setting it up. Davies's meetings with Ye and Zhou occurred on his first trip to Yan'an in October 1944. The trip had been quickly planned because Davies had just returned to China from meetings in Washington, DC. He arrived in Chongqing only two days before Joseph Stilwell's departure. Both Stilwell and Davies thought it would be a good idea for Davies to head to Yan'an and prevent Chiang Kai-shek from shutting down the Dixie Mission. The day after Stilwell left Chongqing, Davies got a seat aboard the "Wounded Duck" C-47 and flew to Yan'an.

Sources disagree on whether the initial idea for cooperation came from the Americans or the Chinese, but by the time Davies visited it was a two-way conversation. Davies recalled a long memo from Jack Service about a meeting held with Mao that raised the idea of US cooperation. Davies took the chance to have face-to-face conversations with the CCP leaders on their home turf to flesh out what form such cooperation might take.[2] The CCP, the G-2, and the

OSS had all been mulling over the possibility of a military operation at a port city in northeastern Jiangsu province called Lianyungang.[3] If it became strategically necessary for the Allies to mount an amphibious invasion of the Japanese islands, the United States would need a base area from which to stage it. Could Lianyungang become that base? At Davies's prodding, Ye sketched out what might be required for such a military engagement.

Ye relayed that the CCP generals estimated around two and a half Japanese divisions (around 50,000 men) would be stationed at Lianyungang if the United States attempted an amphibious landing there. Japan would then likely rally another five divisions in less than a week if fighting heated up. The CCP leaders thus estimated that the United States would require about five divisions for the fight. The CCP generals thought they could contribute 50,000 regular troops plus support the American troops with food and labor by mobilizing the local population. Elsewhere in the vicinity, up to 600,000 CCP regulars would "engage the enemy and cut his lines of communications." Davies recorded what he had heard in a two-page "Top Secret" memo. He addressed it to Albert Wedemeyer, Joseph Stilwell (now back in Washington, DC), and John Carter Vincent, then chief of the China Division at the State Department. "I heard nothing in response," Davies recalled in his memoir.

Based on their positive views of how the CCP was fighting Japan during their first few months of investigation at Yan'an, the American observers advocated providing American assistance to the CCP leaders and troops. Service, Davies, and Charles Stelle all believed Patrick Hurley's mediated negotiations between the Guomindang and the CCP were doomed to fail. In their view, providing US support for the CCP was the only way to keep the party from turning to the Soviets for aid to defend themselves against the Japanese. However, they disagreed on how to provide the support, the extent to which the United States should aid the Communist fighters, and which agency should take the action and the credit. These plans were at the heart of the conflict and the disagreements that consumed the Dixie Mission in early 1945.

Cooperating with the CCP on operations was not part of the sprawling initial orders for the Dixie Mission, but the participants still present investigated the possibility as though it were a legitimate and justifiable part of their work. Several factors probably made these efforts seem natural to the Dixie Mission cohort. First among them was their own personal histories and background in China. They had the "Can Do" spirit of the Fifteenth Infantry and as expatriates were used to some level of autonomy in decision-making. Furthermore, their distance from guiding managers in their organizations and the logistical restrictions on correspondence with them empowered their sense of autonomy. Third, they collectively harbored a total commitment to the goals of the broader

Allied war and were willing to employ just about any means to achieve its ends. Fourth, the original Dixie crew shared Stilwell's views of Chinese military and leadership capabilities, believing the CCP to be more flexible and potentially more capable for the mission they were designing. Taking cues from Stilwell, they suspected Chiang Kai-shek would want to avoid the kind of fight they were planning. This operation never happened, with either CCP troops or Guomindang troops, so it is impossible to know whether it would have worked out. However, historians have used Chinese documents to discredit Stilwell's assessments about Chiang and his troops.[4]

OSS officers at Dixie were under the most pressure to bring operational plans to reality. OSS China headquarters saw such operational plans as one way to gain a competitive edge and prove their worth in China after playing second fiddle for so long to the Army G-2 and the State Department in Chongqing. Secret plans for sabotage with guerrillas was supposedly their bailiwick. This operation was a chance for Stelle, Colling, and Cromley to stake a real claim.

None of the plans for cooperation ultimately came to fruition. On the contrary, it was unthinkable that the United States would partner with the Communists against the strong opposition of Chiang Kai-shek and to the great embarrassment of Patrick Hurley. The very concept of devising such plans resulted in severe consequences for the Americans at Yan'an and helped to sour the intimate rapport Dixie Mission members had been building with the CCP leaders. The operational plans that emerged and the way higher levels within the American government struck them down illustrate the communication problems facing the Americans assigned to the China Theater. The situation was another example of the United States government getting in its own way in China. There was irony in the fact that American officials in China were focused intently on the lack of unity among their Chinese allies, when interagency rivalries, poor intelligence practices and communications, and competing priorities were similarly confusing US policy in China.

THE QUESTION OF US AID TO THE CCP

The members of the Dixie Mission had their disagreements in their first few months at Yan'an, but they did agree that the Communists could achieve gains in the fight against the Japanese. Barrett, Davies, and Service bought into Stilwell's view that the Guomindang appeared to be avoiding confrontation with Japan, biding time for the Allies to get ahead in the war and stockpiling American aid for later use against the CCP. Politically, Stilwell saw that the Guomindang was decentralizing the little political power it could muster, which only encouraged local corruption. Stilwell's view may have been overly simplified, biased, and incorrect, but it was also influential with his subordinates operating in China, particularly those at Yan'an. It is therefore worth explaining how Stilwell saw Chiang.

From Stilwell's perspective, conversations with Chiang proceeded on a loop in 1944 in which Chiang would offer a litany of reasons why he could not do what Stilwell requested. Stilwell recorded these in his papers and journals. The Japanese were too well equipped, and China could not stand a chance in a fight against them, Stilwell recorded Chiang telling him. Chiang argued that if the United States wanted China to fight, Stilwell should give him more materiel, equivalent to what was being given to Britain. Chiang claimed that without this capability he would never achieve victory in the two fights that faced his leadership (Japan and the CCP). Stilwell wrote that Chiang was "bewildered by the spread of Communist influence. He can't see that the mass of Chinese people welcome the Reds as being the only visible hope of relief from crushing taxation, the abuses of the Army and [the terror of] Tai Li's Gestapo."[5] Stilwell resigned himself to the fact that the United States had to work with Chiang: "In time of war you have to take your allies as you find them." Regime change during the emergency of the Japanese invasion was impossible, even if it seemed necessary for China in the long term.[6] Stilwell's paternalism clouded the situation, while many of Chiang's points seem rather reasonable, and Chinese sources have more or less borne them out. It is also not difficult to see in retrospect why these two leaders clashed.

Davies, Service, Barrett, Stelle, and Pinky Dorn had reached the same conclusions as Stilwell, likely based on their loyalty to Stilwell but also on their shared view of China and the world that made them loyal to Stilwell in the first place. The Dixie Mission members held out more optimism than Stilwell that the CCP could help the Allies win the war. The CCP fighters looked very different to them than the Nationalist troops. Davies's visit reinforced for him the growing political confidence the CCP had developed and its support in the countryside. Davies surmised that this confidence would prevent a Communist compromise to Hurley's plans for mediation. In one of the many reports Davies cranked out during his visit to Yan'an from October 22 to November 8, he wrote,

> The United States is the greatest hope and the greatest fear of the Chinese Communists. They recognize that if they receive American aid, even if only on an equal basis with Chiang, they can quickly establish control over most if not all of China, perhaps without civil war. . . . We are the greatest fear of the Communists because the more aid we give Chiang exclusively the greater the likelihood of his precipitating civil war and the more protracted and costly will be the Communist unification of China. . . . If we continue to

> reject them and support an unreconstructed China, they see us as becoming their enemy. But they would prefer to be friends.[7]

Davies ended his visit to Yan'an convinced that local support for the Communists was growing, inspired by the CCP's confidence in negotiations and its capabilities in governance and military actions within its base regions. Davies perceived that Chiang Kai-shek was not winning domestic hearts and minds the way the CCP was, which cast doubt on the emerging White House policy toward China.

Service fully agreed with Davies and argued that the time had come for the United States to deal more harshly with Chiang Kai-shek. On October 10 Service sent a detailed policy memo to the top leaders of US China policy, which still included Stilwell. Service noted that Roosevelt had to weigh in and decide what was to happen next. In a passive way, FDR eventually did. Service argued that the Guomindang government was "in crisis" and experiencing political "bankruptcy," pointing out that the Guomindang needed the American support but that this dependency was not mutual.[8] Service explained that the United States need not "fear the collapse" of the Guomindang government or be held back by any sense of obligation or gratitude to Chiang: "We cannot hope to solve China's problems (which are now our problems) without consideration of the opposition forces—Communist, provincial and liberal," Service wrote. "More than ever, we hold all the aces in Chiang's poker game. It is time we started playing them."

Barrett also supported US aid for the CCP guerrillas, though he resisted going into as much detail on the politics for his reasoning as is found in the messages by Davies and Service. Although Barrett had known and served Stilwell far longer than Davies and Service, he took a more measured view of military affairs in China. From his perspective as a military officer, he supported giving the CCP guerrillas some form of tangible military aid that would enhance their effectiveness and encourage their cooperation with US efforts. In fact, one of his first reports to Stilwell about the Communists had made a cautious recommendation about providing small arms, such as handguns. In the report Barrett conveyed his firm belief that the CCP and the United States were fighting the same enemy—Japan—and that the CCP soldiers' commitment to the cause made them "worthy" of US aid in the form of "ammunition, weapons, pack artillery, and signal equipment" that "would bring immediate results" and, if it did not, "we would have lost very little."[9]

Barrett added some important caveats. He weighed the logistical limitations of the US observers at Yan'an compared to the urgency of the war effort and suggested that the military aid be provided to the CCP right away rather than waiting "until we have sent out observers to cover areas from which reports cannot be received for a long time." Seemingly anticipating surprise at his suggestion, Barrett noted that he had "long regarded with a jaundiced eye the reports of the many foreigners who have gone all out in the support of the Chinese Communists" and believed that his "sales resistance to any cause in China is as high as that of any observer who wishes to be fair minded." Despite weaknesses in the CCP military organization, staff work, and what he called "how masterfully the Chinese can present a cause when they really put their hearts into it," Barrett was still convinced of the CCP guerrillas' entitlement to a limited amount of US military aid. He later wrote that his recommendations at the time were "carefully considered" in light of the opposition they would raise from the Nationalists. The possibility that the CCP fighters might eventually use the weapons against the Nationalist troops "would have to be accepted as a calculated risk."[10]

Stelle's opinions focused less on the politics of arming the CCP and more on the potential results. Stilwell's recall to Washington had prompted a shakeup in OSS personnel postings within China. John Coughlin was promoted to OSS head for CBI. In November 1944 Stelle wrote to him about the CCP's capabilities:

> Observations in the field confirm previous belief that the potential of these people for large scale demolitions is practically unlimited. If the negotiations in Chungking make it possible for us to bring in explosives and gadgets, I don't think there is any doubt that we could build up one of the biggest and most effective SO [Special Operations] jobs of this war. If the negotiations break down and official OK is lacking for supplies being brought up here, there may still be the possibility of a fairly large scale "clandestine" SO operation.[11]

Stelle's hint at clandestine or covert plans to arm the CCP through the OSS later led to considerable controversy.

MISSION CREEP

The fundamental task of the Dixie Mission was to gather information, but by the end of the first six months the interest of Dixie participants drifted toward operational activities. In some of their earliest reports they hinted at ways that the US government could assist the Chinese Communists. They argued that these incentives would serve both the strategic interests of the United States and the near- and long-term intelligence-collection interests of the Army, the OSS, and the State Department. By the time Wedemeyer took control of the China Theater for the United States, the Yan'an observers had already traveled to some of the far-flung areas where CCP guerrillas operated. Pete Peterkin's group did not return from their excursion to fully debrief until January, after Barrett had left Yan'an, but telegrams from them had begun to trickle in from the field. Other Americans had accompanied CCP fighters on closer-in and shorter trips. Firsthand observations only fortified Barrett's resolve to help the CCP troops, and in late November he specifically recommended through Army channels that the United States should help arm a CCP guerrilla force of up to 5,000 fighters.[12]

Around the same time, the OSS's John Colling was conferring with guerrillas from the CCP's Eighteenth Group Army about their demolition capabilities. Colling was an expert in sabotage operations and demolition, and he had been offering his CCP hosts various demonstrations of the equipment and techniques on which the US military relied. On November 18 Colling wrote to Wedemeyer to advise that his CCP military contacts could easily be trained to use American demolition techniques and put them to good use against Japanese targets in North China. He recommended that demolition equipment be provided to the Eighteenth Group Army to assist in its extensive efforts to disrupt Japanese communications.[13] Colling never received a specific written reaction to this memo, possibly due to personnel changes in the US delegation in Chongqing or because the US personnel in Chongqing were sorting through a variety of other strategic decisions about China policy at the time.

The most controversial plan for cooperation between the CCP and the US military involved discussions that occurred between November 1944 and January 1945 about combining Davies's Lianyungang operation ideas with the OSS's APPLE operation. Many in the Allied leadership in 1944 believed an Allied invasion of the Japanese islands would eventually be necessary to end the war. A perch in North China could be the launchpad the US forces needed. Given the potential of such a plan to upset Chiang Kai-shek and derail diplomatic efforts the United States had underway with the Chinese central government, Davies recommended that the OSS secretly pursue the potential arrangements without allowing Chiang's government to discover the plans yet. Under Stilwell, this arrangement might have worked had communications about it moved through Army G-2 "channels." Davies either did not consider how these plans would go over with the new leadership in CBI headquarters (Wedemeyer) or the US embassy (Hurley), or he may have thought the plans were important enough to take the chance.

OSS LEADERS' VIEW OF CHINA OPERATIONS

The OSS officers at Yan'an showed the most enthusiasm among all the Dixie Mission participants for proposals that supported the CCP. The individual

OSS officers posted to Yan'an had skills for war-planning operations and they wanted to use them to achieve strategic ends. They also wanted to stake a claim for the agencies they represented, and their training had prepared them to operate in the field without micromanagement. They sought to carry the ball as far as they could.

OSS China had three different projects running as of October 1944: cooperating with Chinese government officials in Chongqing on intelligence work sanctioned by SACO, cooperating with the Fourteenth Air Force in Kunming under the cover of the AGFRTS organization, and planning operations still in the works at Yan'an.[14] Many American officials in China believed SACO to be a huge policy failure that served only to constrain US intelligence operations in China according to the whims of the Guomindang. OSS officers operating out of Kunming also made little progress on their operations. The Fourteenth Air Force, under the direction of General Chennault, a loyal supporter of Chiang Kai-shek, experienced regular and heavy contact with various Chinese Army and Guomindang-controlled National Government components and reported all OSS actions back to Chongqing. Such action effectively blew the AGFRTS cover that OSS had previously enjoyed and brought all future OSS operational plans from that base under the SACO umbrella.

Of the three outposts, the Dixie Mission showed the greatest potential by far for the type of cutting-edge intelligence work that General Donovan wanted the OSS to do. Donovan sought to use stories of successful operations to persuade Roosevelt and others in Washington of the need for an independent peacetime strategic intelligence organization in the United States after the war's end. Donovan and his subordinate OSS managers were particularly keen on achieving dramatic operational intelligence successes in China through Yan'an-based activities and cooperation with the CCP. The fact that Chiang and the National Government had no jurisdiction over US intelligence operations in Communist-held areas encouraged Donovan. Not only did the OSS face the least amount of foreign government restrictions on their operations at Yan'an but the CCP also offered guerrilla capabilities and unique access to Japanese vulnerabilities.

As early as September 1944, the OSS officers at Dixie had several operations in the works of the kind that could please Donovan, some of which involved direct collaboration with the CCP. Donovan supported all plans for operations in North China. The OSS proposed a radio development project codenamed YENSIG to supply CCP guerrillas with sophisticated radio equipment to connect communications across all fourteen noncontiguous Communist-held base areas in North China.[15] Dixie's OSS officers had also been working on plans to develop intelligence agents and assets throughout northern China through the program codenamed APPLE. By the end of 1944, the OSS had renamed APPLE the North China Intelligence Project. It sought to train Allied agents in Yan'an and send them behind the Japanese lines into North China, Manchuria, and the Korean peninsula, similar to OSS operations that were being conducted successfully in Europe. When Davies kicked the Lianyungang landing idea over to the OSS, Donovan thought it meshed nicely with the North China Intelligence Project plans already in the works. While visiting China, Donovan intended to discuss with various US and Chinese officials the proposals for US cooperation with the CCP in North China.

Beyond Yan'an, responsibility within CBI offices in Chongqing for working with the CCP to cooperate in North China fell to Wedemeyer's newly appointed "China intelligence czar," the director of OSS China, Col. Richard Heppner. Donovan planned to arrive in China for meetings on December 26. Heppner assumed that the OSS director would expect a briefing on the operational plans. He tasked one of his new subordinates, Lt. Col. Willis Bird, who had previously served under Heppner as deputy chief for the OSS office in China, to take the lead in pursuing the plans for landing US paratroopers in Shandong and other unconventional warfare operations run by the OSS in the area. The army's tentative plan involved potentially sending up to 5,000 American paratroopers to the Lianyungang area. OSS would prepare 25,000 CCP guerrillas and provide pistols to the CCP as well.[16]

On December 15, 1944, Barrett escorted Bird to Yan'an for talks with the senior CCP leadership. Bird's trip occurred with the blessing of Gen. Robert McClure, Wedemeyer's deputy. At the time, Wedemeyer was away from Chongqing. Historical records are contradictory about who approved Bird's trip to Yan'an. McClure appears to have kept the trip a secret from Hurley. Bird intended to talk with CCP leaders about the Lianyungang landing idea. He also knew the OSS had long been eager to find a way to penetrate the Japanese territory in China's northeast, acting with its own intelligence agents and assets. If the topic of developing intelligence operations in North China were to come up, Bird would not shy away.

From a military perspective, the discussions of a Shandong landing for US troops represented sound strategic planning based on the information available to those at the level of Wedemeyer and McClure in January 1945. Having plans already in place that could be implemented when necessary was better than developing such plans at the last minute. The development of the nuclear weapons that ultimately helped hasten the end of the war with Japan was a closely held secret, not something the US military leadership in China nor the Chinese Communist Party leaders could have anticipated or might have predicted. From the information they had, envisioning that the United States might implement a Normandy-style attack on Japan to bring about the end of the war was logical, and such an action could not be spontaneous. Precise timing was unknown and contingent upon a series of events in Europe and the Pacific. The CCP's idea about offering Shandong and the US officials' enthusiasm for it is consistent with the types of activities the Yan'an Observer Group had been established to develop. The problem was politics.

Given the delicate situation that Roosevelt was navigating with Chiang Kai-shek through Hurley, in political terms both the plan and its timing were disastrous. OSS proposals to combine the landing agreement with a laundry list of other risky intelligence operations only added complication, and leaving Hurley out of the discussions made the situation even more volatile.

Bird's discussion with the CCP leaders about collaboration elicited enthusiasm from the CCP. Bird reported that he participated in five hours of meetings with Zhu De and Ye Jianying. They drafted a list of recommendations (as Bird described them in internal communication channels, using informal language), which they intended to deliver to Chongqing via US Army officials. They sought approval for the plans from the Chinese government and the United States leadership. The list from Bird's cable is worth quoting in its entirety:

> If the government approves, the following is tentative agreement:
> a. destroying Jap[anese] communications, airfields and blockhouses, and to generally raise hell and run.
> b. To fully equip units assisting and protecting our men in sabotage work.
> c. Points of attack to be selected in general by Wedemeyer. Details to be worked out in co-operation with Communists in that territory.
> d. To provide complete equipment for up to twenty-five thousand guerrillas except food and clothing.
> e. Set up school to instruct in use of American arms, demolitions, communications, etc.
> f. Set up intelligence radio network in co-operation with Eighth Route Army.
> g. To supply at least one hundred thousand Woolworth one shot pistols for Peoples Militia.
> h. to receive complete co-operation of their army of six hundred fifty thousand and Peoples Militia of two and half million when strategic use required by Wedemeyer.[17]

Bird dispatched the description of his agreements to CBI headquarters through OSS channels in December 1944. Word of the agreements did not reach Wedemeyer, who was away from China, until January, when aides presented him a portion of Bird's cable in his Pentagon meetings. In the meantime, through December the G-2 and OSS officers in Chongqing quietly developed Bird's plans. McClure dispatched Barrett on what ended up being Barrett's final trip to Yan'an on December 27, to inform the CCP leaders that Bird's plan had been accepted. Barrett recalled McClure sending him to gauge the attitude of Mao and Zhou about supervising a US paratroop division in a Communist area of Shandong if, after the defeat of Germany, the United States moved them from Europe to China "to take part in the final attack on the Japanese islands."[18] Barrett emphasized to the CCP leaders that the decision to send troops had not been made for certain, but if it did happen, the US would need help from the CCP to support the paratroopers until US supply chains could be established. McClure's response in December and his dispatch of Barrett to Yan'an implied to Barrett that Wedemeyer had given the authority for his trip. Wedemeyer later denied authorizing the trip. Barrett recalled that Mao and Zhou agreed to help, but they did not seem as excited about the plan as he expected, and he speculated that this was out of concern for their ability to support 28,000 American paratroopers, should such troops turn up.[19]

BIRD'S SNAFU

Discussion of Bird's "secret" plans—a poorly kept secret, to be sure—emerged in Chongqing by mid-January, and the topic surfaced in part at the instigation of the Communists. The main concern of the CCP leaders after meeting with Bird was the potential for the plan to be approved by senior US leaders and executed without their participation. They believed Chiang would not agree to US support for the Communists' efforts, which would be required under the terms of the SACO agreement. They also doubted that the United States would go behind Chiang's back in blatant violation of the agreement to support them. To encourage the plan's acceptance, Zhou Enlai offered to travel to Washington, and he made attempts to secure his own meeting at the White House. As rumors of Zhou's request began to swirl in Chongqing, specific reports of Bird's secret plans also began to leak out of the OSS and Army G-2 channels, probably through the ONI officials or Mary Miles, who had endured a troubled and competitive relationship with the army and OSS counterparts in China since 1942.[20] The leaked reports led Hurley to learn of the Bird/Barrett Yan'an trip for the first time in January 1945. His resulting anger reportedly reached an intensity that his staff at the embassy had not previously thought possible.

Hurley informed Roosevelt about what he had learned in an explosive January 14 memo and strongly urged the president to refuse any attempts by the CCP leaders to communicate with him directly. Hurley said he believed that the legitimacy and optimism CCP leaders would gain through contact with the US president would undermine his ability to entice the CCP leaders to negotiate with Chiang Kai-shek—the course of diplomatic action on which Hurley and Roosevelt had agreed. Hurley's memo also asked Roosevelt not to inform anyone in the State Department about his recommendations because Hurley doubted their loyalty.[21] Hurley's comments were sufficiently consistent with Roosevelt's existing attitude about both the State Department and US-China relations that Hurley succeeded in preventing the CCP from gaining any access to the president before his death a few months later.

Hurley's January 14 memo to the White House unsurprisingly precipitated demands from the White House and General Marshall for immediate explanation. Wedemeyer at first attempted to play down the seriousness of the plans. When his efforts failed to defuse the situation, he ultimately blamed the actions on the OSS and the pressure that OSS officials in China had been under to prepare for Donovan's visit. This approach, along with considerable contrition and deference throughout the remainder of the war, allowed Wedemeyer to patch up a working relationship with Hurley. It cost him respect and trust from the OSS and triggered significant concessions in the administration and function of the Dixie Mission, beginning with the replacement of David Barrett.

By the end of the year Barrett's term as head of the Dixie Mission had officially ended. Because Hurley was unable to penalize someone as high-ranking as Wedemeyer, Barrett became something of a scapegoat for the entire affair. As Barrett put it, "Early in January the roof fell in on me."[22] Most tellingly, he was denied a promotion to general that most army officers who knew him believed he had earned. George Marshall had nominated Barrett for lieutenant general in November 1944, a promotion that was permanently withheld. Instead, Barrett was shuttled off to serve as McClure's chief of staff in the new China Combat Command based in Kunming. Barrett bitterly said he was just following orders. Neither Wedemeyer nor McClure ever stepped forward to shield him from Hurley's wrath.

Barrett was old friends with his replacement in the Dixie Mission command position, Morris DePass; both had served in the Fifteenth Infantry Regiment in Tianjin. Before his brief move to Yan'an, DePass had been attaché in the US embassy.[23] Among the diplomatic community in China, DePass cultivated a reputation as a friend of the Chinese Central government intelligence officers in 1943 and 1944, which clearly set him apart from Barrett in terms of his administration of the Dixie Mission.[24]

Barrett's men at Yan'an liked DePass but believed him a poor choice for the job, and the G-2 staff presumably agreed. Years later Peterkin and Raymond Ludden exchanged letters discussing Dixie because both were working on writing their memoirs. Peterkin and Ludden recalled that when Barrett departed they were both away from Yan'an all winter on their guerrilla field trip. When the topic of DePass came up, Ludden recalled to Peterkin, "Joe Dickey [head of G-2 in China] would rather have shot his Old Aunt Hattie than put Morry DePass in command of Dixie."[25]

Hurley's rage over the Lianyungang plans extended to his own embassy staff as well. In early 1945 he officially ended the connection of the Foreign Service with the Dixie Mission. He sent Davies back to Washington and had him permanently transferred out of China. Jack Service made a final trip to Yan'an in March 1945. Soon after that Service became embroiled in a controversy over accusations that sympathy for the CCP had caused him to deliberately leak sensitive official files to the liberal media in the United States. Gone from Yan'an for most of the period from October 1944 to February 1945, Ludden did not return to Washington until later in the spring of 1945. He was the last Foreign Service Officer to be a part of the Dixie Mission.

THE OSS STRUGGLES TO OPERATE FROM YAN'AN

In late 1944 the OSS strategy for developing intelligence-collection programs in North China relied on plying the CCP leaders to develop a web of clandestine intelligence assets that could collect answers to the intelligence questions the OSS had gathered. Whereas OSS officials in European operations had occasionally relied on well-trained US agents to enter enemy and occupied territory under deep cover, such operations had been nearly impossible for the OSS to execute in China, where physical characteristics and language barriers prohibited most American agents from blending in with the Chinese population sufficiently well for clandestine operations or espionage. Instead, the OSS staff in Dixie relied on methods and networks of people that CCP guerillas had already developed for moving back and forth across Japanese lines of communication. Such plans comprised the North China Intelligence Program (codenamed APPLE).[26] However, events of January 1945 set OSS China operations on a slightly different course. After the diplomatic disaster that erupted from Bird's meeting with the CCP leaders in mid-January, Wedemeyer's aversion to the potential political blowback that could result from any US efforts to provide aid to the CCP, even secretly, largely ended the OSS's ability to pursue operations in Communist areas.

Wedemeyer was rightfully concerned about the predictable confusion and misunderstanding that would result from the complicated and disorganized communications protocols within US government channels in China. Communication between field areas such as Yan'an and Chongqing, which crossed agency lines, was particularly problematic. Wedemeyer consequently centralized all US intelligence operations in China under his control via Richard Heppner, who was the head of OSS China and whom Wedemeyer had personally selected. Wedemeyer formalized his proposed changes in an operational directive issued on February 6, specifying that the responsibility of OSS officials in China was to coordinate all operational activities with counterparts from the army's G-2 (intelligence) and G-3 (operations) divisions in Chongqing.[27]

Wedemeyer's order covered the broadest possible scope of OSS activities in China. It specified the "most important" functions of the OSS that required coordination included any operations "designed to affect the physical subversion of the enemy," "the delay and harassment of the enemy," "the collection of secret intelligence by various means including espionage and counterespionage," morale operations, and "the accumulation, evaluation and analysis of economic, political, psychological, topographic and military information concerning the enemy and enemy occupied territories, and the preparation of appropriate studies embracing these subjects."[28] The fact that the army physically controlled communications infrastructure for US installations in Chongqing ensured that it was difficult for OSS officials to evade or ignore the directive. Under the new arrangement, OSS officials in China had much less flexibility to sidestep the parameters of the SACO agreement than they had previously enjoyed.

General Donovan became concerned that Wedemeyer's reorganization would ruin his plans to accelerate OSS operations in China by using a group of clandestine agents who would infiltrate occupied China through the Communist networks. Donovan perceived the OSS plan for operations based out of Yan'an to be a key element in his efforts to persuade Roosevelt of the postwar relevance of the OSS.[29] By October 1944 he and his staff had begun working on proposals for a peacetime version of the OSS that would become the first independent intelligence agency in the United States. This kernel of an idea became the Central Intelligence Agency in 1947. Donovan so strongly desired the OSS expansion in China that he was willing to negotiate with the army on the exact terms. In February 1945 he and Wedemeyer reached a compromise that allowed the OSS to pursue its operations to develop a network of Chinese and Japanese clandestine agents in North China, but instead of relying on CCP networks, the OSS would partner with Guomindang guerilla units near Xi'an.[30] The OSS leaders in Chongqing felt no particular loyalty to working with the CCP, leading the OSS presence at Yan'an to diminish and eventually disappear.

Wedemeyer's centralization of intelligence operations in the China Theater under army auspices was a predictable move for a leader with his considerable expertise in military planning and organization. Consolidating intelligence-collection resources in this way streamlined communications and enhanced efficiency. Wedemeyer's change resulted in a significant expansion for OSS operations in China, except in Yan'an, where China's central government strongly opposed the OSS's activity.

By limiting the use of US strategic intelligence collectors in areas beyond Guomindang control, Wedemeyer's change gave Chiang Kai-shek and the

Guomindang much greater influence on the information about China that US policymakers received. As a relative newcomer to Chinese domestic politics who spoke no Chinese, Wedemeyer may not have realized the full implications of his decision. His top position in the army hierarchy in China probably limited opportunities for subordinates to provide any input on his plan before its implementation.

The increase in cooperation with the Guomindang introduced a new set of challenges for OSS officials in Chongqing and Yan'an. Heppner, the head of OSS operations in China who had a keen awareness of Chinese domestic politics, foresaw some of the difficulties. However, OSS operational planners in Washington ignored his protests; they were trying to hold together the patched-up relationship with Wedemeyer.[31] In the end the OSS operations in North China in collaboration with the Guomindang mirrored most of the organization's earlier efforts in the country: a great expenditure of funds and resources for very little return, punctuated by a few extremely humiliating international incidents.

The most notable of these incidents that emerged from the new OSS human asset operations in North China was the famous case of John Birch, a US Army captain cooperating with GMD troops and the OSS to collect intelligence, who was killed in a conflict with CCP guerillas in late August 1945.[32] The Birch incident resulted from a highly complicated set of diplomatic and military factors, ranging from simple bad luck and poor communication between Chinese troops to poor discipline among the untrained irregular CCP guerrillas. Reports of the affair that had been simplified to the point of bias quickly became a cause célèbre for the anti-Communist movement and China Lobby in the United States that persisted throughout the Cold War.

EMBASSY STAFF MUTINY

After further reducing the potential for the US intelligence officers in Yan'an to collect and disseminate useful political intelligence on the CCP, tensions between Hurley and his embassy staff in Chongqing continued to mount from December 1944 through the spring of 1945. Hurley's arrogant and not particularly erudite style of leadership paired with his ignorance of and disinterest in Chinese civilization provoked severe distrust and disagreement from the embassy's diplomatic staff. In a vicious cycle, US Foreign Service Officers serving under Hurley began to express doubts about his policy and political assessments, and Hurley became defensive and paranoid about their loyalty

Many career diplomats who comprised the staff of the US embassy to China objected to Hurley's close and unquestioning relations with Chiang Kai-shek and his negative assessments about the capabilities and interests of the CCP leaders. Some in the embassy agreed with Davies and Service that Hurley's plan to withhold US aid from the CCP in order to drive them to the negotiating table would backfire and encourage the CCP leaders to pursue assistance from the Soviet Union.[33] Behind his back the diplomats criticized Hurley's position, which they believed was not sufficiently neutral and would be unable to preserve the potential for US mediation efforts to successfully assist political actors in China with forming a true coalition government—the ultimate goal of US policy in China in the 1940s.

HURLEY CRACKS DOWN

Knowing that embassy staff disagreed with him and aware that many shared the views of the US officials in Yan'an that had so angered him, Hurley lost all trust in his staff. He expressed deep concern about the potential for them to undermine his policies. Hurley reportedly forbade embassy staff from sending critical messages to Washington and demanded his review of all messages to Washington before they left Chongqing so he could scrub them for material that he thought could humiliate him with the White House or threaten his policy direction.[34]

This level of personalized micromanagement significantly slowed the pace of work at the US embassy, which similarly affected the Dixie Mission staff, who could not dispatch reports through the embassy in any timely fashion. It also terrified Hurley's staff into submission. In one frequently cited and extreme example, Arthur Ringwalt, a career diplomat who served in the US embassy in China in 1945, claimed that Hurley threatened him with a gun over a critical report. Ringwalt had submitted it to Washington through internal State Department channels, and Hurley thought it might have cast a shadow on elements of the policy he advocated. According to Ringwalt's account, Hurley reportedly brandished a pistol while informing Ringwalt "he had killed men for less than this."[35] Ringwalt never discovered whether the pistol had been loaded, but he claimed he also never wrote another derogatory word while serving under Hurley.

Ringwalt's specific anecdote is impossible to corroborate, but historical records of the embassy reveal a clear change in tone as the building morphed into a toxic work environment. Before Hurley's arrival embassy political officers such as Service and Davies frequently published warts-and-all accounts of Chinese politics, including candid assessments of Chiang Kai-shek and his domestic policies. Reports that reached Washington from the embassy political officers in Chongqing in 1945 tend to adhere to much more banal topics, such as reports of inflation in the Chinese countryside supported by detailed lists relating the prices of groceries.

With the dilution of diplomatic and intelligence reporting emerging from China, Roosevelt had no reason but to continue and fortify his policies in negotiations with other Allied leaders in the months before his death. Unlike his policy toward European allies, Roosevelt's condescending approach to China focused almost exclusively on near- and long-term US interests, often with little regard for how China itself might fare. As historian Warren Cohen succinctly describes the situation, "Roosevelt's East Asian policies gave Americans no cause for grievance—and the Chinese no cause for gratitude."[36] Roosevelt's behavior at the Yalta Conference provided further evidence. Without Chinese voices or input, Roosevelt, Winston Churchill, and Joseph Stalin negotiated agreements designed to entice Soviet entrance into the war against Japan that would significantly affect Chinese sovereignty and territory, particularly in Manchuria.[37] Hurley and Wedemeyer traveled to Washington for talks with Roosevelt and other top US leaders about policy implementation in early March 1945.

Taking advantage of Hurley's absence from China, the embassy staff in Chongqing prepared a report explaining their view of the problems with Hurley's China policy and suggested alternate recommendations. The diplomats argued that as a result of US policy and other events in China, circumstances "have combined to increase greatly Chiang's feeling of strength and have resulted in unrealistic optimism on his part and lack of willingness to make any compromise."[38] Furthermore, because the CCP determined the United States to be definitely "committed to the support of Chiang alone, and that we will not force Chiang's hand in order to be able to aid or cooperate with them," CCP leaders were taking steps for "self-protection" that would move China closer to civil war. They claimed that without a drastic change in US policy, "chaos in China will be inevitable and the probable outbreak of disastrous civil conflict will be accelerated," which would be dangerous to American interests both "from a military standpoint" and "from a long-range point of view." The diplomats suggested that the controversy over initial plans to support the CCP's military efforts had resulted in clarity over particular elements of US China policy: "The Generalissimo and his Government will not at this time on their own initiative take any forward step which will mean loss of face, prestige or personal power. The Communists will not, without guarantees in which they have confidence, take any forward step which will involve dispersion and eventual elimination of their forces upon which their present strength and future political existence depend." The diplomats timed the report's release to take advantage of the presence of both Wedemeyer and Hurley in Washington, which they believed could provide "a favorable opportunity for discussion" of US relations with the political parties in China and plans to aid the CCP guerrillas. The authors also clarified that the document represented the consensus of all the diplomats in Chongqing and Wedemeyer's chief of staff.

The report arrived in Washington on February 28, 1945, just before Hurley himself arrived there. Unsurprisingly, Hurley perceived the document as a mutinous personal attack on his leadership. Its wide distribution around Washington deeply embarrassed him and led to what historian Warren Cohen has aptly called a showdown between Hurley and his staff.[39] After lengthy discussions of the matter at the State and War Departments, Roosevelt sided firmly with his friend, Ambassador Hurley. Thus, the CCP would receive no assistance from the United States unless Chiang approved it, and US policy in China aimed only to "sustain and reform" Chiang's regime.[40]

CHANGES IN CHONGQING AND YAN'AN

Hurley initiated significant changes to the personnel at the embassy and their relationships with other US government organizations operating in China, effectively silencing dissent from his subordinates until he resigned as ambassador in November 1945. By then diplomats in the embassy had faced Hurley's draconian censorship and loyalty exercises. They were shocked to see what happened to Service and Davies, career diplomats that they viewed as coming under attack simply for doing their jobs. These factors strongly discouraged other foreign service officers to report information about the CCP that could in any way be perceived as charitable, whether or not it reflected what they had observed. Thus, in 1945 and early 1946 sensitive political analysis on the CCP ceased to be broadly available to US foreign policy decision-makers, except for reports the Nationalists provided, which universally portrayed the CCP in a negative light. When Hurley's replacement, John Leighton Stuart, was sworn in on July 4, 1946, he changed the tone in the embassy. By this time negotiations that Roosevelt and Hurley had insisted on between the Nationalists and the Communists were underway, and policymakers had an artificially narrow view of events on the ground. Few reports about Chinese Communists or the plans and intentions of the CCP appear in official State Department records from this time, even though from April 23 to June 11, 1945, the CCP leaders in Yan'an held their Seventh Party Congress, which historians today consider to be among the most important conferences in CCP history because it consolidated the power of Mao Zedong.[41]

Separate from but simultaneous to the tumult over US diplomatic personnel transitions in China, Secretary of State Cordell Hull became ill and ultimately resigned in late November 1944. Although Roosevelt had restrained Hull's influence throughout World War II, Hull made an indelible mark on the administrative culture of the State Department while serving as its head from 1933 to 1944, and his exit left the organization reeling. A significant portion of the US diplomatic corps in 1944 had never served under another secretary. One of Hull's deputies, Roosevelt crony and businessman Edward Stettinius Jr., succeeded Hull and served in the role for only six months. President Truman replaced Stettinius with James Byrnes in July 1945, who served as secretary until George Marshall took the job in January 1947.[42] These years were a period of tremendous fluctuation for the US national security regime and for US-China relations.

DISTRUST AND INSTITUTIONAL RIVALRIES DISTRACT US INTELLIGENCE COLLECTORS IN YAN'AN

In terms of being able to close the US government's intelligence gap regarding the CCP and providing intelligence that could help explain the intricacies of Chinese domestic politics to US leaders, limiting the ability of the OSS to cooperate with the CCP was a definite setback. Like US military officials based at Yan'an, OSS officials at the CCP base refrained from reporting any intelligence about CCP politics for broad dissemination within the government because they had no orders or mandate to do so. Apart from a handful of internal analytic reports that circulated within the OSS R&A Branch, OSS China never weakened the monopoly that State Department officials had on providing political assessments about the CCP within the US government.[43] Hurley's fear of disloyalty and policy criticism prevented Foreign Service Officers in China from exercising their authority to report on the CCP. Washington received almost no information on the CCP at this time except what was conveyed through contacts in the Guomindang—the CCP leaders' main domestic political opponents.

Continued competition for budgetary resources in Washington trickled down to personnel in field offices in the form of waylaid approvals for interagency operations and destructive secrecy between agencies that were supposedly collaborating. On the level of organizational culture, strong personal identifications with the agencies that employed them often encouraged US intelligence officials in Yan'an and their closest colleagues in Chongqing and Kunming to feel confidence bordering on arrogance regarding the efficiency of their own bureaucratic processes and disdain for other agencies. These perceptions contributed to their willingness to duplicate efforts and their reluctance to share information with or delegate duties to other agencies. Heppner described dealing with such issues as a matter of course in a letter to Donovan dated February 17, 1945: "I have been forced to sit on the SI Branch very sharply because of excessive branch-mindedness and an attempt by them to emasculate AGFRTS. I had expected this sort of thing, however, and I know how to deal with it."[44]

Personnel changes and the departure of the close-knit group of China experts that had comprised the initial Dixie Mission opened the door for ingrained institutional rivalries to surface, impeding efficiency at Yan'an starting in 1945. Barrett never returned to Yan'an after he was replaced. Peterkin stepped up to help DePass lead, and he soon became the leader himself for a time.

NOTES

1. John Paton Davies Jr., *China Hand: An Autobiography* (Philadelphia: University of Pennsylvania Press, 2012), 219.
2. Memo, John Davies, "Chinese Communist Preliminary Estimate of Cooperation Which They Could Offer a Hypothetical American Landing at Lienyunkang," November 3, 1944, US National Archives and Records Administration (hereafter NARA), RG 493, box 7, folder: "Radios-Eyes Only—Communists, Wires." For a detailed explanation of the Dixie Mission's discussion with the CCP leaders regarding a potential invasion of Japan, see Maochun Yu, *OSS in China: Prelude to Cold War* (Annapolis, MD: Naval Institute Press, 1996), 183–85.
3. The Chinese name of the place is 连云港, which is romanized as "Lienyunkang" in many records from the 1940s.
4. See Hans van de Ven, *War and Nationalism in China, 1925–1945* (London: RoutledgeCurzon, 2003) and *China at War: Tragedy in the Emergence of the New China, 1937–1952* (Cambridge, MA: Harvard University Press, 2018); and Hsi-sheng Ch'i, *The Much Troubled Alliance* (Singapore: World Scientific, 2015).
5. Joseph W. Stilwell, *The Stilwell Papers* (New York: William Sloane, 1948), 317.
6. Stilwell, *The Stilwell Papers,* 321.
7. Memo, John Paton Davies, "The Chinese Communists and the Great Powers," November 7, 1944, NARA, RG 226, entry 148, box 7, folder 104.
8. John S. Service, *Lost Chance in China: World War II Despatches of John S. Service,* ed. Joseph E. Esherick (New York: Random House, 1974), 161–66.
9. John N. Hart, *The Making of an Army "Old China Hand": A Memoir of Colonel David D. Barrett* (Berkeley: University of California, Center for China Studies, 1985), 42.
10. David D. Barrett, *Dixie Mission: The United States Army Observer Group in Yenan, 1944* (Berkeley: University of California, Center for China Studies, 1970), 91.
11. Memo, Charles Stelle to John Coughlin, November 22, 1944, NARA, RG 226, entry 148, box 7, folder 104.
12. Hart, *The Making of an Army "Old China Hand,"* 53.
13. Memo, John Colling to Albert Wedemeyer, November 18, 1944, NARA, RG 226, entry 148, box 7, folder 104: Dixie Intelligence Reports.
14. Yu, *OSS in China,*170.
15. Yu, 167.
16. R. Smith, *OSS: The Secret History of America's First Central Intelligence Agency* (Berkeley: University of California Press, 1972), 272–73.
17. Charles F. Romanus and Riley Sunderland, *Time Runs Out in CBI* (Washington, DC: US Army Center of Military History, 1959), 252.
18. Barrett, *Dixie Mission,* 77.
19. Barrett, 78.

20. See Milton E. Miles and Hawthorne Daniel, *A Different Kind of War* (New York: Doubleday, 1967). Miles represented the ONI in China in 1942 and served from 1943 to 1945 as SACO deputy director. His memoir drips with vitriol for Stilwell, the Dixie Mission, and the entire G-2 perspective.
21. Ambassador in China [Hurley] to FDR, January 14, 1945, *Foreign Relations of the United States, Diplomatic Papers 1945: The Far East, China,* vol. 7, accessed May 1, 2022, https://history.state.gov/historicaldocuments/frus1945v07/d135.
22. Barrett, *Dixie Mission,* 78.
23. Memo, Patrick Hurley to Embassy Staff, February 2, 1945, NARA, RG 493, entry UD-UP 252, box 30, folder: Messages 1945 201 D. The memo explains replacement of attaché Col. Morris DePass with Col. Charles W. Mason.
24. Michael Schaller, *The U.S. Crusade in China, 1938–1945* (New York: Columbia University Press, 1979), 226–28.
25. Letter, Raymond Ludden to Wilbur Peterkin, March 12, 1971, Hoover Institution, Personal Papers of Wilbur J. Peterkin.
26. Official OSS records about the APPLE operation, including correspondence and multiple drafts of the proposal, are preserved at NARA, RG 226, entry NM-54 1, box 23, folder: China.
27. Memo, Richard Heppner to William Donovan, February 17, 1945, NARA, RG 226, entry 148, box 14, with attached Directive, Acting Chief of Staff by command of Albert Wedemeyer, "Operational Directive No. 4," February 6, 1945.
28. Memo, Heppner to Donovan, February 17, 1945.
29. Historian Maochun Yu describes the evolution of Donovan's attitudes and the resulting operations in *OSS in China,* 214–18.
30. Yu, 216–17.
31. Yu, 215.
32. Carolle J. Carter records one of the most objective descriptions of the incident in *Mission to Yenan: American Liaison with the Chinese Communists, 1944–1947* (Lexington: University Press of Kentucky, 1997), 173–76.
33. For more on Hurley's disagreements with the career diplomats who staffed the US embassy in Chongqing in early 1945, see Warren I. Cohen, *America's Response to China: A History of Sino-American Relations,* 5th ed. (New York: Columbia University Press, 2010), 159–65.
34. For the full anecdote in Ringwalt's own words, see Schaller, *The U.S. Crusade in China,* 208.
35. Schaller, 208.
36. Cohen, *America's Response to China,* 147.
37. Cohen, *America's Response to China,* 157–58. For a summary of the Yalta Conference from the US perspective, see official statement of the US Department of State Historian at https://history.state.gov/milestones/1937–1945/yalta-conf (accessed October 14, 2015).
38. Memo, Charge in China George Atcheson to the Secretary of State, Chungking, February 28, 1945, *FRUS, Diplomatic Papers 1945: The Far East, China,* 242.
39. Cohen, *America's Response to China,* 160.
40. Cohen, 160.
41. Alexander V. Pantsov with Steven I. Levine, *Mao: The Real Story* (New York: Simon & Schuster), 2007.

42. See List of Secretaries of State, accessed February 15, 2022, https://www.state.gov/former-secretaries-of-state/.
43. OSS R&A official Charles Stelle, who served in Yan'an from when the first Dixie plane touched down until spring 1945, often included detailed observations and shrewd analysis of intentions and attitudes of CCP leaders in long reports to his counterparts, such as Joseph Spencer in Chongqing. Stelle's reports are preserved in NARA, RG 226, entry 190.
44. Heppner to Donovan, February 17, 1945.

8

LEAVING YAN'AN BEHIND

革命不是请客吃饭…
[A revolution is not a dinner party…]
—Mao Zedong

The dinner parties and dances at Yan'an were over, at least for the Americans. The last view of Yan'an that Col. John Sells saw was of CCP soldiers setting charges and blowing up the old airstrip. It was the morning of March 11, 1947. Three days earlier Gen. Zhu De had warned Sells and the few remaining Americans at Yan'an that the CCP needed to remove the airstrip to keep his people safe. With the airfield serving as one of the few visible targets for Guomindang bombers, the CCP leaders had decided to destroy it.

All US efforts to mediate the civil war in China had failed. The US Observer Mission to Yan'an had officially ended in April 1946, but its last commander and Zhou Enlai had agreed to keep a skeleton crew stationed there. Zhou requested that the United States send a person of at least colonel rank to remain at Yan'an to maintain basic communications and help provide consular support to American journalists, downed US pilots, and UN aid workers passing through the area.[1] The army designated Sells to fill the role. His main assignment had been oversight of the physical relocation of CCP leaders and their dependents to Yan'an from Guomindang-held areas, such as Chongqing. However, Sells reportedly approached his work with considerable bitterness and a possible alcohol dependence problem that prevented efficacy in the role.[2] Chiang Kai-shek's air attacks on Yan'an made it necessary to close this last open connection between the CCP and the United States. The little that was left of the Dixie Mission was permanently in the hands of the CCP leaders from that point on, as the plane carrying Sells lifted off.[3]

The post-Barrett Dixie Mission personnel had little momentum to build upon after the setbacks and personnel shifts that occurred between October 1944 and January 1945. Patrick Hurley proceeded with vengeance, gutting the Yan'an group's interagency focus. Meanwhile, Albert Wedemeyer's interest in smoothing over the jagged edges that Joseph Stilwell had left behind resulted in the US post in Yan'an becoming a standard army intelligence and liaison outpost. In this single-agency capacity, the US Observer Group at Yan'an unexpectedly outlasted both World War II and the OSS.[4] However, the limits taken on in 1945 and 1946 were well beyond what John Davies and Jack Service had imagined when they thought up the mission.

HURLEY'S REVENGE

Hurley had an undeniable and stifling influence on the Dixie Mission in the final months of World War II. Hurley's anger over the mission's efforts to unilaterally arrange cooperative military agreements with the CCP in late 1944 led him to impose severe limitations on the types of intelligence that US officials in North China could collect. In retrospect this seems like cutting off his nose to spite his face. Hurley enjoyed little respect among US career diplomats and other prewar military intelligence officials such as David Barrett. He was President Roosevelt's friend dispatched to fix China. Hurley's subordinates thus lacked the power to protest his actions. However, they believed he did not understand China the way they did. Hurley got along well enough with Chiang Kai-shek, even though he approached the relationship with the same attitude of condescension that Stilwell exhibited to the Chinese leader. He just communicated it differently. Hurley's revenge-driven efforts to smother the cooperation between US intelligence agencies at Yan'an succeeded. Considering the longer-term view of US intelligence on the CCP, the move was extremely poor form, and the US government lost an opportunity for a deeper understanding of the CCP.

In the face of Hurley's explosive anger over OSS and G-2 actions in December 1944, plans for Dixie Mission officials to cooperate with the CCP on covert military operations were terminated. No vestiges of the plans remained in force by February 1945. Hurley might have withdrawn US presence from Yan'an altogether, but because Stilwell had arranged it as an army operation, ending it was a tricky endeavor. Albert Wedemeyer still found the Yan'an outpost useful for military purposes and wanted to avoid squandering the resources that had gone into establishing the collection capabilities there. To help smooth interagency relations between Hurley and the army, General Wedemeyer released a sternly worded statement in January 1945 regarding army support of US policy in China, which was briefed to all US Army personnel in China, including and especially those at Yan'an, to whom it was particularly directed.[5] Wedemeyer's statement reminded all army subordinates that they were in China "to implement the policy of the United States, not to formulate or discuss that policy," and that US policy specified "wholehearted cooperation with the present Chinese National Government headed by Generalissimo Chiang Kai-shek."

Rather than leaving these initial statements to interpretation, Wedemeyer then spelled out his meaning in terms that required no sophisticated analysis:

> Officers in China Theater will not assist, negotiate or collaborate in any way with Chinese political parties, activities or persons not specifically authorized by the Commanding General, US Forces, China Theater. This includes discussing hypothetical aid or employment of US resources to assist any effort of an unapproved political party, activity or persons. This also forbids rendering local assistance or making loans or gifts of arms, ammunition or other military materiel or equipment to such groups, activities or persons by an individual or organization of the United States Forces in the China Theater.

No evidence has ever surfaced that US Army personnel in Yan'an raised the topic of cooperation with the CCP after Wedemeyer's message. The high hopes that OSS had held for operations in North China were dashed.

In his fury over the actions of Robert McClure and the Dixie Mission participants in meetings with CCP leaders, Hurley withdrew all State Department officials from Yan'an. On January 7, 1945, Wedemeyer received a telegram from the Secretary of State marked secret, ordering the "release of any or all Foreign Service Officers" detailed to the army's China Theater Headquarters, specifically John Paton Davies.[6] Hurley had insisted that State Department headquarters issue the order to Wedemeyer, but ambiguity within the telegram suggests that in Washington support for Hurley's personnel decisions was not unanimous. Specifically, after issuing the order for the release of the Foreign Service Officers from General Staff work, the telegram states, "Secretary of State indicates Embassy staff in Chungking can assist you there although he believes it advantageous to have Foreign Service officers in Communist Area at Yenan." The telegram then offers the continued work of Ray Ludden as a political adviser to the military intelligence officers.

Ray Ludden continued his Foreign Service career focused on China and East Asia from 1945 on, but he never returned to the Dixie Mission staff. Jack Service and John Emmerson continued working on China-related issues from both Chongqing and Washington in spring 1945. Service made a final temporary visit to Yan'an in March 1945. The American group at Yan'an never had State Department contact after that.

Hurley's inability to overcome his anger and disappointment with what he perceived to be the disloyalty and insubordination of John Paton Davies meant permanent assignment away from China affairs for Davies. This was a huge blow to Davies, who had a personal connection to the Dixie Mission and lifelong roots in China. Although Davies had never been officially assigned to the Dixie Mission, he had in many ways orchestrated the group's establishment and vehemently defended its work to others within the US government.[7] Davies vocally disagreed with Hurley's China policy in late 1944 and early 1945, and the State Department acquiesced. Secretary of State Edward Stettinius had held his title an even shorter time than Hurley.[8]

Foreseeing a falling out with Hurley, Davies had started searching for a position outside China in fall 1944 after Stilwell's recall. In his memoirs Davies claims he wanted "a transfer to the embassy in Moscow from which to observe the Soviet entry into the war against Japan, Soviet relations with the Chinese Communists, and Moscow's approach to the Chinese civil war, which I believed would follow on the heels of Japan's defeat."[9] Davies's queries landed him a position at the US embassy in Moscow. He left China for Moscow in early January 1945 to work with George Kennan, observing and assessing the start of the Cold War.[10]

Davies's career and reputation after his time in China was a roller coaster. In 1948 he received the Medal of Freedom for actions taken to save himself and others after a plane crash in Myanmar in 1943. In the 1950s Davies was a target of Joseph McCarthy's loyalty hearings due to his CCP-friendly reports from Yan'an. Numerous trials all failed to prove he was a Communist. Nonetheless, Secretary of State John Foster Dulles gave into political pressure and fired Davies in 1954. The US government exonerated Davies from the charges in 1969 after years of legal battles. By that time he and his wife had established an award-winning furniture business based in Peru.[11]

THE ARMY GENERAL STAFF STRIKES BACK

In 1945 the US Army still valued the unique military intelligence and liaison capabilities available at and through the Yan'an base. The ambassador's exclusion of both the OSS and the State Department from performing any innovative strategic intelligence work from CCP headquarters left the army's G-2 in charge of setting the agenda for the group at Yan'an. The top priority of the Dixie Mission during the spring of 1945, as General Wedemeyer conveyed it to officials in Yan'an, was collecting logistical information that the army could immediately act upon to win the war, keeping political issues entirely out of it. Americans at Yan'an began collecting the sort of US military intelligence officials felt comfortable processing. This military intelligence was immediately useful to the army but did little to increase policymakers' strategic understanding of the domestic political situation in China or improve White House China policy. The initial Dixie Mission crew had brought to Yan'an an innovative approach to intelligence-collection efforts and area expertise about Chinese politics (along with a hefty dose of Stilwell's brand of Open Door paternalism). These elements were gone by March 1945.

Peterkin's Moment

The spring of 1945 marked a turning point for the Dixie Mission in several respects. Hurley and Wedemeyer had made so many personnel changes that the base looked completely different than when Pete Peterkin had left for the countryside. Shortly after his return to Yan'an in January, he noted in his journal that only seven of the original Dixie Mission members were still in Yan'an: he and Ray Cromley, Louis Jones (Army Air Corps), Charles Stelle, Anton Remenih, Walter Gress, and George Nakamura were all that remained.[12] Morris DePass lasted only a few weeks as commander of the unit; he departed Yan'an shortly after the Chinese New Year festivities in February. Peterkin made rank and led the group through the summer. Peterkin was a dedicated officer who had been in Yan'an from the beginning. Barrett had mentored him in the few years he had served in China, but he lacked Barrett's depth of experience.

Life at Yan'an physically became a bit easier for US personnel that spring. One of Barrett's last acts had been to organize a team to manage an overland delivery of vehicles and other mechanical supplies, giving the Americans access to new tools. There was less need to rely on the CCP's sad antique lorry. They were able to bring General Marshall from the airstrip to the Dixie buildings in greater comfort and style than Hurley had experienced in his visits. The convoy had also brought electric generators that provided power for lights to the American offices and the newly fortified brick mess hall. The team named the refurbished building Whittlesey Hall, in honor of their fallen comrade.[13]

Peterkin noted in his memoir how quickly things changed at Yan'an after Wedemeyer got in trouble over the APPLE affair and Willis Bird's exuberant plans for North China. When Peterkin took charge of the Observer Group in February, his orders for the installation had been downscaled to disseminating weather reports, continuing to collect order of battle information on Japan, military (but not political!) liaison with the CCP headquarters, and support for rescued Allied fliers.[14] Each of these goals involved a steady flow of new US personnel rotating into the mission, some permanent assignments and some temporary. Many of the new officials had no particular expertise in Chinese affairs or language but were technical experts participating in the installation of advanced radio or weather technology.

Although the potential for the collection of new political information on the CCP diminished under Hurley's rules, other resources improved. Yan'an had more US personnel, and the military resources available expanded significantly.

In its first months many Dixie personnel spent their time learning about the CCP and drafting politically focused intelligence reports for US audiences. By the time Harry Truman took office, almost all American efforts at Yan'an had shifted to focus on basic military and intelligence liaison activities and the construction of operational infrastructure, such as radio communications systems and weather monitoring equipment. Information collected in these efforts mainly served specific military purposes. Military intelligence of this sort had little influence on US policy in China generally or on the ongoing US efforts to broker a truce between the CCP and Guomindang.

The Yan'an post continued to collect copies of Japanese periodicals and captured Japanese documents and attempted to convey these into other parts of the US government where they would be useful. Administrative and logistical challenges with interagency communications were at their height at this time. The Japanese materials typically failed to reach the relevant analytic personnel in Chongqing and Washington in time to be of immediate use for the war.

Slow Technological Expansion

Throughout 1945 US officials at Yan'an continued to call for the development of more effective radio networks in the CCP base areas. Without sophisticated radio technology and established protocols for its use, intelligence collection from these remote areas was simply not feasible. Plus, physically transporting time-sensitive intelligence documents by air was impossible for several reasons. To start, Japanese troops often occupied the areas between the geographically discontinuous CCP base areas, making planes flying between them vulnerable. But this concern was minor compared to the other logistical issues preventing such transportation. Few airstrips or fuel depots existed in the northern parts of China. Building these assets would be time-consuming and expensive, particularly because the area also lacked reliable and efficient roadways, transportation vehicles for construction equipment and resources, and, in many cases, the necessary fuel infrastructure for heavy vehicles. The same issues prevented moving the materials by road, particularly considering that the most important intelligence had to be delivered immediately. The month it took to travel across the Chinese countryside made the details of attack plans, troop movements, or weather data obsolete long before their arrival. Thus, for the US intelligence officials in Yan'an to be able to collect and disseminate any useful intelligence, they needed to use radio technology to transmit the most important details.

Although the need for this radio equipment was obvious to all involved in the war in China, procuring equipment suitable for use in rural north China, where power supply issues were severe, and dispatching it to where it was needed, was frustratingly slow. The same poor conditions and terrain in remote northern

China during World War II that made the transport of intelligence information by ground or air unfeasible also stalled the development of the radio network. The first American intelligence officials to reach Yan'an had assessed in August 1944 that they needed radio equipment and trainers. Cromley had submitted the necessary requests and justifications.

Once approved, these requests wended their way through the military and OSS bureaucracies and the first planes carrying equipment and trainers arrived in late 1944. However, according to a memo from OSS officer Burton Fahs, director of R&A Branch for the Far East who visited Yan'an temporarily in December 1944 to assess the status of intelligence collection in China, many of the radio sets sent to Yan'an and intended for field use were completely unsuitable in the actual physical conditions in China. Climate, transportation, and power supply challenges prevented the equipment from being used as it had been used in the European conditions for which it was designed.[15]

OSS officers working throughout China to establish a reliable radio network had specifically complained about receiving radios with rechargeable batteries, which often required up to ten hours of steady power supply to recharge. In January 1945 one OSS official serving in eastern China explained to headquarters that the power infrastructure in Shanghai, one of the most developed cities in China at the time, operated only ten days of each month. The supply probably would have been reduced further out of concerns for fuel conservation.[16] Remote areas or cities smaller than Shanghai had no electricity at all. Thus, American intelligence officials serving in China specifically requested radios powered by dry-cell batteries. The replacement equipment needed at Yan'an finally arrived in mid-February 1945 along with eight signal corps radio operators to build and operate a network and train CCP counterparts in the use of the equipment.[17]

Along the same lines, the first Dixie Mission officials had observed a need for microfilm equipment to facilitate the processing of and dissemination to Washington the huge volumes of captured documents and difficult-to-find Japanese publications to which CCP guerrillas had access. The Dixie Mission routinely received copies of the *Tokyo Asahi* daily newspaper within ten days of publication via the CCP communication networks throughout North China, according to Barrett. He explained: "As everyone who knows anything about intelligence work is well aware, a daily newspaper, even though published under the strictest of wartime security regulations, is one of the best sources of military information in the world."[18]

Despite the usefulness of these sources, they lacked the immediacy of intelligence transmitted via radio. Moreover, a further challenge in transporting printed materials was their volume. Cargo space on planes into Yan'an was reserved for supplies, people, mail, and sensitive documents. Without microfilm equipment, the only way to transport mass media and other nonsensitive publications to US base areas in southwest China was overland, typically on the backs of mules, a time-consuming affair during which the documents were vulnerable to loss, damage, and exposure to poor weather that could render them useless, if they even arrived in the hands of US intelligence officials in time to be of use. Converting the materials to microfilm in the field would have significantly accelerated the pace at which they could be distributed as well as the volume that could be sent from Yan'an to Chongqing. The weekly flight between the two cities could easily carry microfilm.[19]

US intelligence officials at Yan'an recognized that the United States had to provide the microfilm equipment and supplies as well as the American personnel who could train the CCP members to use it. US personnel established an effective microfilm lab at Yan'an in 1945. They also intended to set up additional outposts in the countryside, but plans progressed too slowly before the end of the war.[20] Once they obtained the required equipment, the US officials at Yan'an also created a photography lab and trained a Chinese technician to operate it.[21] US officials arranged for Japanese agents who were loyal to the CCP to travel to Beijing, where they purchased Japanese publications not generally available to the US government elsewhere. Once the agents had transported the periodicals overland back to Yan'an, the Chinese technician photographed them and printed them onto microfilm for easy transport to Chongqing by plane. From Chongqing, officials with OSS and the army's G-2 forwarded the film to intelligence analysts and policymakers in Washington via the diplomatic pouch system. This method of conveyance worked more efficiently than sending paper documents.

FROM AREA EXPERTS TO TECHNICAL EXPERTS AT YAN'AN

The original idea for the Dixie Mission sought to sidestep some of the biggest inefficiencies in interagency intelligence work. Though Stilwell and Davies had recruited capable personnel who could work as a team, Hurley and Wedemeyer identified Stilwell's informal network as a threat to their interests and policies. The delegation of Americans based at Yan'an consequently experienced three changes of commanding officer and two name changes in the twelve months of 1945 alone—extremely jarring transitions from an administrative standpoint for an outpost as tiny and remote as Yan'an.[22] In January 1945 Peterkin had noted that only six of the original members of the Dixie Mission remained with him in Yan'an, and by October 1945 these six had all left as well.[23] The rapid and substantial personnel turnover among US officials working on CCP intelligence collection in both Yan'an and Chongqing decimated the remaining vestiges of knowledge and institutional history behind the Dixie Mission's creation. Few reminders of the original Dixie participants remained at Yan'an beyond Whittlesey's name on the chow hall.[24]

Personnel turnover within the Dixie Mission also reduced the instances of informal interagency communication. Prior to the recall of Stilwell and the resignation of Amb. Clarence Gauss, many of the US intelligence officials serving at Yan'an shared a professional interest in Chinese affairs and a connection to Stilwell that facilitated deep trust and open communication. A tangible example of this network's circumvention of bureaucratic constraints occurred in January 1945, when one OSS China Morale Operations Branch (MO) official secretly received a copy of a report Davies had written after his visit to Yan'an titled "China and the Kremlin." His cover letter to the report specifies that Davies passed it to OSS in confidence, and "it would be most unfortunate if there was any leak on this."[25] In 1945, systems for interagency communication were calcifying. Meanwhile, the number of intelligence personnel was increasing, and many of the newcomers to the unit were also new to China. They had no connection to the cohort of US diplomats and attachés from the 1920s and 1930s. Instances of unauthorized interagency information-sharing were almost nonexistent.

WANING US INTELLIGENCE COLLECTION ABOUT THE CCP

Having no US diplomats, the mission at Yan'an could not have met its original goal of filling in the gaps of information about Chinese domestic politics even if Hurley had allowed it. At this time the State Department was tasked with fulfilling a unique role within the US executive branch. Even with OSS on the scene, State was the only agency providing political assessments and intelligence reporting on social, economic, and political topics directly into the White House and other executive branch agencies. US diplomats in the 1940s did not frequently use the term "intelligence" to describe the products of their work, but the information they provided meets the basic definitions of intelligence used today: US diplomats collected nonpublic information about foreign affairs that was relevant to the policy interests of the United States. At Yan'an, political assessments about the CCP and information gleaned from political discussions with the CCP leaders on behalf of the US government had been the sole responsibility of the Foreign Service Officers, particularly Jack Service.

Other agencies with personnel operating in China did not generally engage in the production of political assessments. Intrinsic competition for resources and influence between the agencies responsible for foreign policy and strategic issues had resulted in strict divisions of labor between diplomats and attachés prior to World War II. Roosevelt established the OSS in part because the combined efforts of the State Department and military intelligence organizations were failing to meet the more sophisticated intelligence demands that World War II had presented. However, OSS officials found it extremely difficult to break through established administrative norms and work within the bounds of the SACO agreement to establish effective political intelligence reporting mechanisms from China during the war.[26]

Thus, the complete withdrawal of State Department participation in US intelligence efforts at Yan'an early in 1945 significantly reduced the capacity of the Dixie Mission to provide political intelligence reporting on the CCP. Without Foreign Service Officers to observe the CCP leaders and compile their observations in contextualized reports, the American officials who remained at Yan'an would have found it difficult to succeed their State Department colleagues in their duties, even if Hurley had not forbidden it.

US officials serving in remote forward areas such as Yan'an tended to be extremely cautious about exceeding the mandates of their prescribed professional responsibilities, since doing so would create unnecessary tension between colleagues serving under often arduous conditions and cause controversy with management in rear areas, all of whom tended to be geographically located together in US embassy compounds like the one in Chongqing. Barrett's memoirs frequently refer to this phenomenon of respect for organizational specialization. At one point Barrett explicitly notes that his reports were "all on military subjects, as the political side was covered by Jack Service and Ray Ludden."[27] Barrett further specifies the list of topics that he considered to be within his purview: "Estimates of the strength of the Communist forces—on these I had to accept generally the figures given me, as there was no way to check them—and their tactics, equipment, training, discipline, and morale. I also did my best to make a fair assessment of the contribution they had made in the past to the war effort in general and what they were likely to be able to contribute in the future."[28] Although the frequency of his personal contacts with CCP leaders and his years of service in the military attaché's office in China would have qualified Barrett to provide at least somewhat constructive commentary on the CCP leaders' politics, the norms and protocols of bureaucratic behavior prevented him from engaging in such activity. Political reports simply exceeded the scope of Barrett's position, if not his officially acknowledged expertise. This phenomenon ceased to be an issue after 1945, when few American personnel newly dispatched to Yan'an possessed expertise on Chinese politics.

YEATON TAKES CHARGE

The appointment in July 1945 of Col. Ivan D. Yeaton as commanding officer of the Yan'an group effectively ended the mission's potential to evolve into a cooperative and productive base for interagency strategic intelligence collection on the CCP. Yeaton arrived in Yan'an only a few days before the United States destroyed two cities in Japan with its newly developed nuclear weapons, hastening the end of the war. President Truman's long-term US policy goals in China, which had mostly been simple extensions of Roosevelt's policies, had not been achieved by August 1945.

Truman's appointed representatives in China met little success in implementing the disjointed US policy in China, which required US diplomats to continue their attempts to mediate in political negotiations between the Guomindang and the CCP while simultaneously offering public support to Chiang Kai-shek's regime. Truman's attention was on other issues besides China, and he focused on China policy with reluctance. Historians seeking details on his thinking about the Chinese Civil War must dig deep; files at the Truman Library labeled "China" deceptively hold only the records related to the place settings ordered for the White House by First Lady Bess Truman. Following Patrick Hurley's abrupt and unexpected resignation from the role of ambassador to China in November 1945, Truman appointed Gen. George Marshall to be his special representative in China, personally overseeing all negotiations.[29] Fearing the loss of continuity in the US delegation to China, Truman also convinced Wedemeyer to accept a one-year stint as US ambassador to China starting in May 1946, after Wedemeyer's duties as theater commander in China were completed.[30] Marshall's talks ultimately failed—perhaps the only time Marshall failed at anything.[31]

Despite the lack of progress in negotiations, Truman continued to advocate the creation of a US-friendly coalition government in China, under the leadership of Chiang, and the US government continued to hope—however vainly—that it could help prevent an all-out Chinese civil war. Wedemeyer, Marshall, and Truman's White House aides all advised the president that maintaining a US connection to the CCP leaders via the group at Yan'an could facilitate negotiations at minimal cost to the United States. Thus, the American contingent remained in Yan'an into early 1947. Yeaton's tenure in charge of the American mission at Yan'an lasted into the spring of 1946; he departed when it started to become dangerous for Americans to be at Yan'an, which was frequently coming under GMD air attack.

Yeaton had no specific expertise on China, but he did have a significant career with military intelligence, all under US Army auspices. He had served in intelligence roles for most of a long career in the army, and the army considered him a top expert on Russia and communism—a credential he proclaimed with frequency while in China. Yeaton's first experience in the army in 1919 and 1920 had been as a staff officer in the American Expeditionary Force in Siberia, aiding the White Russians who were fleeing persecution by the rising Bolsheviks.[32] Subsequent training and education in Russian language and Communist philosophy, including an abbreviated master's degree program at Columbia University in the 1920s, had prepared Yeaton for a position in the US attaché's office in the Moscow embassy in the 1930s. He eventually served as US military attaché to Russia in Moscow and was among the US personnel evacuated from that city prior to the Battle of Moscow (1941–42). Following this return to Washington, Yeaton served in the pool of G-2 intelligence analysts preparing orders of battle for European forces to aid Allied strategic planning.

Yeaton's education on Communist philosophy and his experience living in Stalin's Moscow had granted him considerable respect within the broader army staff as an expert on communism, especially among those focused on Europe (i.e., most of the General Staff). His experiences also imbued him with a legendary hatred for Communist regimes and a blanket vehement opposition to Communist ideology, which he perceived to be a threat to individual freedom designed solely for the goal of global domination and controlled globally by Soviet leaders, particularly Joseph Stalin. Yeaton held a commonly held view at the time that Communist movements beyond the Soviet Union, such as the one in China, were exclusively Soviet puppet regimes, lured into the ideology by the insidious propaganda and proselytizing of the Soviet Comintern. According to Yeaton, "The expansion of communism under Soviet hegemony by military power to enslave small nations would be directed at us some day, when we were no longer powerful enough to defend ourselves successfully. On that basis I reasoned that the Soviet Union was our enemy."[33] With Yeaton's selection to lead the Yan'an group, the CCP leaders would have certainly perceived a chilling effect on their relationship with the Truman administration.

Yeaton had received orders to China after Wedemeyer repeatedly requested the services of an intelligence official with expertise on Communism. According to Yeaton's recollection, after hearing Yeaton discuss his background during a dinner with Chiang Kai-shek, Hurley recommended that Wedemeyer send Yeaton to head the Yan'an mission instead of making him chief of intelligence at theater headquarters in Chongqing to replace Joseph Dickey, as had been expected.[34] Yeaton's selection to command the Yan'an group was part of a broader trend of populating open leadership positions in the China Theater with army staff officers previously assigned to the European Theater. With the end of the war in Europe in May 1945, success in the Pacific War immediately became the top priority for US military leaders. The palpable shift in policymaker attention from Europe to Asia, which began as early as the start of Operation Overlord (D-Day) in Europe in June 1944, caused some barely repressed bitterness among army officials such as Yeaton, who had spent years learning European languages and studying European politics and who saw posts in East Asia as career suicide.

Prior to World War II only a small fraction of American diplomats or military officials had served in East Asia, and the region had a reputation as a backwater. Most lower-ranking US officials who served in East Asian positions did so for the duration of their careers, and they often had personal connections to the region, similar to Davies and Service. Higher-ranking personnel posted to East Asia tended to be outcasts from the central currents of the Washington elite, if not before they achieved their posts in East Asia then almost certainly after. Roosevelt had contributed to this perception by using posts in Asia to dispense with problematic friends and cronies to whom he owed political favors but who he believed could not be trusted with posts that he perceived to be more important. Career diplomats such as Davies viewed Roosevelt's appointments of Hurley and Donald Nelson, Chiang Kai-shek's personal representative on economic matters, to be of this variety. Davies despaired that China was becoming a dumping ground for ranking officers and friends of the president who needed to be assigned to positions where Roosevelt thought they could not do too much damage. "China is apparently to the American political scene what Siberia is to the Russians. Only Roosevelt's technique is quicker and more humane."[35] All the original Dixie Mission members saw the trend continue into the Truman era, and Yeaton was their evidence.

The Army Intelligence Branch's Far East unit had a particularly undesirable reputation within G-2 circles, especially compared with the branch's more successful record on European intelligence during the war. Perhaps reflecting the strain that World War II had placed on the underdeveloped US intelligence capabilities, many Army General Staff officers perceived the G-2 itself to be dysfunctional, disorganized, and mismanaged throughout the war. Yeaton quoted Dwight D. Eisenhower, who replaced Marshall as chief of staff of the army in 1945, as remarking that the "G-2 did not even know how to organize itself."[36] Similarly, Yeaton likened the G-2 in 1944 and 1945 to Humpty Dumpty, "desperately trying to put itself back together again after someone had pushed it off the wall."[37] Within the G-2, the elements focused on the Far East had the worst reputations, and of these, the ones focused on China were perceived to be the worst of the worst. Yeaton and fellow European intelligence analysts had high regard for G-2 Japan analysts, particularly those in the cutting-edge cryptography unit who were working with MacArthur to develop and utilize their findings, codenamed MAGIC. Other than this exception, army officials within the broader G-2 looked down their noses at their colleagues who served in China.

Despite being written thirty years after the events he describes, Yeaton's memoirs clearly convey his passionate resentment at being diverted from his focus on Europe and sent to China. Yeaton opposed the abrupt shift of US policymaker attention away from Europe toward Asia. Prior to the summer of 1944, Yeaton was among the G-2 staff officers in Washington who worked intently on the detailed intelligence required to support the successful US military campaigns in Europe, particularly Operation Overlord. Yeaton describes how he and his colleagues who worked on Overlord within the G-2 became locked out of efforts to follow up on the progress of their plans, claiming that "overnight our orientation was shifted 180 degrees from Europe to the Far East. The why was only one of the several questions that were never answered."[38] Yeaton's memoirs rail against Roosevelt's strategic planners, particularly Harry Hopkins, and showcase his low esteem for Marshall and any of Marshall's perceived cronies, most especially Stilwell and Barrett.

Perhaps most important, Yeaton's memoirs reveal his assumptions about the reorganization of the G-2 in 1944 as the US government intensified efforts to end the Pacific War. Yeaton criticized the reorganizations for removing area experts such as himself from their core area of expertise and seeking to deploy them as a more fungible workforce of intelligence officials wherever a surge of personnel was needed. He claimed that intelligence work within the US government and other countries such as Great Britain had been organized by region with good reason. He astutely ascribed the lack of attention to such organizational effort to the Roosevelt administration, which he argued did not want to see intelligence experts grow powerful enough to criticize foreign policy. Yeaton observed firsthand that the Roosevelt White House was not open to critiques of US-Soviet policy and suggested that the surge staffing within the army in 1944 made the United States more vulnerable to the Soviet geopolitical machinations that eventually devolved into the Cold War after V-E Day.[39]

Yeaton's points regarding how to use area experts in intelligence work are somewhat ironic because Yeaton confidently assumed that his expertise on Russia and Soviet Communism would make him more capable than his Chinese-speaking predecessors in Yan'an at determining the CCP leaders' intentions. Yeaton had a low opinion of the intelligence work that US officials had performed at Yan'an and of the base's contribution to the war effort. He made his opinion of the Dixie Mission completely clear in his memoirs:

> From a military intelligence standpoint, the "Dixie Mission" was ill-conceived, organized without reconnaissance, dispatched without concrete directives, overstaffed with personnel unfamiliar with communist ideology, tactics or methods, and located in an area inaccessible except by animal transport. Moreover, the mission was a guest of a rebel government, no longer interested in the war against Japan and seeking United states recognition and lend-lease supplies only to continue the civil war, after the Japanese surrendered. How many strikes are "out" in this ball game?[40]

Yeaton assessed the first six months of the Dixie Mission to be an unmitigated disaster, insidiously designed by Zhou Enlai, who seduced Barrett, Service, and Davies into positive impressions of CCP activities, taking advantage of the Americans' ignorance of Communist ideology and tactics. He argued that "only trained eyes" such as his own "would recognize the sheathed claws and unctuous manner of the communist when he is in trouble and needs help."[41]

Relations between CCP leaders and the Americans at Yan'an retained a hollow civility after Yeaton's arrival in Yan'an, but Yeaton maintained a profound suspicion of both his CCP hosts and the Americans who had previously served at the base. Yeaton noted what he perceived to be lax security procedures around Yan'an and communications likely to be vulnerable to monitoring by Soviets. In his eagerness to point to connections between the Soviets and CCP leaders, Yeaton claimed to have spotted two uniformed Soviet NKVD Signal Corps officers sitting in the corner of the room where Yeaton first met Mao Zedong. But Yeaton was almost certainly confusing the uniforms of two Guomindang liaison officers stationed at Yan'an with his memory of the Soviet intelligence service uniforms.[42] Peterkin claimed that he knew of Guomindang liaison officers appearing at Yan'an, but he had never seen any Soviet presence there. The debate over this issue occurred in writing in the late 1970s when Yeaton, Peterkin, and many other former Dixie participants wrote and published memoirs. Without verification from CCP records that have yet to see the light of day, it is impossible to confidently assess whether the people Yeaton said he saw were Guomindang, NKVD, or imaginary. The debate itself, and the fact that these men were waging it decades later, speaks to the level of passion Dixie Mission members felt about their time at Yan'an and the spectrum of ideological difference between the 1944 group and those who came after Roosevelt's death.

Yeaton displayed little interest in interagency cooperation or innovative intelligence collection. His condescending attitude toward the existing personnel at Yan'an and his lack of curiosity about the group's prior activities made him unpopular with his subordinates. Peterkin described Yeaton during their first encounter as "Very unfriendly!" and the situation never improved before Peterkin permanently left Yan'an in mid-August 1945.[43] Peterkin attempted to follow his orders from Dickey, head of the G-2 for China, to brief Yeaton on active programs at Yan'an. According to Peterkin, Yeaton said "he was an expert on communism and there was nothing I could tell him that he didn't already know."[44] As Peterkin packed to leave the base on August 12, he recorded in his diary that most of the Dixie Mission personnel had visited him, "asking for transfers, stating that they did not want to serve under Yeaton."[45]

In another telling example of the differences in leadership of Dixie from 1944 to 1945, Yeaton described discovering twenty-five radios and two generators that OSS officials had transported to Yan'an but never used after he had settled in and surveyed the situation in the building spaces the American officials occupied. In Yeaton's telling, rather than arranging for the equipment to be utilized for intelligence work in North China or returned to Chongqing, he installed one of the generators in his living compound to power electric lights and movies for the comfort of his army subordinates.[46] Peterkin and Ludden read Yeaton's memoirs when the book was published and wrote each other about all the factual errors they found. The story of the generators was top of the list. Peterkin vehemently disputed that the generators were unused.[47] Historians may never know whether Yeaton or Peterkin had the story correct, but the debate itself is revealing.

If Yeaton's story was the accurate one, his use of the generator may have inadvertently fostered more cordial relations with CCP leaders. The top CCP leaders did enjoy private screenings of American films that arrived on the weekly planes from Beijing throughout 1946. Mao Zedong reportedly particularly relished films that featured Laurel and Hardy, which Sidney Rittenberg watched with him at weekend dinners.[48] Rittenberg, an American who defected to China, after 1949 served as the director of the official English language news agency in the People's Republic when he was not imprisoned on suspicion of being an American spy. He arrived at Yan'an in 1946 and remembered the excellent parties the Dixie Mission held. Yeaton's men also made sure that supplies arrived on the plane for a full Thanksgiving feast that year, which was a novelty that none of the CCP leaders took lightly, according to Rittenberg.

LIMPING ALONG AS LIAISON

By the time Yeaton settled into his role in charge of the American group at Yan'an, the base had fully transformed from its original function as an experiment in interagency strategic intelligence collection to a basic army outpost for wartime military intelligence gathering. However, the Japanese surrender and end of the war made such military intelligence irrelevant. By the fall of 1945 the American intelligence activities at Yan'an had sharply declined, even though the US government always maintained a presence of fifteen to twenty US officials from various agencies. Some of them supported ongoing negotiations between CCP and Guomindang leaders, though these talks were failing, and relations between the two parties steadily deteriorated. American officials at Yan'an also participated in plans to develop transportation infrastructure in North China, particularly improving access to fuel, which would facilitate continued US efforts to aid the Chinese central government with reconstruction and the demobilization of Japanese troops. Reflecting the group's changes in function and its sharply declining status within the US government, the name of the group itself was also officially changed at this time from Yan'an Observers Group to Yan'an Liaison Group.[49] From the fall of 1945 until the last Americans left Yan'an in spring 1947, US intelligence-collection activities at Yan'an dwindled.

Meanwhile, Truman and his national security advisers in Washington were busy assessing how to meet the new demands the outcome of the war had placed on the US national security infrastructure without sacrificing the preservation of democratic values and concern for civil liberties that had prevented the development of US intelligence capabilities prior to the war. Truman dismantled the OSS in the fall of 1945. Via executive order effective October 1, 1945, Truman assigned the well-respected OSS R&A Branch to the State Department and assigned the War Department to administer elements of the OSS offices that had previously handled clandestine intelligence collection and counterintelligence.[50] The War Department referred collectively to the new offices as the Strategic Services Unit (SSU). The executive order rendered the rest of the OSS functions, including its nascent covert action capability, defunct and left Roosevelt's crony William Donovan without a position in the government. Nonetheless, Truman acknowledged Donovan's arguments that the United States needed a capable and coordinated intelligence regime to address Stalin's brazen occupation of Eastern Europe and prevent analytic catastrophes such as the Japanese surprise attack on Pearl Harbor.[51]

Recognizing the inadequacy of the national security bureaucracy for the postwar role of the United States in global security, Truman and his staff conceptualized a massive reform of the US national security regime. White House and executive branch personnel began a bureaucratic adaptation process that culminated in the National Security Act of 1947, which established the Central Intelligence Agency, the National Security Council, the Joint Chiefs of Staff, and the Air Force. It also dramatically restructured the civilian military leadership structure, creating the Department of Defense with a civilian secretary overseeing the Departments of the Army, the Navy, and the Air Force.

The reform process was far from a smooth or direct path for Truman and his aides. Rather, the White House found itself mediating between strong personalities who were defending deeply entrenched bureaucratic interests and each of whom held passionate opinions about the best way for the United States to protect its national security interests and develop modern intelligence capabilities. The executive branch organizations that previously had partial and ad hoc responsibilities for intelligence activity all had opinions about how postwar US intelligence capabilities should be developed and administered. These agencies included the Departments of State, War, Navy, and Army as well as the Federal Bureau of Investigation. Legendary disagreements on the topic between US Army Secretary Ferdinand Eberstadt and US Navy Secretary James Forrestal alone have captivated historians for decades. A major source of disagreement in late 1945 focused on which agency would have overall administrative (and budgetary) control of intelligence capabilities. After reviewing several plans, Truman created an independent organization called the Central Intelligence Group (CIG), which at first operated with a skeleton crew and no designated budget.[52] The CIG eventually became the CIA.

World leaders and events abroad that affected US security interests did not pause and wait for Truman and his aides to resolve their plans for a new intelligence regime in 1945 and 1946. On the contrary, Stalin's strategic decisions hinted at the beginning of the Cold War, and the deterioration of stability in China accelerated at this time. While debates over intelligence reform played out among the highest levels of leadership in Washington, lower-ranking civilian and military officials in the US government who had responsibilities for intelligence and security issues continued working and attempted to keep pace with the organizational changes occurring above them. Work at the US Embassy in China continued, as did intelligence operations that were underway throughout North China and liaison activities still in progress at Yan'an.

By late 1945 intelligence reporting from Yan'an had slowed to a trickle. Leonard Meeker, chief of the Research and Intelligence Service Branch of the SSU in China, submitted one of the most revealing reports about the true state of the Yan'an Liaison Group in late October 1945.[53] Meeker made a short trip to Yan'an in early October 1945 to confer with Yeaton and survey the intelligence work of the unit, and his report to the SSU Research and Intelligence Service headquarters chief in Washington, classified secret at the time, is remarkable for its candor. Compared with the reports OSS officials such as Stelle sent from Yan'an in October 1944, Meeker's report demonstrates the dramatic transition that the section had experienced in one year in terms of intelligence collection and operations.

Meeker began his report by firmly dispelling the apparently rife rumors in Washington that the Soviets had constructed airfields in North China near Yan'an and were supplying the CCP with weapons and resources. Instead, Meeker described the absence of any visible airfields, including the one at which his party attempted to land.[54] Meeker explained that his pilot had flown back and forth across Shaanxi province for over an hour in search of Yan'an. They finally located the small landing space for a plane at a location north of the Wei River where the Yan'an base was supposed to be. Fortunately, the space was the correct location—the grave-pocked rudimentary airfield into which pilot Jack Champion had crash-landed the Wounded Duck in July 1944. The difficulty in locating Yan'an made a deep impression on Meeker, who argued that his experience "made perfectly clear to me that the reports of Communist airfields constructed around Yenan and receiving large amounts of Russian supplies were entire fabrications." Moreover, he wrote, "no plane can come in there without the whole population, including the Americans, knowing it. So whatever dealings the Russians may have been having with the Chinese Communists elsewhere, it seems definite that they have not had any in north Shensi." The rumors swirling in Washington about Soviet contact with the CCP and the fact that Meeker, a short-term visitor to Yan'an, had to be the one to dispel them hints at the poor state of communication channels from Yeaton and the American contingent based at Yan'an by the final months of 1945.

In the same report Meeker bluntly articulated this failure: "From conversation at Yenan and with G-2 personnel here in Chungking, I judge that the Observer Group is largely engaged in servicing itself, with a little liaison function and very little intelligence thrown in. . . . This is of course discouraging, in view of what seem to me the great opportunities for valuable intelligence work there at the present time." Meeker diagnosed the problem as the terrible reputation of OSS China among the still G-2–dominated section of American officials based at Yan'an. He believed that the poor OSS reputation partially stemmed from specific personality conflicts. Many G-2 officials had found it impossible to cooperate with the OSS's Ray Cromley, who was notoriously arrogant, inflexible, and unwilling to participate in the army chain of command for communications. The problems also evolved from severe misjudgments by OSS operations in North China, performed unilaterally without proper clearance from the G-2 leadership of the group or from the CCP hosts. Nonetheless, Meeker argued that it would be worth sending a new intelligence official to Yan'an to develop opportunities in the postwar environment. He surmised, "What it takes essentially is someone with active interest and moderate qualifications; there is just about no one like that at Yenan now. It seems to me that if R&A can possibly spare someone for the job it would be a tremendously good investment." However, the few new personnel who rotated into Yan'an in 1946 came from the army, not from the SSU. US strategic intelligence collection on the CCP or the CCP-held areas in North China never regained its strength.

In 1944 and 1945 the US government had a significant intelligence gap about the CCP that some American officials working in China admitted but which senior leaders in Washington failed to recognize. This distinction became more pronounced and problematic in 1945, as people lacking expertise on Chinese politics rotated into the top positions in the American delegation to China. Personnel who had spent careers working in China feared US policymakers' lack of understanding of the intricacies of Chinese politics, including negative aspects of Chiang Kai-shek's leadership, as potentially undermining the ability of US policy to support US interests in China. These lower-ranking officials faced the major bureaucratic hurdle of having to deliver their observations and assessments to policymakers who could calibrate US foreign policy in a format that the policymakers would accept. With suspicions of Stalin's policies and global ambitions mounting in Washington, US policymakers were rightfully resistant to intelligence from China that appeared to be overly sympathetic to Communist viewpoints.

During their first six months in Yan'an the initial Dixie Mission participants had attempted to supersede what they perceived to be obsolete bureaucratic procedures that prevented interagency cooperation on strategic intelligence collection about the CCP. Mutual professional connections to Stilwell and the protection of his authority facilitated the limited trust and shared sense of purpose between US intelligence officials from various agencies. However, the results in Yan'an suggest that the risks of circumventing government channels and oversight to perform intelligence work probably outweighed the benefits, given the high stakes of intelligence work in terms of information and operational security and diplomatic sensitivities. Moreover, the changes that began occurring in the composition and functions of the American base in Yan'an by early 1945 destroyed its initial spirit of collaboration and rendered its most productive features impossible for the remainder of the American operations at CCP headquarters. For purely political reasons the experiences—positive and negative—of the US intelligence officials in North China failed to be factored into the debates in Washington over the design of the new postwar US national security regime.

THE END OF THE US MISSION TO YAN'AN

American activities at Yan'an had been winding down for months in advance of the final plane's departure, with Yeaton heading to another more promising army staff position in April 1946. Yeaton ceded interim control of the Yan'an post's continuing support for US radio communications in North China and development of transportation infrastructure in the area to his chief of staff, Maj. Clifford Young. US leaders claimed that transportation development in North China had the short-term benefit of facilitating US aid to China as it recovered from Japanese occupation and decades of war. Similarly, the development of fuel resources, from oil wells to pipelines, assisted the US in short-term aid projects. Both road-building and fuel development activities could assist the long-term interests of US corporations who sought to operate in China if China's domestic political conflict were to be resolved in the Americans' favor, in the form of a liberal democracy and capitalist economy.

On the morning of March 11, John Sells, along with the last American officials and journalists who had remained at the CCP headquarters, flew to Nanjing, where the Chinese central government had reconstituted its capital following Japan's defeat. The airstrip that had allowed the first team of US officials to engage with the CCP on their own turf returned to dust. The last C-47 departure formed a tangible symbol of the ultimate acceptance by the United States of its failed attempts to intercede in China's domestic political conflict.

NOTES

Epigraph: Mao Zedong, "Report on an Investigation of the Peasant Movement in Hunan," March 1927. The full translated quote reads, "A revolution is not a dinner party, or writing an essay, or painting a picture, or doing embroidery; it cannot be so refined, so leisurely and gentle, so temperate, kind, courteous, restrained, and magnanimous. A revolution is an insurrection, an act of violence by which one class overthrows another."

1. Telegram, Central Committee of the Communist Party of China to Zhou Enlai regarding the retreat of the US Military Observation Team, April 7, 1946, Central Archives Collection, *Zhongyangdang anguancang Mei Jun Guan chazu dangan hui bian*/Compilation of Archives of the US Army Observer Group (Shanghai: Shanghai Zhousuo Chuban She, 2018), 2:248.
2. Sidney Rittenberg, an American who served as a translator for the CCP news agency and who lived in Yan'an in 1946 and 1947, describes Sells as an alcoholic. Rittenberg states that each week the US supply plane would bring seven bottles of whiskey for Sells and collect seven empty bottles from the previous week. Author in-person interview of Sidney Rittenberg, Scottsdale, Arizona, February 2013.
3. Carolle J. Carter, *Mission to Yenan: American Liaison with the Chinese Communists* (Lexington: University Press of Kentucky, 1997), 197–98.
4. Truman dissolved the OSS by executive order effective October 1, 1945.
5. Statement, Albert Wedemeyer, January 30, 1945, NARA, RG 493, entry UD-UP 635: Yenan Liaison Group, box 143.
6. Secretary of State to Albert Wedemeyer, January 7, 1945, NARA, RG 493, General Staff, G-2 Intelligence Section, entry UD-UP 252, box 30.
7. In their correspondence in the 1970s Peterkin and Ludden noted that Yeaton's book was incorrect on this account. Davies never had a formal assignment to Dixie. Letter, Wilbur Peterkin to Ray Ludden, June 15, 1976, Hoover Institution, Personal Papers of Wilbur J. Peterkin. See also Ivan D. Yeaton, *Memoirs of Ivan D. Yeaton, 1919–1953* (Stanford, CA: Hoover Institution on War, Revolution, and Peace, 1976).
8. Roosevelt had appointed Hurley to be US ambassador to China on November 17, 1944; he appointed Stettinius to replace Cordell Hull as secretary of state on December 1, 1944.
9. John Paton Davies Jr., *China Hand: An Autobiography* (Philadelphia: University of Pennsylvania Press, 2012), 210.
10. Davies departed for Moscow in the first week of February 1945, according to a telegram he sent to John Service via G-2 channels on January 30, 1945. See NARA, RG 493, General Staff, G-2 Intelligence Section, entry UD-UP 252, box 30.
11. Davies's exoneration within the State Department is so complete as to now be lionized. The department has even created a traveling exhibit that includes Davies's artwork and his official biography. See "John Davies Jr." installation, Art in Embassies, Department of State, https://art.state.gov/personnel/john_davies_jr/.

12. W. J. Peterkin, *Inside China, 1943–1945: An Eyewitness Account of America's Mission in Yenan* (Baltimore: Gateway, 1992), 63.
13. Letters, Wilbur Peterkin to Ray Ludden, May 19 and June 15, 1976, Hoover Institution, Personal Papers of Wilbur J. Peterkin.
14. Peterkin, *Inside China, 1943–1945*, 118.
15. Burton Fahs, "Intelligence from China: Opportunities and Needs," December 16, 1944, NARA, RG 226, entry NM-54 53, box 4.
16. Memo, Squires to Monroe, January 31, 1945, NARA, RG 226, entry 148: Field Station files, box 2.
17. William P. Head, *Yenan! Colonel Wilbur Peterkin and the American Military Mission to the Chinese Communists, 1944–1945* (Chapel Hill, NC: Documentary Publications, 1987), 84.
18. David D. Barrett, *The Dixie Mission: The United States Army Observer Group in Yenan, 1944* (Berkeley: University of California, Center for China Studies, 1970), 35.
19. Memo, Ray Cromley to OSS China Headquarters, December 16, 1944, NARA, RG 226, entry 148, box 7, folder 103: Dixie.
20. Memo, Charles Stelle to Richard Heppner, April 12, 1945, NARA, RG 226, entry 190, box 581.
21. For more on use of microfilm by US intelligence officials at Yan'an, see Carter, *Mission to Yenan*, 74. In addition to the declassified OSS documents on this topic available to researchers at the US National Archives, extensive interviews with former Dixie Mission personnel inform Carter's descriptions.
22. Commanding officers changed from Morris DePass (January 1945) to Wilbur Peterkin (February–July 1945) and then to Ivan Yeaton (July 1945–April 1946). The name of the group changed from the US Army Observer Group in Yan'an to the US Liaison Group in Yan'an. The official name of the Dixie Mission changed frequently and is often unclear in the archival records. Name changes were not documented until Yeaton's arrival at Yan'an. Clear references to a changed name for the unit reflects the solidification of norms for postwar staff work.
23. Original members present in February 1945 included Wilbur Peterkin, Ray Cromley, Louis Jones, Charles Stelle, Anton Reminih, Walter Gress, and George Nakamura. John Emmerson, who was successfully developing psychological operations from Yan'an with help from the CCP and Japanese POWs held there, joined the Dixie Mission in the fall of 1944 but is generally associated with the first group of Dixie officials. Peterkin verified the personnel 1945 rosters in interviews with his biographer and official documents from his personal papers. See William P. Head, *Yenan! Colonel Wilbur Peterkin and the American Military Mission to the Chinese Communists, 1944–1945* (Chapel Hill, NC: Documentary Publications, 1987), 82.
24. Head, *Yenan!*, 84.
25. Letter, Harley C. Stevens to John Davies, cover to Memo, "China and the Kremlin," January 6, 1945, NARA, RG 226, entry NM-54 1, box 23, folder: China.
26. Maochun Yu, *OSS in China: Prelude to Cold War* (Annapolis, MD: Naval Institute Press, 1996), 160–71.
27. Barrett, *Dixie Mission*, 36.
28. Barrett, 36.

29. For more on Truman's personnel decisions in China in 1945, see Warren I. Cohen, *America's Response to China: A History of Sino-American Relations,* 5th ed. (New York: Columbia University Press, 2010), 192–93.
30. Carter, *Mission to Yenan,* 178.
31. For more on America's role in the Chinese Civil War, see Daniel Kurtz-Phelan, *The China Mission: George Marshall's Unfinished War, 1945–1947* (New York: Norton, 2018); and Kevin Peraino, *A Force So Swift: Mao, Truman, and the Birth of Modern China, 1949* (New York: Penguin Random House, 2017).
32. Ivan D. Yeaton, *Memoirs of Ivan D. Yeaton, 1919–1953* (Stanford, CA: Hoover Institution on War, Revolution and Peace, 1976), 4–8.
33. Yeaton, 64.
34. Yeaton, 98.
35. Davies included this remark in a letter he wrote to his wife, commenting on the appointment of Patrick Hurley as US ambassador to China. See Davies, *China Hand,* 197.
36. Yeaton, *Memoirs,* 55.
37. Yeaton, 55.
38. Yeaton, 61.
39. Yeaton, 60–63.
40. Yeaton, 88.
41. Yeaton, 90.
42. Yeaton, 103. Peterkin refutes Yeaton's statement that NKVD officers were at Yan'an during Yeaton's tenure, based on the rosters of foreign personnel in Yan'an that Peterkin maintained throughout the summer of 1945. Peterkin, *Inside China,* xi.
43. Head, *Yenan!,* 103.
44. Head, 103.
45. Head, 104.
46. Yeaton, *Memoirs,* 107.
47. Letters, Wilbur Peterkin to Raymond Ludden, May 19 and June 15, 1976, Hoover Institution, Personal Papers of Wilbur Peterkin.
48. Rittenberg interview.
49. Michael Schaller, *The U.S. Crusade in China, 1938–1945* (New York: Columbia University Press, 1979), 228.
50. Michael Warner, ed., *The CIA under Harry Truman* (Washington, DC: CIA Center for the Study of Intelligence, 1994), xi–xii.
51. Warner, xi–xii.
52. For more on the formation of the CIG, see William M. Leary, ed., *The Central Intelligence Agency: History and Documents* (Tuscaloosa: University of Alabama Press, 1984); and Arthur B. Darling, *The Central Intelligence Agency: An Instrument of Government to 1950* (University Park: Pennsylvania State University Press, 1990).
53. The activities of the SSU's R&A Service were somewhat duplicative of those being carried out by the OSS R&A Branch, which the State Department had absorbed. Deconflicting the roles of these organizations was on the agenda of Truman's aides and senior executive branch administrators in Washington at the time.
54. Report, Leonard Meeker to SSU R&A Service Chief, October 23, 1945, NARA, RG 226, entry NM-54 53, box 4.

CONCLUSION

Jack [Service] called last night to let me know that Dave Barrett died yesterday. He didn't go into any detail, but the immediate cause was kidney failure. For my money, David died some years ago of a broken heart.

—Ray Ludden to Wilbur Peterkin, February 5, 1977

Ray Ludden and Pete Peterkin continued to correspond for many years after the last American plane departed Yan'an. Their correspondence hints at the intensity of emotion the original members of the Dixie Mission felt toward each other, the work they did in China, and the outcomes of their contributions. Ludden and Peterkin, roommates at Yan'an whom David Barrett had dispatched to verify CCP intelligence reports on the four-month trek through CCP-held forward areas, maintained a friendship that lasted until their respective deaths, corresponding monthly via thoughtful letters. By all accounts, including thoughts expressed in his own memoir, Barrett suffered lifelong career repercussions from his participation in the Dixie Mission, and understandably he felt great bitterness about the fate of US-CCP relations. Barrett left Yan'an in December 1944, and his friends, including Service and Ludden, frequently recalled thinking that he never really moved on. Barrett experienced the failure of the Dixie Mission to achieve its goals as a personal failure—like heartbreak. Evidence of the short- and long-term burdens that participation in the Dixie Mission created for those originally involved is eminently visible in the records they left behind.

In the same way that December 1944 was a personal turning point for Barrett and other original participants in the American intelligence mission to Yan'an, the events of that time were a public turning point for the Dixie Mission itself. Prior to that December, American intelligence officials stationed at Yan'an formed relationships with their CCP hosts based on their shared passion for developing effective, if unconventional, methods to defeat the Japanese. A few Americans who arrived in Yan'an later formed cordial relationships with the CCP leaders but they were held at a greater distance; events had disrupted the trust that the first Americans in Yan'an had incubated. The initial Dixie

Mission crew stretched the limits of their vague operational mandate to learn about and cooperate with CCP fighters. Just as they had begun to implement cooperative operations with the CCP, the administrative pillars supporting their plans began to shift.

Joseph Stilwell and his network of State Department aides, who conceived the idea for the Dixie Mission, represented a cohort of American subject matter experts on China that were unique to the pre–World War II period. They operated on norms and values that differed in some respects to those of other parts of the US government operating outside China. Before the war, Americans in China were accustomed to operating outside administrative boundaries when it was necessary to achieve their ends, and they frequently lacked precedents for the work they were doing. Stilwell and his cohort recognized an intelligence gap on China's domestic political situation. Their ideological motivations reflected paternalism that was characteristic of many Americans in China at the time. Stilwell's interest in the CCP was selfishly tied to his childish argument with Chiang Kai-shek, a Chinese leader who did not want to cede his troops and power to yet another Western leader who had come along. In the face of the conflict between Stilwell and Chiang, Stilwell's staff as early as 1943 deemed information on the CCP necessary to develop and implement effective US strategy. Stilwell and OSS representatives bonded over feeling hamstrung by SACO oversight, which limited the ability of US officials to independently gather intelligence in China. Together Stilwell and OSS China attempted to circumvent the SACO agreement with an army-led interagency solution: the Dixie Mission. Stilwell's network applied this ad hoc approach and their knowledge of Chinese politics, society, and language to the work at Yan'an during the first months of Dixie.

The initial Dixie Mission crew gathered old and new intelligence officials into one team. They did cooperate across interagency boundaries to the best of their ability, and they attempted to report accurate impressions of the CCP's capabilities and intentions. However, the initial Dixie participants suffered from a dangerous analytic myopia. They not only formed relationships with CCP leaders but also saw promising signs in CCP leadership that fed their prejudices about how China's politics ought to be. These factors predisposed them to having charitable views of the CCP. They gave the CCP the benefit of the doubt, which in turn diluted the impact of their intelligence messages with US officials beyond Yan'an, who were increasingly suspicious of the Communists' ideology as the mission continued. Their views and recommendations also risked the US relationship with Chiang and other actors within the Chinese central government, who opposed US interest in and even implicit recognition of the CCP.

Moreover, the deeply implicit assumption of superiority at the heart of American Open Door imperialism made it more difficult for the first Dixie

Mission members to recognize the agency CCP members had in shaping their impressions of Yan'an. The longer the initial Dixie Mission members stayed at Yan'an, the more the CCP won them over. At the end of September 1944, a few weeks before Stilwell's recall, Barrett reiterated his positive assessment of CCP efforts fighting the Japanese: "To sum up, I am convinced that the Communist forces can be of immediate assistance to the Allied war effort in China, and that this assistance can save American lives, and speed up the ultimate victory. The amount of use which can be made of the Communist forces will in general be in direct proportion to the assistance which we can give them in arms, equipment, and training."[1] Even today, with the advantage of so many contemporary historical records to review, it is difficult to tell whether Barrett's assessment was accurate or the result of CCP persuasive efforts and what Barrett and his team wanted to see.

The assumption of superiority of the Open Door imperialism was a subconscious reality for Barrett, Davies, Service, and other Americans at Yan'an, and it may have made it more difficult for them to recognize the true aims of the CCP. CCP leaders had significant incentives to manipulate American officials and the means to do so. American observers, often entering into relationships with CCP leaders founded on an attitude of paternalistic service, frequently overlooked the possibility of being subject to manipulation, or worse, overlooked the possibility that their counterparts even had the ability to enact such influence.

The experiences of Americans in the Dixie Mission corroborate other recent studies that have shown how effective the CCP leaders were at conducting public relations in the 1940s. Julia Lovell has argued that the CCP under Mao deliberately groomed its image among visiting foreigners, particularly with famous foreign writers such as Agnes Smedley, Anna Louise Strong, and, in particular, Edgar Snow.[2] Snow's experience in Yan'an, while collecting material for his international bestseller *Red Star over China*, showcased the "international PR genius of the CCP from its early days, and the way Mao's ideas and persona traversed territories, languages, and classes, and attracted international cheerleaders."[3] Lovell's detailed genealogy of Snow's book reveals a pattern for how "Mao and his lieutenants built and manipulated international networks of support from the 1930s to the present day—networks that changed the course of China's civil war and the Cold War, and influenced Mao's own political thought and practice."[4]

The Yan'an that the Dixie Mission experienced was no Potemkin village; the effect was much more subtle. If Soviet influence efforts toward foreigner observers were a heavy cleaver, CCP pursuits in the same vein were a scalpel. Lovell describes Snow's presentation of the CCP to the world as "persecuted innocents, as appealing underdogs: as patriots first and Communists second, willing and able to fight the Japanese, constrained only by Nationalist repression."[5] The initial roster of Americans in the Dixie Mission had read *Red Star,* and they were skeptical. Nonetheless, their reports, even after months at Yan'an, parallel Snow's account. The evidence that the CCP in the 1930s and 1940s was cultivating its image deliberately to help strengthen its legitimacy, appeal, and popularity suggests that the Dixie Mission participants may have been unwittingly persuaded.

Reflection on the activities of US intelligence officials in China's Communist base areas in the 1940s is significant because it reveals how individuals experienced and participated in two major historical changes in US foreign policy: taking a side in China's civil war and developing a system for foreign intelligence that could support America's perceived global responsibilities. The evolution of this narrative exposes the fact that US personnel were not of one mind through these changes, and their differences likely influenced the outcomes. Lacking an established administrative structure for interagency communication on intelligence matters, the unilateral actions of American intelligence officials in a remote but strategically significant area such as Yan'an, China, could (and did) lead to counterproductive diplomatic disasters.

Throughout the lifespan of the American presence in Yan'an, military intelligence officials, specifically army intelligence officers, commanded the mission. Although army intelligence officials stationed in the CBI Theater generally possessed expertise on China, they were unprepared to provide actionable strategic intelligence to US policymakers back home. The OSS officials at Yan'an, particularly Charles Stelle, recognized a need to develop such methodologies, but the army's influence and hierarchical dominance over the Dixie Mission drowned the voices and influence of other agencies.

Disorganized, new, and lacking the necessary influence in China, the OSS repeatedly encountered obstacles to developing effective and professional intelligence operations in China, particularly in Yan'an. Their work within the bounds of SACO guidelines was more productive, but it was effective only in bringing about an end to the Japanese occupation of China. This outcome was well underway by the time the OSS in Yan'an could have been most helpful to it. Conversely, the OSS's departure from Yan'an—a result of their own mistakes within the US legation—limited US policymakers' awareness of CCP intentions as the new Harry Truman administration attempted to mediate the Chinese Civil War.

By December 1944, Dixie Mission participants found themselves at the center of a clash between the policy priorities of new top American representatives in China—Patrick Hurley and Albert Wedemeyer—and the interests of their predecessors. Hurley and Wedemeyer performed a predictable course correction for the implementation of US policy in China based on the substantial gap that existed between their own perceptions of China and the messages they were receiving from the original Dixie Mission participants. Regardless of their skills or evidence supporting their policy advice, the relatively low-ranking American officials based at Yan'an in December 1944 could not influence their administrative superiors. Under the supervision of Hurley and Wedemeyer in 1945, the US mission to Yan'an transformed into an exercise in benign and inconsequential military intelligence collection operations.

The shift that occurred in the priorities of the American presence at Yan'an after 1945 had two important implications for US intelligence on China in the late 1940s. First, the changes eliminated the unique and unprecedented potential for productive interagency collaboration and cooperation that had existed in the Dixie Mission's first few months. Second, Hurley's suggestion that Communist sympathies had biased the US intelligence officials at Yan'an tainted perceptions of the achievements and shortcomings of the entire US intelligence project. The immediate politicization of the Dixie Mission fundamentally altered assessments of operational "lessons learned" from the engagement.

The zeal with which David Barrett, Jack Service, Ray Ludden, John Davies, Charles Stelle, and others reported on CCP intentions and capabilities made it easy for US leaders who were less familiar with Chinese politics to discount their reports and sideline them as Communist sympathizers. Hurley's vengeful accusations about them have since been discredited, but the power structure of the US government in the 1940s took Hurley's comments quite seriously. Hurley's vindictive public questioning of the ideological loyalties and potential Communist sympathies of the initial Dixie Mission participants almost certainly facilitated perceptions among some in Washington that Communist sympathizers within the US government were responsible for the shortcomings of US intelligence operations in Yan'an, and to some extent even the shortcomings of broader US policy toward the CCP.

Introducing ideological loyalty issues into the evaluations of the Dixie Mission had the effect of temporarily exonerating Hurley from the effects of his obstinate behavior and poor decision-making. But it also distracted attention from structural inadequacies in the US intelligence process that prevented US personnel at Yan'an from effectively conveying their observations and assessments to others in the US government who needed the information. By the end of 1945, strengthening anti-Communist elements in American politics had emerged as an influence on the American intelligence efforts in Yan'an in a new way. Undertones of ideological conflict were unmistakable. Opposition to Communism and loyalty to American liberal political ideology superseded regional expertise in the selection of Dixie's final leaders.

The diplomatic fallout from the Dixie Mission's greatest shortcomings occurred in 1945 and 1946, synchronous to the negotiations in Washington,

DC, among Truman's senior advisers and executive appointees over the creation of the postwar US intelligence regime. Hurley's political tactics encouraged the White House to disregard the difficulties and pitfalls of the American intelligence experience at Yan'an as an unfortunate aberration. They consequently disregarded the American experience in Yan'an as an instance of alarming Communist sympathy within the US government ranks, instead of perceiving it as a cautionary tale of the challenges of conducting ad hoc foreign intelligence activities in remote and unknown areas.

The case of the Dixie Mission foreshadowed several challenges of foreign intelligence practices that plagued the US national security regime in the 1950s and 1960s. For example, the experience of the American intelligence officials at Yan'an emphasized potential pitfalls of combining intelligence collection with uncoordinated and improvised covert military operations under the direction of leaders with little regional expertise, such as Hurley, Wedemeyer, and Ivan Yeaton. Similarly, the fate of the original Dixie Mission participants is an early example of the potentially dangerous consequences of politicization of intelligence operations. Political decisions about diplomatic appointments and the personal preferences of the White House, particularly during FDR's presidency, distorted their perceptions of the Dixie Mission reports. The Dixie Mission case also reveals why the professionalized collection of strategic foreign intelligence requires a sophisticated bureaucracy to succeed in efficiently providing policymakers with useful and timely information.

The Dixie Mission case clarifies that simply placing capable experts in the field to collect information is not nearly sufficient to achieve the goal of arming policymakers with the information they require. Intelligence officials in the field must be actors in a functional bureaucracy in which the relevant organizations have clearly established jurisdictional boundaries and are capable of and motivated to work together instead of competing against one another. Effective intelligence collection requires logistical conditions that allow for the information to be safely and quickly disseminated to headquarters offices, analyzed and contextualized by experts and distributed to policymakers before the information becomes obsolete. Policymakers too must recognize the information as being useful to them and trust the process by which it is produced. They must understand the scope and limits of the information presented to them through the intelligence process and be prepared to receive undesirable messages without "killing the messenger." Between 1944 and 1947, when the Dixie Mission operated, the United States had not yet established an intelligence community that was achieving these requirements, and the outcome of the US Observer Mission to Yan'an highlights the potential consequences of that reality.

The Dixie Mission case is particularly helpful for its ability to humanize the ambiguity of the political, ideological, philosophical, and strategic questions intelligence officials operating in remote areas in the 1940s faced daily. Examples from this mission display the effects of subconscious cultural attitudes, such as the Open Door paternalism common to US officials stationed in China during this era. Moreover, the experiences of individual US intelligence officials operating in Communist-held north China during World War II reveal both the vulnerabilities and potential policy costs of dysfunctional administrative norms for US intelligence activity. In the Dixie Mission case, intelligence examples display evidence of a failure to move beyond outdated bureaucratic protocols and political competition among and between institutions, even in the face of changing security demands and the highest possible stakes for national and global security. The problems are evident even when highly capable personnel are in place as intelligence collectors. In Yan'an, replacing the expert personnel with technical generalists exacerbated the problems. The commitment of China's major domestic opposition party to communist principles further facilitated the lack of policymaker attention to the North China examples.

NOTES

Epigraph: Letter from Ray Ludden to Wilbur Peterkin, February 5, 1977, Hoover Institution, Personal Papers of Wilbur J. Peterkin, box 2.

1. John N. Hart, *The Making of an Army "Old China Hand": A Memoir of Colonel David D. Barrett* (Berkeley: University of California, Center for China Studies, 1985), 42.
2. Julia Lovell, *Maoism: A Global History* (New York: Vintage, 2019), chap. 2.
3. Lovell, 60.
4. Lovell, 60.
5. Lovell, 75.

Initial members of the Dixie Mission, who arrived in Yan'an, China, on the first US plane in July 1944, with Chinese Communist officials. (*Seated, left to right*): Vice Chairman Zhou Enlai, Gen. Peng Dehuai, Col. David Barrett, Gen. Zhu De, John Service, and unidentified Chinese official. (*Standing, left to right*): Two unidentified Chinese officials, Capt. Charles Stelle, Capt. Jack Champion, Capt. Paul Domke, Lt. Henry Whittlesey, unidentified American (*behind Whittlesey*), Maj. Ray Cromley, Capt. John Colling, Sgt. William Cady, Sgt. Walter Gress, Sgt. Anton Remenih, and Maj. Melvin Casberg. *Harrison Forman Collection, American Geographical Society Library, University of Wisconsin–Milwaukee Libraries*

Cave dwellings in Yan'an, 1944. Dixie Mission quarters were built in caves like these. *Harrison Forman Collection, American Geographical Society Library, University of Wisconsin–Milwaukee Libraries*

The US Army C-47 plane that brought the first Dixie Mission officers to Yan'an. Dixie Mission members referred to the plane as the "Wounded Duck" due to the clearly visible damage it sustained on its first landing in Yan'an. *Harrison Forman Collection, American Geographical Society Library, University of Wisconsin–Milwaukee Libraries*

Mao Zedong (*second from right*) talks with Dixie Mission medic Melvin Casberg (*far left*), Henry Whittlesey (*second left*), and Charles Stelle (*back to camera*), along with two Western journalists at a dinner party in Yan'an, 1944. *Harrison Forman Collection, American Geographical Society Library, University of Wisconsin–Milwaukee Libraries*

Mao Zedong (*left*) and Peng Dehuai with US Army Air Corps weather intelligence officer Maj. Charles R. Dole in Yan'an. *Harrison Forman Collection, American Geographical Society Library, University of Wisconsin–Milwaukee Libraries*

The first leader of the Dixie Mission, Col. David Barrett, jokes with Chinese Communist Party officials at a dinner party in Yan'an, 1944. *Harrison Forman Collection, American Geographical Society Library, University of Wisconsin–Milwaukee Libraries*

Mao Zedong (*second from left*), Zhou Enlai (*right*), and top military leaders of the Chinese Communist Party host US Ambassador Patrick J. Hurley (*center*) in Yan'an in August 1945. *US Army Signal Corps, National Archives and Records Administration*

SELECTED BIBLIOGRAPHY

UNPUBLISHED US GOVERNMENT DOCUMENTS

NARA: National Archives and Records Administration, College Park, MD

RG 59 Records of the US Department of State
RG 165 Records of the War Department General and Special Staffs
RG 226 Records of the Office of Strategic Services (OSS)
RG 319 Records of the US Army Staff
RG 493 Records of US Forces in the CBI Theater of Operations

FDRL: Franklin D. Roosevelt Presidential Library, Hyde Park, NY

American War Production Mission in China Collection
Departmental Files
Diplomatic Correspondence
Map Room File
President's Official Files
President's Personal File
President's Secretary's File

HSTL: Harry S. Truman Presidential Library, Independence, MO

Chronological File
National Security Council Files
President's Secretaries' Files
Subject File
Truman Official Files
White House Confidential File

PERSONAL PAPERS

Bancroft Library, University of California at Berkeley, CA

Papers of John S. Service

FDRL: Franklin D. Roosevelt Presidential Library, Hyde Park, NY

Papers of Earnest Cuneo
Papers of Charles Fahy

Papers of Harry L. Hopkins
Papers of Isador Lubin
Files of James S. Lanigan
Papers of James Roosevelt
Papers of Vice President Henry A. Wallace, 1941–1945
Papers of Sumner Welles

Hoover Institution, Stanford University, Stanford, CA

David D. Barrett Collection
Melvin A. Casberg Collection
O. Edmund Clubb Collection
Papers of Lauchlin Currie
Paul C. Domke Collection
Papers of Frank Dorn
John N. Hart Collection
Personal Papers of Wilbur J. Peterkin
Laurence E. Salisbury Collection
Philip D. Sprouse Collection
Joseph W. Stilwell Collection
Albert C. Wedemeyer Collection
Ivan D. Yeaton Collection

HSTL: Harry S. Truman Presidential Library, Independence, MO

Papers of Sally Cahalan
Papers of Clark M. Clifford
John Paton Davies Collection
Papers of George M. Elsey
Papers of Edwin A. Locke Jr.
Papers of Forrest McCluney
Papers of John F. Melby
Papers of John H. Ohly
Papers of Samuel I. Rosenman
Papers of Sidney Souers
Papers of John Stewart Service and Charles Edward Rhetts
Papers of Ralph N. Stohl

INTERVIEWS AND CORRESPONDENCE

Sidney Rittenberg, February 2013
Kellogg Stelle, 2021–2022

MEMOIRS AND PUBLISHED PRIMARY SOURCES

Memoirs

Barrett, David D. *Dixie Mission: The United States Army Observer Group in Yenan, 1944.* Berkeley: University of California, Center for China Studies, 1970.

Carlson, Evans Fordyce. *Twin Stars of China*. New York: Dodd, Mead, 1940.

Colling, John C. *The Spirit of Yanan: A Wartime Chapter of Sino-American Friendship*. Beijing: Foreign Languages Press, 2004.

Davies, John Paton, Jr. *China Hand: An Autobiography*. Philadelphia: University of Pennsylvania Press, 2012.

———. *Dragon by the Tail: American, British, Japanese, and Russian Encounters with China and One Another*. New York: W. W. Norton, 1972.

Dorn, Frank. *Walkout with Stilwell in Burma*. New York: Pyramid, 1973.

Emmerson, John K. *The Japanese Thread: A Life in the U.S. Foreign Service*. New York: Holt, Rinehart and Winston, 1978.

Epstein, Israel. *Unfinished Revolution in China*. Boston: Little, Brown, 1947.

Fairbank, John King. *Chinabound: A Fifty-Year Memoir*. New York: Harper & Row, 1982.

Ickes, Harold L. *The Secret Diary of Harold L. Ickes, Vol. 2: The Inside Struggle, 1936–1939*. New York: Simon & Schuster, 1954.

Langer, William L. *In and Out of the Ivory Tower: The Autobiography of William L. Langer*. New York: N. Watson, 1977.

Miles, Milton. *A Different Kind of War: The Little-Known Story of the Combined Guerrilla Forces Created in China by the U.S. Navy and the Chinese during World War II*. Garden City, NY: Doubleday, 1967.

Peterkin, Wilbur J. *Inside China, 1943–1945: An Eyewitness Account of America's Mission in Yenan*. Baltimore: Gateway, 1992.

Service, John S. *Lost Chance in China: The World War II Despatches of John S. Service*. Edited by Joseph E. Esherick. New York: Random House, 1974.

Stilwell, Joseph W. *The Stilwell Papers*. Arranged and edited by Theodore H. White. New York: William Sloane, 1948.

Wedemeyer, Albert C. *Wedemeyer Reports!* New York: Henry Holt, 1958.

Yeaton, Ivan D. *Memoirs of Ivan D. Yeaton*. Stanford, CA: Hoover Institution on War, Revolution, and Peace, 1976.

Published Primary Sources

Central Archives Collection. *Zhongyangdang anguancang Mei Jun Guan chazu dangan hui bian* [Compilation of Archives of the US Army Observer Group]. Vols. 1 and 2. Shanghai: Shanghai Zhousuo Chuban She, 2018.

Chiang Kai-shek. *Xian zongtong Jiang gong sixiang yanlun ji* (di 21 juan) [Collected speeches and thoughts of President Chiang Kai-shek, vol. 21]. Edited by Qin Xiaoyi. Taipei: Zhongguo Guomindang Zhongyang weiyuan hui dangshi weiyuan hui, 1984.

Guofang bu junishi qingbao ju. *Zhongmei hezuo suo zhi* [Annals of the Sino-American Cooperative Organization]. Taipei: Guofang bu junshi qingbao ju, 2011.

Kuo, Warren. *Analytical History of the Chinese Communist Party*. 4 vols. Taibei, China: Institute of International Relations, 1968.

US Department of State. *The China White Paper, August 1949: United States Relations with China*. Stanford, CA: Stanford University Press, 1967.

———. *Foreign Relations of the United States: Diplomatic Papers 1936, Vol. 4 (The Far East)*. Washington, DC: Government Printing Office, 1954.

———. *Foreign Relations of the United States: Diplomatic Papers 1937, Vols. 3–4 (The Far East)*. Washington, DC: Government Printing Office, 1954.

——. *Foreign Relations of the United States: Diplomatic Papers 1938, Vol. 3–4 (The Far East).* Washington, DC: Government Printing Office, 1954.

——. *Foreign Relations of the United States: Diplomatic Papers 1939, Vol. 3 (The Far East).* Washington, DC: Government Printing Office, 1955.

——. *Foreign Relations of the United States: Diplomatic Papers 1940, Vol. 4 (The Far East).* Washington, DC: Government Printing Office, 1955.

——. *Foreign Relations of the United States: Diplomatic Papers 1941, Vols. 4–5 (The Far East).* Washington, DC: Government Printing Office, 1956.

——. *Foreign Relations of the United States: Diplomatic Papers 1942, China.* Washington, DC: Government Printing Office, 1956.

——. *Foreign Relations of the United States: Diplomatic Papers 1943, China.* Washington, DC: Government Printing Office, 1957.

——. *Foreign Relations of the United States: Diplomatic Papers 1944, Vol. 6 (China).* Washington, DC: Government Printing Office, 1967.

——. *Papers Relating to the Foreign Relations of the United States, Japan 1931–1941, Volume 1: The Far East, China.* Washington, DC: Government Printing Office, 1969.

US Senate. *The Amerasia Papers: A Clue to the Catastrophe of China, Vols. 1–2.* Washington, DC: Government Printing Office, 1970.

Wang Jianying. *Zhongguo gongchandang zuzhi shidashijishi, 1921.7–1937.7* [Major events in the organizational history of the Chinese Communist Party, July 1921–July 1937]. Guangzhou: Guangdong People's Press, 2003.

——. *Zhongguo hong jun ren wu zhi* [Biographies of Red Army members]. Guangzhou: Guangdong People's Publishing House, 2000.

——. *Zhongguo gongchandang lishi dashiji, 1919.5-1987.12* [Chronicle of Chinese Communist Party history, May 1919–December 1987]. Beijing: People's Press, 1989.

White, Theodore H., and Annalee Jacoby. *Thunder Out of China.* New York: William Slone, 1946.

White, Theodore H., ed. *The Stilwell Papers.* New York: W. Sloane, 1948.

Zhu De. "From the Nanchang Uprising to Going up the Jinggang Mountain [Memoir]." Xinhua News Service, July 31, 1982. Translated by the Foreign Broadcast Information Service August 3, 1982.

SECONDARY SOURCES

Aldrich, Richard J. *Intelligence and the War against Japan: Britain, America, and the Politics of Secret Service.* Cambridge, UK: Cambridge University Press, 2000.

Ameringer, Charles D. *U.S. Foreign Intelligence: The Secret Side of American History.* Lexington, MA: Lexington, 1990.

Andrew, Christopher. *For the President's Eyes Only: Secret Intelligence and the American Presidency from Washington to Bush.* New York: HarperCollins, 1995.

Barrett, David D. "The Guest of a Chinese War Lord: A Side-Light on War in China." *Coast Artillery Journal* 75, no. 1 (January–February 1932): 119–22.

——. "Solders of Misfortune." *Society of American Military Engineers* 357 (January–February 1962).

Bianco, Lucian. *Origins of the Chinese Revolution, 1915–1949.* Stanford, CA: Stanford University Press, 1971.

Bidwell, Bruce W. *History of the Military Intelligence Division, Department of the Army General Staff: 1775–1941*. Frederick, MD: University Publications of America, 1986.

Benton, Gregor. *Mountain Fires: The Red Army's Three-Year War in South China, 1934–1938*. Berkeley: University of California Press, 1992.

Bergin, Bob. "The Dixie Mission in 1944: The First US Intelligence Encounter with the Chinese Communists." *Studies in Intelligence* 63, no. 3 (September 2019): 11–30.

Bernstein, Richard. *China 1945: Mao's Revolution and America's Fateful Choice*. New York: Knopf, 2014.

Blankfort, Michael. *The Big Yankee: The Life of Carlson of the Raiders*. Boston: Little, Brown, 1947.

Buhite, Russell D. *Patrick J. Hurley and Americana Foreign Policy*. Ithaca, NY: Cornell University Press, 1973.

Carter, Carolle J. *Mission to Yenan: American Liaison with the Chinese Communists, 1944–1947*. Lexington: University Press of Kentucky, 1997.

Ceplair, Larry. *Anti-Communism in Twentieth-Century America: A Critical History*. Santa Barbara, CA: Praeger, 2011.

Challou, George, ed. *The Secrets War: The Office of Strategic Services in World War II*. Washington, DC: National Archives and Records Administration, 1992.

Chen Jian. "The Myth of America's 'Lost Chance' in China: A Chinese Perspective in Light of New Evidence." *Diplomatic History* 21, no. 1 (Winter 1997): 77–86.

Ch'i, Hsi-sheng. *The Much Troubled Alliance: U.S.-China Military Cooperation during the Pacific War, 1914–1945*. Singapore: World Scientific, 2015.

Cohen, Warren I. *America's Response to China: A History of Sino-American Relations*. 5th ed. New York: Columbia University Press, 2010.

Corke, Sarah-Jane. *US Covert Operations and Cold War Strategy: Truman, Secret Warfare and the CIA, 1947–53*. London: Routledge, 2008.

Cornebise, Alfred E. *The United States 15th Infantry Regiment in China, 1912–1938*. Jefferson, NC: McFarland, 2004.

Corson, William R. *The Armies of Ignorance: The Rise of the American Intelligence Empire*. New York: Dial, 1977.

Darling, Arthur B. *The Central Intelligence Agency: An Instrument of Government, to 1950*. University Park: Pennsylvania State University Press, 1990.

Dirlik, Arif. *The Origins of Chinese Communism*. New York: Oxford University Press, 1989.

Dorwart, Jeffrey M. *Eberstadt and Forrestal: A National Security Partnership, 1909–1949*. College Station: Texas A&M University Press, 1991.

Drea, Edward J. *MacArthur's ULTRA: Codebreaking and the War against Japan, 1942–1945*. Lawrence: University Press of Kansas, 1992.

Dreyer, Edward L. *China at War, 1901–1949*. London: Longman, 1995.

Eastman, Lloyd. "Nationalist China during the Sino-Japanese War, 1937–1944." In *The Nationalist Era in China, 1927–1949*, edited by Lloyd Eastman, Jerome Chen, Suzanne Pepper, and Lyman P. Van Slyke, 115–76. Cambridge, UK: Cambridge University Press, 1991.

Fairbank, John King. *The United States and China*. 4th ed. Cambridge, MA: Harvard University Press, 1981.

Feis, Herbert. *The China Tangle: The American Effort in China from Pearl Harbor to the Marshall Mission*. Princeton, NJ: Princeton University Press, 1953.

Frank, Richard B. *Tower of Skulls: A History of the Asia-Pacific War, July 1937–May 1942.* New York: W. W. Norton, 2020.

Fredman, Zach. *The Tormented Alliance: American Servicemen and the Occupation of China, 1941–1949.* Chapel Hill: University of North Carolina Press, 2022.

Gilbert, James L. *World War I and the Origins of U.S. Military Intelligence.* Lanham, MD: Scarecrow, 2012.

Goodall, Alex. *Loyalty and Liberty: American Countersubversion from World War I to the McCarthy Era.* Urbana: University of Illinois Press, 2013.

Guillermaz, Jacques. *A History of the Chinese Communist Party, 1921–1949.* Translated by Anne Destenay. New York: Random House, 1972.

Gurman, Hannah. "'Learn to Write Well': The China Hands and the Communist-ificiation of Diplomatic Reporting." *Journal of Contemporary History* 45, no. 2 (2010): 430–53.

Harrison, Henrietta. *The Making of the Republican Citizen: Political Ceremonies and Symbols in China, 1911–1929.* Oxford: Oxford University Press, 2000.

Hart, John N. *The Making of an Army "Old China Hand": A Memoir of Colonel David D. Barrett.* Berkeley: University of California, Center for China Studies, 1985.

Head, William P. *Yenan! Colonel Wilbur Peterkin and the American Military Mission to the Chinese Communists, 1944–1945.* Chapel Hill, NC: Documentary Publications, 1987.

Hogan, Michael, *A Cross of Iron: Harry S. Truman and the Origins of the National Security State, 1945–1954.* Cambridge, UK: Cambridge University Press, 1998.

Hollinger, David. *Protestants Abroad: How Missionaries Tried to Change the World but Changed America.* Princeton, NJ: Princeton University Press, 2017.

Hunt, Michael H., *The Making of a Special Relationship: The United States and China to 1914.* New York: Columbia University Press, 1983.

Jeffreys-Johns, Rhodri. *The CIA and American Democracy.* New Haven, CT: Yale University Press, 1989.

Jespersen, T. Christopher. *American Images of China, 1931–1949.* Stanford, CA: Stanford University Press, 1996.

Jing Tsu. *Kingdom of Characters: The Language Revolution That Made China Modern.* New York: Riverhead, 2022.

Joiner, Lynne. *Honorable Survivor: Mao's China, McCarthy's America, and the Persecution of John S. Service.* Annapolis, MD: Naval Institute Press, 2009.

Kahn, E. J. *The China Hands: America's Foreign Service Officers and What Befell Them.* New York: Viking, 1976.

Katz, Barry. *Foreign Intelligence: Research and Analysis in the Office of Strategic Services, 1942–1945.* Cambridge, MA: Harvard University Press, 1989.

Klehr, Harvey, and Ronald Radosh. *The Amerasia Spy Case: Prelude to McCarthyism.* Chapel Hill: University of North Carolina Press, 1996.

Kurtz-Phelan, Daniel. *The China Mission: George Marshall's Unfinished War, 1945–1947.* New York: Norton, 2018.

Lary, Diana. *China's Civil War: A Social History, 1945–1949.* Cambridge, UK: Cambridge University Press, 2015.

Leffler, Melvyn, *A Preponderance of Power: National Security, the Truman Administration, and the Cold War.* Stanford, CA: Stanford University Press, 1992.

———. *The Specter of Communism: The United States and the Origins of the Cold War, 1917–1953.* New York: Hill and Wang, 1994.

Li, Xiaobing. *A History of the Modern Chinese Army.* Lexington: University Press of Kentucky, 2007.

Lovell, Julia. *Maoism: A Global History.* New York: Vintage, 2019.

Lowenthal, Mark. *Intelligence: From Secrets to Policy.* 2nd ed. Washington, DC: CQ, 2003.

MacKinnon, Stephen R., and Oris Friesen. *China Reporting: An Oral History of American Journalism in the 1930s and 1940s.* Berkeley: University of California Press, 1987.

Mayers, David A. *FDR's Ambassadors and the Diplomacy of Crisis: From the Rise of Hitler to the End of World War II.* Cambridge, UK: Cambridge University Press, 2013.

McLaughlin, John J. *General Albert C. Wedemeyer: America's Unsung Strategist in World War II.* Havertown, PA: Casemate, 2012.

Menand, Louis. "Wild Thing: Did the O.S.S. Help Win the War against Hitler?" *New Yorker,* March 14, 2011, 69.

Messer, Robert. "Roosevelt, Truman, and China: An Overview." In *Sino-American Relations, 1945–1955: A Joint Reassessment of a Critical Decade,* edited by Harry Harding and Yuan Ming, 64–67. Wilmington, DE: SR, 1989.

Miles, Milton E., and Daniel Hawthorne. *A Different Kind of War: The Unknown Story of the U.S. Navy's Guerrilla Forces in World War II.* New York: Doubleday, 1967.

Mitter, Rana. *Forgotten Ally: China's World War II, 1937–1944.* Boston: Houghton Mifflin Harcourt, 2013.

Moran, Christopher, and Andrew Hammond. "Bringing the 'Social' in from the Cold: Towards a Social History of American Intelligence." *Cambridge Review of International Affairs* 34, no. 5 (2021): 616–36.

Niu, Jun. *From Yan'an to the World: The Origin and Development of Chinese Communist Foreign Policy.* Translated by Stephen I. Levine. Norwalk, CT: Eastbridge, 2005.

O'Donnell, Patrick K. *Operatives, Spies, and Saboteurs: The Unknown Story of the Men and Women of World War II's OSS.* New York: Free Press, 2004.

Oseth, John M. *Regulating U.S. Intelligence Operations.* Lexington: University Press of Kentucky, 1985.

Oyen, Meredith. *The Diplomacy of Migration: Transnational Lives and the Making of U.S.-Chinese Relations in the Cold War.* Ithaca, NY: Cornell University Press, 2015.

Pantsov, Alexander V. *Mao: The Real Story.* New York: Simon & Schuster, 2012.

———. *Victorious in Defeat: The Life and Times of Chiang Kai-shek, China, 1887–1975.* Translated from Russian by Steven I. Levine. New Haven, CT: Yale University Press, 2023.

Peattie, Mark, Edward J. Drea, and Hans J. van de Ven, eds. *The Battle for China: Essays on the Military History of the Sino-Japanese War.* Stanford, CA: Stanford University Press, 2010.

Peraino, Kevin. *A Force So Swift: Mao, Truman, and the Birth of Modern China, 1949.* New York: Penguin Random House, 2017

Persico, Joseph E. *Roosevelt's Secret War.* New York: Random House, 2001.

Plating, John D. *The Hump: America's Strategy for Keeping China in World War II.* College Station: Texas A&M University Press, 2011.

Pomfret, John. *The Beautiful Country and the Middle Kingdom: America and China, 1776 to the Present.* New York: Picador, 2016.

Reynolds, Nicholas. *Need to Know: World War II and the Rise of American Intelligence.* New York: Mariner, 2022.

Romanus, Charles F., and Riley Sunderland. *United States Army in World War II: China, Burma, India Theater.* Washington, DC: Office of the Chief of the Army, US Department of Defense, 1953.

Saich, Tony, ed. *The Rise to Power of the Chinese Communist Party: Documents and Analysis.* Armonk, NY: M. E. Sharpe, 1996.

Schaller, Michael. *The U.S. Crusade in China, 1938–1945.* New York: Columbia University Press, 1979.

Sheng, Michael M. "Chinese Communist Policy toward the United States and the Myth of the 'Lost Chance,' 1948–1950." *Modern Asian Studies* 28, no. 3 (July 1994): 475–502.

Shewmaker, Kenneth E. *Americans and Chinese Communists, 1927–1945: A Persuading Encounter.* Ithaca, NY: Cornell University Press, 1971.

Sims, Jennifer E., and Burton Gerber, eds. *Transforming U.S. Intelligence.* Washington, DC: Georgetown University Press, 2005.

Smist, Frank J. *Congress Oversees the United States Intelligence Community, 1947–1994.* Knoxville: University of Tennessee Press, 1994.

Smith, Bradley F. *The Shadow Warriors: O.S.S. and the Origins of the C.I.A.* New York: Basic, 1983.

Smith, Richard Harris. *OSS: The Secret History of America's First Central Intelligence Agency.* Berkeley: University of California Press, 1972.

Smith, Stephen A. *Like Cattle and Horses: Nationalism and Labor in Shanghai, 1895–1927.* Durham, NC: Duke University Press, 2002.

Snow, Edgar. *Red Star over China.* New York: Random House, 1938.

Spengler, Henry M. "American Liaison Groups." *Military Review* 27 (1947): 61.

Strauss, Julia. "Introduction: In Search of PRC History." *China Quarterly* 188 (December 2006): 850–79.

Stuart, Douglas T. *Creating the National Security State: A History of the Law That Transformed America.* Princeton, NJ: Princeton University Press, 2008.

Sutter, Robert G. *U.S.-Chinese Relations: Perilous Past, Pragmatic Present.* Lanham, MD: Rowman & Littlefield, 2010.

Sutton, Michael Avery. *Double Crossed: The Missionaries Who Spied for the United States during the Second World War.* New York: Basic, 2019.

Tanner, Harold M. *Where Chiang Kai-shek Lost China: The Liao-Shen Campaign, 1948.* Bloomington: Indiana University Press, 2015.

Taylor, Jay. *The Generalissimo: Chiang Kai-shek and the Struggle for Modern China.* Cambridge, MA: Belknap, 2009.

Thomson, James C., Jr., Peter W. Stanley, and John Curtis Perry. *Sentimental Imperialists: The American Experience in East Asia.* New York: Harper and Row, 1981.

Troy, Thomas F. *Donovan and the CIA: A History of the Establishment of the Central Intelligence Agency.* Frederick, MD: University Publications of America, 1981.

Tuchman, Barbara. *Stilwell and the American Experience in China, 1911–45.* New York: Macmillan, 1970.

Vafts, Alfred. *The Military Attaché.* Princeton, NJ: Princeton University Press, 1967.

van de Ven, Hans J. *China at War: Tragedy in the Emergence of the New China, 1937–1953.* Cambridge, MA: Harvard University Press, 2018.

———. *From Friend to Comrade: The Founding of the Chinese Communist Party, 1920–1927.* Berkeley: University of California Press, 1991.
———. "Stilwell in the Stocks: The Chinese Nationalists and the Allied Powers in the Second World War." *Asian Affairs* 34, no. 3 (2003): 243–59.
———. *War and Nationalism in China, 1925–1945.* London: RoutledgeCurzon, 2003.
van de Ven, Hans, Diana Lary, and Stephen R. MacKinnon, eds. *Negotiating China's Destiny in World War II.* Stanford, CA: Stanford University Press, 2015.
Wakeman, Frederic, Jr. *Spymaster: Dai Li and the Chinese Secret Service.* Berkeley: University of California Press, 2003.
Waller, Douglas. *Disciples: The World War II Missions of CIA Directors Who Fought for Wild Bill Donovan: Allen Dulles, Richard Helms, William Colby, William Casey.* New York: Simon & Schuster, 2015.
Warner, Michael, ed. *The CIA under Harry Truman.* Washington, DC: CIA Center for the Study of Intelligence, 1994.
———. "Prolonged Suspense: The Fortier Board and the Transformation of the Office of Strategic Services." *Journal of Intelligence History* 2, no. 1 (2002): 65–76.
———. *The Rise and Fall of Intelligence: An International Security History.* Washington, DC: Georgetown University Press, 2014.
Westad, Odd Arne. *Cold War and Revolution: Soviet-American Rivalry and the Origins of the Chinese Civil War, 1944–1946.* New York: Columbia University Press, 1993.
———. *Decisive Encounters: The Chinese Civil War, 1946–1950.* Stanford, CA: Stanford University Press, 2003.
Whitson, William W. *The Chinese High Command: A History of Communist Military Politics, 1927–71.* New York: Praeger, 1973.
Wilford, Hugh. *America's Great Game: The CIA's Secret Arabists and the Shaping of the Modern Middle East.* New York: Basic, 2013.
Xiang, Sunny. *Tonal Intelligence: The Aesthetics of Asian Inscrutability during the Long Cold War.* New York: Columbia University Press, 2020.
Yu, Maochun. *The Dragon's War: Allied Operations and the Fate of China, 1937–1947.* Annapolis, MD: Naval Institute Press, 2006.
———. *OSS in China: Prelude to Cold War.* Annapolis, MD: Naval Institute Press, 1996.
Zegart, Amy. *Eyes on Spies: Congress and the United States Intelligence Community.* Stanford, CA: Hoover Institution Press, 2011.
———. *Flawed by Design: The Evolution of the CIA, JCS, and NSC.* Stanford, CA: Stanford University Press, 1999.

INDEX

ABOUT THE AUTHOR

SARA B. CASTRO is an associate professor of history at the US Air Force Academy in Colorado Springs, Colorado, and president of the Society for Intelligence History. Her work has been published in the *Journal of Military History*, the *Journal of Chinese Military History*, and the *International Journal of Intelligence and Counterintelligence* as well as in various refereed volumes and online publications. She serves on the editorial board of the *International Journal of Intelligence and Counterintelligence*. Castro previously worked as an intelligence analyst for the US government.